Book 3

Transcending the Climate Change Deception

Toward Real Sustainability

Mark Keenan

Former scientist at United Nations Environment Division
and at the UK Department of Energy and Climate Change

Exclusion of Liability:

The author respects all people and religions and therefore rejects any kind of racist, anti-Christian, anti-Jewish, anti-Islamic (etc.) prejudice and propaganda. When certain aspects of big corporations, banking, religions, political and corporate institutions, and extremely wealthy individuals or families are scrutinised in this book it is solely meant to find a higher platform of mutual understanding (beyond ideological, denominational and dogmatic antagonism).

The author has gathered and evaluated all information presented in this book to the best of his knowledge. Nevertheless, he invites all readers to examine his sources and arguments with a critical mind. The author rejects any responsibility for all forms of unintended conclusion and reaction on the part of the reader that might be induced by a superficial, incomplete or biased reading of this book.

16th June 2022

Copyright Mark Keenan

All rights reserved.

This book is available on www.amazon.com and at www.mkeenan.ie

ALL GLORIES TO GOD

HARE KRISHNA

OM NAMO VASUDEVAYA

Table of Contents

Table of Contents 3

Foreword 8
   The corporate super-entity 15

1. Climate change deception and other false UN narratives 21

Manmade climate change is a convenient lie – not caused by CO_2 or by methane from livestock/cows 21
The modern green movement is far removed from the original principles of environmentalism 24
Evidence from renowned scientists that demolishes the fake climate change hysteria 27
Temperatures were higher in the 1930s than today, but the UN ignores that data 28
UN IPPC committee chairman resigned in protest at UN IPPC lies and false information 30
Most of the scientists that say climate change is a problem are on perpetual government grants 31
UN IPPC cherry picks data, uses flawed modelling and scenarios not remotely related to the real world ... 32
Financialization of the world economy based on a life-killing net-zero emissions strategy 34
Central bankers are entirely funding and controlling the advancement of the worldwide climate change 'project' 34
Central bankers hijacked the real environmental movement in 1992 creating the fake climate change agenda 36
Key players that promoted the climate crisis agenda 38
The Chicago Climate Exchange and the trillion-dollar money-generating hoax 39
Deceptive narratives on covid-19, UN agenda 2030, climate change, and the WEF reset 40
Renewable energy is not a viable solution to the world's energy problems 42
The nonsense of electric cars 44
The failure of the industrial agriculture 'green revolution' 46
Desertification - UN incorrectly state that animal livestock is a cause – it is actually the solution 47
Farmers have been given wrong information by governments 48
What is the UN really? 49
Real environmentalism was hijacked by deceptive UN political schemes 51
30 years of UN-defined sustainable development has not solved the real environmental and human wellbeing problems that exist worldwide – and was not designed to 54
Decoding the real objectives behind the UN 17 'New Sustainable Development Goals' 55
UN Agenda 21/2030 is an agenda of control – it is the opposite of real sustainability 60
UN Agenda 2030 smart cities - smart for them, but not smart for you 61
The trick of world heritage sites and 'rewilding' 62

Communism disguised as sustainability - Local Governments for Sustainability stakeholder councils 63

2. WEF 'reset' attempt sold as a solution to climate change and covid-19 65

Smart devices, 5G and electromagnetic frequency technologies 67
Geo-engineering and the technology they use to pollute the skies......68

3. Summary of the climate change and sustainable development deceptions 69

The way forward to a 'real' sustainable and resilient society 74

4. The UN climate hoax required a single controlling world influence 75

A single group controlling the world's mega-corporations and mega-banks?......75
Who owns the banks and asset management companies that own and control the world?......76
Blackrock - the company that owns most of the world......76
Study proves one corporate 'super-entity' owns/dominates the world economy and resources 77
The private banking cartel owns and controls the corporate super-entity 78
Who owns the mega-banks that own and control the world?......78
The central banking system exerts vast control over the world economy 79
How did a private banking cartel gain ownership of the world's wealth and resources?......79
1913 to 2019 - a private banking elite gained control of the world's wealth/ resources 80
100 years of private banking leaves all nations in vast debt + bankers owning the world 82
The end result is the system, or the 'matrix', we all live in and were born into 83
2019 - mathematical end-phase of a world financial system that was always flawed/ fraudulent 83
The UN / WEF and international bankers needed a smokescreen for the economic reset 84
WEF/UN marketing of a technocratic world reset – unelected one world government......86
The private banking cartel purchased and controls the world's corporate media......88
Six corporations own 96% of the media - testimonies the media is controlled by world bankers 88
The Tavistock Institute - a history of media manipulations and social engineering 90
The financial pyramid of power and control......93
Representative democracy as currently implemented in much of the world is an illusion......95
The constraints of the new world order 'scientific dictatorship' 96
Key historical trends in the system 97
The Jewish question......98
Is pattern recognition antisemitic? 101

5. 1913 - 2019: Private banking control and the corporate super-entity 103

6. UN sustainable development is a problem wrapped up as a solution – what about the real sustainability challenge? 107

The Earth we all depend on – what about real pollution to land, air and water?......107
The sustainability squeeze and the real sustainability challenge......109
Sustainable development – a problem wrapped up as a solution 112
30 years of 'UN-defined sustainable development' has not solved the real environmental problem......114
SD perpetuates the problem - does not address root causes of instability in the system 115

The UN Brundtland definition enabled 'polluting' forms of GDP growth to continue..............................116
The word 'sustainable' was hijacked...117
The failure/flaws of decoupling, resource substitution or eco-efficiency strategies...............................120
International policies for 'sustainable development' incorrectly endorse GDP growth............................124
Green economy/green growth strategy is destructive globalisation painted green..................................125
The UN incorrectly promote GDP growth thus causing environmental impacts 126
Blaming population growth rather addressing the root causes..127

7. Globalisation – a destructive paradigm 129

The tragedy of the commons and the privatization of everything..129
Corporations prioritize profit above all else...131
Corporate globalisation – a design for mega-corporate rule of the world's resources 132
The World Bank and the IMF – terrorist organisations devastating the developing world.......................136
Corporate control of the food supply 137

8. The flaws of the GDP growth system 140

9. Contemporary economics is a flawed ideology / pseudo-science......................141

10. Systemic problems, oil dependency, constraints to growth, and collapse 142

The serious implications of oil availability – constraints to GDP growth..142
Analysis published by the Foundation for the Economics of Sustainability 144

11. Modern day attempts to scientifically define 'real' sustainability 146

The problem of reductionism..146
The precautionary principle has been ignored in science...148
Balancing material flows with nature's capacity via sustainable design..151
Cradle to Cradle design 152
Sustainable design, eco-efficiency or eco-innovation has failed – it is not enough 153
Born in the unsustainable matrix – ideological delusion (not fact) in education and politics 154
Real sustainability should not be labelled with any 'political' ideology..156

12. A sustainable retreat – creating resilient local systems....................................157

Discarding false narratives and starting anew...157
A sustainable retreat is needed not so-called 'UN sustainable development' 158
Is it possible to re-align the current 'system' toward 'real' sustainability...158
Sustainability or Collapse? – the risk of societal collapse 159
Resilience planning and creating sustainable communities/regions..161
The wisdom of E.F. Schumacher..164
The bio-char solution to soil management and desertification...166
Re-discovering the power and dynamics of horses...167
Natural house construction 168
A transition to a gift economy? - the moneyless manifesto 169

Vedic communities and ancient knowledge for thriving in balance with nature 169
Rediscovering the splendour of ancient forest villages 170
Ancient Vedic culture – a thriving God-conscious society in balance with nature 171
Bible (Genesis 1:26) 173
A Vedic perspective on the importance of cows in self-sufficient communities 174
The need for traditional farming decoupled from a government-controlled system 175
Consciousness and dharma in a spiritual civilisation of wellbeing for all 177
A metaphorical 'mountain of success' – a 'successful society of higher quality' 178

13. The trap of the materialistic illusion 181
Materialism is not the answer to the problems of humankind 181
The illusion of 'the economy' 184
The fabricated matrix is a system of domination and exploitation 185

14. Beyond material consciousness 189
Are humans capable of 'real' sustainability? 189
Breaking through the matrix of material illusions – transcending un-sustainability 192
Higher consciousness and interconnectedness – the Avatar movie metaphor 192
Beyond the material consciousness - seeking a higher quality 194
Walking a spiritual path 195
The Dao of sustainability / the Tao of quality 196
The refusal of consciousness and denial of God in so-called modern science 198
The satanic consciousness directing the climate change and covid hysteria 201
Is there a reason some people can see through the fake agendas, but most cannot? 203
The 'new normal' and the 'old normal' are not normal 204
The infiltration and manipulation of religious institutions 206
The programming of consciousness and how to transcend it 207

15. Transcending the world power game – wisdom from ancient scriptures 208

Endnotes 209

Acknowledgements - A Note of Thanks

I am very grateful to the world-renowned climate science experts, scientists in various fields, and authors that are quoted in this book for their diligent work. Thank you to the authors that provided kind permission to quote their writings. Thank you to the Irish Climate Science Forum for their diligent work in presenting analysis by world climate science experts. Thank you to my family and to friends for their support and assistance over the years. May God be with you all.

Foreword

Hello dear reader. As I write this I can see the Atlantic Ocean from my window and the beautiful sunlight that is sparkling across the waves, and I thank God for the beauty and purity of creation. That sense of wellbeing, purity and perfection in nature is in stark contrast to 'un-reality' that is beamed out from the TV set in the corner. This 'speaking plastic box' has been trying to sell me an electric car so I can 'save the planet'. Yet, as a former scientist at the UK government, Dept. of Energy and Climate Change, I know that climate change is a political scam, and that the production of electric cars causes a lot of 'real' pollution. Thousands of other diligent scientists also know this. The climate has always been changing slowly and naturally in its own cycle – climate change is not caused by carbon emissions or methane from livestock, such as cows. So, what is the real story behind the climate change agenda? First, I feel I should tell you a little of my background so here goes.

In 2011, I began working at the United Nations (UN) Environment Division in Geneva. In my role I was the main person responsible for facilitating the worldwide implementation of pollution monitoring and database systems for thousands of pollutants under the Pollutant Release and Transfer Register (PRTR) Protocol, a multilateral environmental agreement. As part of my scientific work, I analysed key aspects of pollution releases to land, air and water systems, and I liaised with governments in over 58 countries. Carbon (CO_2) was also listed as a pollutant in the register, and is the main focus of the UN promoted climate change hysteria that has been rampant among the world's population. However, the reality is that the CO_2 itself is not actually a pollutant. Climate change is not actually caused by CO_2 or by methane from cows. Along with 1,000 other scientists in climate and related fields, I have signed the European Climate Declaration, which asserts "the proclaimed climate crisis exists in computer models only" and asserts the UN climate change narrative is incorrect, see www.clintel.org. I sent this information to the Green Party politicians, but they disagree and are, it seems, rather brainwashed by the UN-promoted cult of manmade climate change.

Real pollution exists, but the problem is not CO_2. The process of industrial globalisation has produced many substances that are registered as pollutants, including thousands of new man-made chemical compounds, toxins, nano-particles and GMOs that are in violation of the scientific pre-cautionary principle. Over the past tens of thousands of years, the human body has never been exposed to these new substances so we do not know the long-term effects. Despite regulations in relation to various substances, the UN environmental law instruments are largely impotent in safe-guarding human health and nature from the vast scale of rampant corporate technological pollution. **Despite the deceptive and fake environmental facade, it has adopted, the vast institutional entity of the UN has fully endorsed environmentally destructive industrial globalisation for the past 70 years.** The UN climate change, sustainable development and green economy policies over the past 30 years are little more than worldwide marketing tricks that have tragically brainwashed two generations of young people who do not understand what the UN actually is.

None of us in school or university were exposed to information about the 'globalist' financial powers, or the unjust privately-owned world banking and debt-money creation systems, that were at the root of the formation of these post-WWII international institutions. Thus, most people, unfortunately, do not appear to realise what the UN actually is, what it really is designed for, and who are the globalist robber barons that control it from the top down, just as they have controlled the world's money creation and supply process. Like the worldwide banking sector, the UN is so big it is hard to see it fully. We are often shown some of its pretty trees (i.e., seemingly noble projects) on our televisions, but we can't see the whole forest, what the forest hides, or who planted it!

Prior to working at the UN, I had been a Science Advisor at the United Kingdom government, Department of Energy and Climate Change in Whitehall, London. At that time although I had studied hundreds of books and academic papers on environment, sustainability and energy, I was unconvinced that climate change, if it was occurring in any unnatural way, was being caused by CO_2. I had an ongoing nagging doubt and scepticism that CO_2 was the problem that the UN claimed – I was 'on the fence' so to speak until I could analyse the evidence for myself.

I soon discovered that the UN climate crisis predictions are not based on physical evidence, they are based on complex computer modelling. One has to decode and analyse the modelling process to ascertain whether or not the models are valid and accurate or whether they have obvious flaws. The vast majority of scientists, economists, politicians and the general public have simply assumed that the UN IPPC models are accurate. This is intellectually lazy and naïve, yet one can imagine that occupied with their own jobs and positions within a reductionist system, very few people have the time or skills to analyse these models, what to mention actually dispute them. Nonetheless, **there were many senior and highly distinguished scientists that did exactly that –**

they claimed the UN narrative was incorrect and that there was no climate emergency. Their voices have been drowned out by a vast money-driven political and media establishment of the globalised 'system'. The vitally important work of some of these renowned scientists is referenced in this book.

> "deeply flawed logic, obscured by shrewd and unrelenting propaganda, actually enabled a coalition of powerful special interests to convince nearly everyone in the world that Co2 from human industry was a dangerous plant destroying toxin. It will be remembered as the greatest mass delusion in the history of the world – that Co2 the life of plants was considered for a time to be a deadly poison."
> – Professor Richard Lindzen, Professor Emeritus of Atmospheric Sciences at MIT.

This globalised system involves the promotion of beliefs that claim to be unchallengeable truths, but are in fact ideologies in which evidence is manipulated, twisted and distorted to prove the 'governing idea', and thus promote its worldwide dissemination. They start with the conclusion they want and then wrench and manipulate what evidence they can to fit that conclusion. Manmade climate change due to anthropogenic carbon emission is a major example of this. **In the world of 2022, objective truth has been replaced to a very large extent by ideology.** The bogus mantra is 'my opinion is as valid as your opinion', in the consequent vacuum of no objective truth, power is what has been dictating reality. The establishment of 'what is real' became a contest, in which those with all the money could easily win the battles. However, the game is not over and truth has a way of surviving and winning the war in the end.

If you have read my previous book you will know that after decades of corporate consolidation, only a few connected mega-corporations now own and control virtually the entire world corporate media system.

> "Secrecy has been maintained because the robber barons have been able to use their monopoly over money to buy up major media, educational institutions, and other outlets of public information. While Rockefeller was buying up universities, medical schools, and the Encyclopedia Britannica, Morgan bought up newspapers... By 1983... fifty corporations owned half or more of the media business. **By 2000, that number was down to six corporations, with directorates interlocked with each other and with major commercial banks**. (See Endnote [1])" – Ellen H. Brown, chairperson of the US Public Banking Institute

The small group of elite interests that own these corporations literally control the corporate-media narrative. The masses are not supposed to think independently about the reality that it served to them by the current TV/corporate media culture. Turning on the TV people are hit with a barrage of news and advertising compelling them to accept what the government says and what the godless cult of corporate scientism tells them to do and to buy. If you disagree with the 'consensus reality', verbal abuse, online bullying or social media censorship is typically used to shut down your argument. This is because the intellectual position of the people hypnotised by the corporate-controlled information 'matrix' is built on sand. This is the reason thousands of truth tellers are banned or suspended on corporate-owned Facebook, twitter and YouTube etc. The 'educated' masses meanwhile are misled by a smile and a charming personality - traits that are often wielded by the narcissist. Former President Obama smilingly told the US population they need to combat climate change – even while the evidence indicated otherwise.

Note that I have no commercial interest in stating the climate change is not caused by CO_2. Some people assume that because I am pointing out this fact, that I must be a supporter of oil and coal usage - this is an intellectually lazy assumption. The vast burning of oil and coal does cause 'real' air pollution problems and my personal preference is that in an ideal world I would prefer that humanity was not using oil and coal in 'polluting ways'. I am fully aware, however, that we do not currently live in an ideal world, and have been born into, and continually shunted into, a globalised polluting system that most people cannot easily step out of. An article of mine was recently fraudulently reworded by a print publication in the UK to make it look as if I was supporting the use of oil, but in truth I am against 'real' pollution, and the reality is that the CO_2 component is not a pollutant. In 2022, many deluded environmentalists are driving around in electric cars, the battery production for which has caused vast amounts of 'real' pollution. In relation to climate change and sustainability this book is about uncovering the truth.

I resigned from these permanent staff member science-based roles in both UK government and in the UN. It had become evident to me that **the manipulation and fraudulent distortion of scientific and economic data had long been used by the UN and complicit governments to promote false and deceptive agendas**. These agendas stem from the top echelons of the international political, mega-corporate and financial system, and those few so-called elites who control it. By fully controlling the source of money creation the money-masters have been able to fund any agenda they wish and, similarly, defund anything they wish. The false narrative that carbon emissions, and methane emissions from livestock or dairy cows, cause climate change is at the top of 'their agenda'. Very few people actually dig into the data or examine the modelling. The masses blindly accept the UN narrative or what the TV tells them to believe. Note that the UN does not focus on the thousands of other real pollutants that corporate industrial globalisation creates.

The cult of 'manmade climate change' is a media and UN politically-promoted 'ideology', that is being used for a wider agenda of the so-called 'elites'. Manmade climate change is not based in evidential fact, and has hijacked 'real' environmentalism. **Institutions, including the UN, the World Economic Forum (WEF), and the World Health Organisation (WHO), are privately-motivated unelected unaccountable organisations** controlled by the source of debt-money creation, i.e., the world private-banking cartel; and are just clever marketing tools and political mechanisms for implementing and maintaining a corrupt worldwide system, **under the clever guise of 'fixing the problems of the world'**. The word sustainable was hijacked decades ago, it is now deceptively used to advance the agendas of globalist mega-corporate interests who couldn't care less about the environment.

The UN Agenda 2030 plan and the Paris Agreement goal to reduce CO_2 emissions by 7% per annum until 2030 is in effect a plan that will disable the traditional resource mechanisms for the food, energy and goods that enable human life and survival. This is being done before humanity has transitioned away from the flawed polluting trans-national industrial economy toward self-sufficient local economies. The aim is to catapult humanity into the arms of UN Agenda 2030 and the WEF 'reset' plan, which are clever marketing plans entirely designed by the so-called elite mega-corporate interests of the Davos group. Whether you believe the 'plug is being pulled' intentionally or not, implementation of these plans would inevitably result in a de-population outcome. The dependency of humanity on a globalised system was intentionally created for decades by an international political corporate hierarchy rampantly promoting and implementing flawed trans-national systems for agriculture, energy and goods, necessary for, and **aligned with a usury economy in which wealth continuously flowed toward the private bankers**. These globalised oil-dependent systems become useless as the availability of oil declines either due to reduced Energy Returned on Energy Invested (EROEI) or geo-political manipulations.

Furthermore, the current green energy/renewable technologies being promoted by the UN and WEF, are not a viable solution for the world's energy supply. The EROEI is much too low - in essence the entire process is mathematically flawed. This is evidenced by the work of Professor David MacKay, Former Regius Professor of Engineering at Cambridge University and former Chief Scientific Advisor at DECC.

The funding of the entire world economy is now based on a life-killing net-zero GHG strategy. **Note that the world's central bankers are at the root of this decision and are fully funding the worldwide climate change 'project'.** The central bankers are the folks that are behind all this nonsense. The Bank for International Settlements created the Task Force on Climate-related Financial Disclosure, which represents the world's mega-banks and $118 trillion of assets globally (that is 118 thousand billion dollars - a huge chunk of the assets of the entire world).

After the so-called **banking crisis in Europe in 2008,** I had authored a blog in 2009, 2010 and 2011, which included analysis and criticism of the flawed globalisation GDP hypergrowth paradigm and associated fraudulent debt-money banking system; how those systems are a root driver of ongoing environmental impacts; and analysis of the bailout of privately-owned banks by the Irish government. This bailout was a historic and unjust event that unjustly transferred vast amounts of private banking debt onto the people of Ireland. This vast debt could, in actuality, never be repaid, but resulted in increased taxes and austerity/cutbacks upon the Irish people. The private international 'bondholders' that should have lost their investments, suddenly found the debts were guaranteed and paid for by the Irish government. These bondholders held wealth over 100 times that of the entire population of Ireland and could certainly afford to lose these investments, yet the Irish population who had nothing to do with the situation had to pay their debts! I felt the architects behind such vast injustice should be exposed. Similar boom-bust-bailout cycles (orchestrated tricks of the international banking system) had occurred in many countries over the decades, as described in my book *Globalism Unmasked: The Truth about Banking and the Reset of Society*.

We live in a corporate moneyocracy and nothing of major importance happens in the world that is not pre-planned by the so-called moneyed elites to happen that way. In 2020, it was clear that **Covid-19 was an excuse for the imposition of a whole new set of government rules**, and was also a smokescreen being used as cover for an attempted economic-reset of the entire world according to the design of these same so-called elites. Twenty years of research proves that from the Federal Reserve coup of 1913 to JFK to 911 to the climate crisis hysteria and covid-19, it is the same line of mechanics at work. The criminal elites promote the term 'conspiracy theorist' as an attempt to dismiss the many people that are realising such truths. The fraudulent covid-19 PCR test is the first key to realising the pandemic hoax. This, and much more, is comprehensively explained in my book '*Transcending the Covid-19 Deception*'.

Over the years the evidence-based research of many people continually led toward an international banking/mega-corporate/political cartel or 'cabal' that appeared to be at the root of the injustices in the world - **'follow the money' and you will find who runs the world.** More and more 'truth-seekers' worldwide were calling out this group, they were called the globalists, the elite central bankers, etc.

After posting evidence-based research on the banking system, I was 'shadow-banned' from Facebook around the year 2011, before I had ever heard the term 'shadow-banned'. My Facebook posts with relevant links on these issues were not being seen by any of the hundreds of online Facebook contacts. Facebook certainly is a clever trick for monitoring and censoring information and worldwide opinion, and I was likely amongst the first cohort of people to leave it. Post 911, millions more people were searching for truth worldwide, I certainly was not alone. However, over the past years of the so-called digital age, **internet censorship algorithms** on corporate platforms, such as Google, Facebook and YouTube, have been routinely de-platforming various 'truths' that the elites don't want you to know about.

The 'climate change is caused by carbon emissions' narrative and covid-19 situation, are **two of the biggest deceptive political and media-driven cons in the history of human kind.** Such narratives have been embedded into the public consciousness, but many people are now seeing through the lies. They are using these well marketed scares, false ideologies, fake crises, and political systems (democracy, communism, socialism, etc.) to control you. Many people are thus in a media-and-government-induced dysfunctional state of confusion, and thus blindly assume their pre-determined role in society under this 'dictatorship of words' without even being aware of it. For example, we now have millions of so-called climate change warriors blind to the fact that climate change is not actually caused by carbon emissions. These aspects are pieces of a jigsaw that create an overall picture of increased freedom killing control under cover of deceptive and unproven political narratives, such as manmade climate change and a pandemic that is so deadly it disappears when you turn off your television! This is all to scare people into accepting totalitarian authority and limitations to their freedom and personal wellbeing.

To better perceive what is 'behind the curtain' of the climate change and covid-19 hoaxes and the totalitarian UN/WEF reset agenda it helps to examine what has happened in the decades beforehand. It is important to perceive the implications of the worldwide fractional-reserve banking scam and the subtle system of debt-slavery that has existed for decades. For many decades the so-called banking and corporate elites have had full control of the source of money creation and its allocation, via the debt-money system, and have therefore, **by default, been able to fund, and increasingly control and manipulate the entire world spectrum of industry, media, government, education, ideological supremacy** and war to their own design, agenda and benefit. Mayer Amschel Rothschild (banker) reportedly said:

> "Give me control of a nation's money supply and I care not who makes its laws." – Mayer Amschel Rothschild (banker)

The criminal banking cartel **usurped control of the Federal Reserve and money creation process in 1913,** and since then have been gathering vast amounts of interest on loans from almost all the governments and people of the world. By 2019, these few people had amassed a majority percentage of the wealth and assets of the world via their banking/financial mechanisms and ownership of mega-corporations. In essence, by owning the source of debt-money creation and with decades of corporate consolidation, **by 2019, a single super-entity or super-corporate-structure existed**, acting under the names of many corporations, but ultimately owned and controlled by 'one' small ultra-wealthy cartel. The cartel includes the private banking families that took historical ownership and control of the money creation process back in 1913 and established a privately-owned world central banking system.

The corporate super-entity

The Covid and Climate change hoaxes could not have been orchestrated without a single controlling world influence over the media, banking, and the corporate/political structure. Who owns the banks and asset management companies that own and control the world? Let's take the example of Blackrock, one of the world's largest asset management companies, which manages funds of over $27 trillion ($27,000 billion) and in effect owns most of the U.S. and large parts of the world. The major shareholders of Blackrock are all mega-banks and financial corporations, in this way we can see that it the private mega-banks that own most of the world.

A study was conducted in 2018 at the Swiss Federal Institute of Technology in Zurich, on the relationships between 37 million companies and investors worldwide, and they concluded there is one 'super-entity' of just 147 tightly knit mega-corporations, and all of their ownership was held by other members of the super-entity. In essence, the worldwide privately owned financial and corporate orthodoxy is one large self-reinforcing super-entity underneath the tentacles of financial mega-corporations, who are themselves pre-dominantly owned by a small coterie of privately owned mega-banks/financial institutions. One corporate 'super-entity' of interlocking ownership literally owns and dominates the world economy, resources, and media.

The private banking cartel owns and controls the corporate super-entity. A small number of mega-banks are among the top ten stock holders of virtually every Fortune 500 corporation. This is why less than 0.001 % of the world's population, i.e., a small number of banking family elites and their networks, own the majority of the world's assets and wealth. It is no coincidence that the founder of the WEF is Klaus Schwab, a son of Marianne Schwab (nee Rothschild) of the banking dynasty.

A systemic ongoing problem with the world economic system, and energy availability, has been manifesting. Various studies now indicate that the energy returned on energy invested for oil has seriously declined, and the days of using oil as a cheap energy source to drive the flawed globalised system and seemingly endless growth may soon be over permanently. The decades old economic Ponzi scheme of the globalists has thus reached its mathematical end-phase, forcing another paradigm shift.

By 2019, virtually every national government of the world owed vast or mathematically unpayable amounts of debt to the international private banking cartel. This decades old system forced people to live in a debt cycle which never ends. Since debt does not really exist (the money was created from nothing by the private banking system), the national debt is a hoax perpetrated by the so-called 'powers that be'. The private central-banks and governments facilitate this worldwide con game that nowadays is hardly ever questioned. President John F Kennedy (RIP) was the last US President to attempt to rectify this.

This system of debt-money slavery had reached its mathematical end-phase by 2019, as the amount of debt on the system was over ten times, in relative, terms than that of the great crash of 1929. In this most serious event in financial history, infinite amounts of quantitative easing were required and sanctioned to keep the system going. Yet hardly anyone knew about this because they were being mentally traumatised by news of a worldwide (fake) pandemic, which is yet more evidence of the total grip the financial elites have over world corporate and government media.

A new system of control was needed and the elites had known this for a long time. **'Climate change due to CO_2' and covid-19 are intentionally created scare tactics intended to propel the world into the arms of the UN Agenda 2030 plan, the Davos Group WEF technocratic 'reset'** and a nefarious bio-pharmaceutical agenda of the corporate controlled WHO. The globalist Davos Group represents the world's ultra-rich – the 2500 richest financial and corporate organisations in the world. The so-called elites that have a controlling interest in the world banking, corporate and economic system, and their political and corporate cohorts, planned and orchestrated the fake climate and covid-19 crises, which only exist on your TV.

(Note: My book *Transcending the Covid-19 Deception* provides comprehensive evidence that covid was a fake pandemic based on a fraudulent PCR test, and thus netted trillions in revenue for vaccine companies. The covid PCR test is not an indicator of anything never mind an indicator of a disease. Courts of law in Portugal, Austria and Germany found that the PCR test cannot detect a covid-19 infection, but governments worldwide continued to ignore this. For example, the High Court of Portugal ruled decisively in a landmark case in 2020 against the local regional health authority on behalf of persons that were tested positive by the PCR. The court ruled that the restrictions can't be supported by the testing because the PCR test is faulty. The ruling states:

> "if someone is tested by PCR as positive when a threshold of 35 cycles or higher is used (as is the rule in most laboratories in Europe and the U.S.) the probability that said person is infected is less than 3%, and the probability that said result is a false positive is 97%.")

These cohorts include top echelons of the UN, the WEF, the WHO, and their witting or unwitting 'yes-men' in subservient national governments. These unelected unaccountable international organisations are fully linked at the top echelons with the privately owned world debt-money banking system. Most people still have no idea that **in March 2020 the world central bankers launched a world economic reset under cover of the pre-planned covid world lockdown**. Viruses, it seems, suddenly became invisible enemies of the world's governments, but it was all pre-planned. The 'climate crisis' and 'covid-19 hoax' was and is a cover/smokescreen for an attempted new worldwide system of societal control. At the exact same time as the lockdown was introduced the world central bankers implemented a world financial reset and transferred trillions of dollars to Blackrock; and the WEF/UN launched a pre-planned technocratic reset of world society aligned with their Agenda 2030 plan.

Additional orchestrated pandemics, crises and orchestrated wars, in which both sides are pawns of the globalists, are likely 'in the pipeline' to further these plans. These and other deceptions are used as excuses for the so-called 'great economic reset', which is in reality a UN/WEF promoted freedom killing new world order, and is now widely exposed worldwide.

The WEF reset/UN Agenda 2030 **moves the elites beyond control of the money system, to control of the people system,** via new rules, track and trace, bio-metrics, vaccine passports, digital IDs, facial recognition, smart cities and blockchain power dynamics. That is not smart for you, it is smart for them. It is all presented in clever marketing language because if people understood it nobody would want it. Humanity urgently needs to take back control of the money creation process, or, at least, function outside of the privately-owned worldwide banking, credit creation and corporate system.

This is ideological subversion plain and simple, there is 'nothing new under the sun', certain narcissistic folks are always seeking power and control. If you are not familiar with these lies/deceptions and are facing these issues for the first time you could be forgiven for thinking 'how can this be? This must be conspiracy theory?'. The first essential fact to realise is that, via the process of corporate consolidation, the worldwide mega-corporate media system is now virtually entirely owned and controlled by one small group of connected mega-corporate interests. Government TV channels, for example, the BBC in the UK, or RTE in Ireland, receive huge lump sum funding from the likes of the EU (a promoter of climate change) and the Bill and Melinda Gates Foundation (the biggest vaccine salesman in the world). These interests have been promoting certain 'ideologies' for decades to advance their corporate and political aims. John Swinton, former chief-of-staff for the New York Times once said: "We are the tools and vassals of rich men behind the scenes... They pull the strings... AND WE DANCE."

It is time for people to replace their window on the world. This starts by turning off the TV. Evidence and opposing views that refute these 'ideologies' have been censored and deleted routinely on corporate-owned media and internet platforms over the past twenty years and more. For example, I was suspended from Twitter in 2020 for posting official VAERS database statistics on Covid-19 vaccine adverse reactions - how can it be anything other than censorship to stop people from quoting official government data? Corporate media platforms use algorithms to censor truth that does not fit the agenda of the corporate elites. YouTube even admits to having deleted over 800,000 videos on the coronavirus subject. **We are in an information war, no** wonder they want us to cover our mouths with masks and social distance. In addition, my website, was subjected to an unusual database 'attack' in 2021. I certainly am not alone, millions of people worldwide are exposing the lies; and many thousands of people, including many prominent scientists and doctors, have not been allowed a voice on corporate and government TV channels and have been censored on social media. These brave people have been exposing the evidence-based truth about the bogus climate change agenda, the fake pandemic and much more.

In summary, the bigger picture is that the top echelons of international organisations including the UN, the WEF, and the WHO have **a cleverly marketed corporate-designed agenda for the entirety of worldwide society to control your entire lifestyle and that of your children for decades to come.** This is being attempted under the excuse or cover of the lie of combatting manmade climate change, protection from a fake pandemic and other scare mongering manipulative tactics. The objective is to advance their own sinister objectives - in fact, these international organisations are merely tools of the criminally fraudulent worldwide banking cartel. At the top level these organisations are fully aligned with the 'source of money', i.e., the worldwide banking cartel/cabal and its various political cohorts. All governments take direction and instruction from these unaccountable unelected international organisations and central bankers. This criminal financial network has been funding and promoting many deceptive ideologies and 'fake truths' for a long time, in fact for a very long time. The history of this network goes back hundreds and even thousands of years and is linked with the history of money creation itself.

People's access to energy and resources is being intentionally reduced via bogus climate change policies, high inflation, ongoing geo-political theatre and intentionally instigated war, in which both 'sides' are acting as pawns for the wider agenda of the punch-and-judy show globalists.

Democracy will not make things better, it is an illusory divide and conquer/control trick. It is just the election of the latest political figure heads, the ins-become-the-outs and the outs-become-the-ins, none of whom have any real power. It is the behind-the-scenes privately-owned world banking cartel that owns the debt-money creation system that has the means to control, own, fund, or de-fund whatever government, corporation or ideology it wishes. Many politicians are the witting, and often un-witting, pawns, of the globalists. Democratic leaders are subservient not to the people but always to international finance. International banking and mega corporations control governments.

The old system was based on debt-slavery of money created from nothing by private bankers, and the new system being pushed is based on technocratic control created from nothing except our consent to cleverly marketed narcissism and lies. **We need a better paradigm, but obviously not the technocratic 'new normal' paradigm the elites have planned for us to keep us under tabs**. Local systems for food, energy, water and services are an essential part of escaping the coming technocratic system that is being cleverly wrapped around us.

As sovereign free peoples, we urgently need to **start planning, connecting with each other and creating much more self-sufficient local communities, towns, and regions free of the globalist controlled corporate, political and monetary system**. If people are not dependent on the system they cannot be controlled by the system. How many people will accept a 'well-marketed system of technocratic control' and how many will maintain their own freedom and create their own local systems? You are part of the answer.

The good news is the truth is gaining ground and this worldwide 'situation' is sparking a greater creative and spiritual awakening that will easily outlive and transcend the current criminal power game of greed and control. A thriving society based on freedom, truth, real knowledge, integrity, real health, happiness, strong people, strong local resilience, expression of the real self, and spiritual realisation is being manifested. We don't need these international money-masters and their 'paid-for' bureaucrats. We don't need to be slaves to their lies, or to their systems of godless fraudulent scientism, medical authoritarianism, fraudulent banking, and international political and corporate totalitarianism. It is time to leave it all behind – to hell with the new normal and to hell with the old normal. The dystopian movie *The Matrix* portrays humans as just batteries, the slave energy to fuel a technocratic dictatorship. How many people will wake up, like the movie character 'Neo' and discover their own power?

We are in a real physical and spiritual war for truth and freedom. Embracing original spiritual knowledge purifies and further strengthens us internally, enabling us to more easily overcome all challenges. A cleansing is coming and to be on the side of good we must act accordingly. God gave us all free will, and our choices at this juncture have major ramifications. It is my hope this book will help you to bypass various deceptions, untruths and traps of the corporate-owned and institutionally-corrupt world-system; transcend the lies; and accelerate your journey toward truth, freedom, success, happiness and spiritual wellbeing.

With best wishes,

Mark Keenan, 16th June 2022

1. Climate change deception and other false UN narratives

Manmade climate change is a convenient lie – not caused by CO_2 or by methane from livestock/cows

In 2018, a UN IPPC report warned that 'we have 12 years to save the earth', thus sending the climate change doomsday cult into a frenzy. However, the reality is that manmade climate change is a convenient lie. It is nothing more than propaganda promoted by the UN, EU, various political and media personalities, and certain government-funded academic institutes. It has involved a political agenda of taxation and policies designed to facilitate UN Agenda 2030 and World Economic Forum corporate plans. Thousands of scientists dispute the UN IPCC theory that greenhouse gases, such as CO_2 or 'methane from cows', cause climate change. Serious flaws, lies and distortions in the UN narrative have been proven to exist.

The UN assertion that 97% of climate scientists agree with the UN narrative is a fraudulent manipulation of statistics. Via analysis, common sense or the human faculty of intuitive intelligence, many millions of people worldwide also know that the UN theory is absurd nonsense. The so-called powers-that-be are creating all the chaotic BS. They are creating all the problems and are telling us that we have to respond to, or pay for, it all. Whatever they are telling us 'is wrong in the world', we are told we have to fix it by becoming humble slaves to their dictates. Meanwhile, as we shall see, they make trillions. It is the tried and tested problem-reaction-solution Hegelian dialectic formula.

I am a signatory of the Climate Intelligence Group (CLINTEL) European Climate Declaration, see Endnote [2], a declaration that has been signed by 1,000 scientists, engineers and other professionals from 33 countries in climate and related fields, that asserts "the proclaimed climate crisis exists in computer models only". I have zero commercial interest in stating this position. This declaration, see Endnote [3], states that climate change is not due to manmade CO_2 emissions. The following is an excerpt:

"European Climate Declaration: There Is No Climate Emergency Date: 24/09/19 Press Release, Climate Intelligence Foundation (CLINTEL) As the latest U.N. climate summit begins in New York, a new, high-level global network of 500 prominent climate scientists and professionals has submitted a declaration that there is no "climate emergency". The group has sent a European Climate Declaration with a registered letter to António Guterres, Secretary-General of the United Nations. Professor Guus Berkhout of The Netherlands, who organized the Declaration, said: "So popular is the Declaration with scientists and researchers worldwide that signatories are flooding in not only from within Europe but also from other countries such as the United States and Canada, Australia and New Zealand." The group's letter warns the U.N. that "the general-circulation models of climate on which international policy is at present founded are unfit for their purpose". The Declaration adds that the models, which have predicted far more warming than they should, "are not remotely plausible as policy tools", in that "they ... exaggerate the effect of greenhouse gases such as CO2" and "ignore the fact that enriching the atmosphere with CO2 is beneficial".

The following is a relevant extract from an open letter from CLINTEL to Bill Gates in 2020:

"One of the questions we are working intensively on is climate sensitivity – how much global warming is natural and how much is caused by our enterprises and industries. Contrary to what current theoretical models project, we have concluded that the actual climate sensitivity to doubled CO2 is far from alarming. Our conclusion fits with all observations that have been made in the past 60 years.... With all respect, your statement that climate change could be worse than the current pandemic, follows the multitude of 'copy-cat' statements by the climate catastrophe consensus claims. The proclaimed "climate crisis" exists in the computer models only. Many scientists have already shown that the most often referred to doom scenario RCP 8.5 is extremely unlikely. Latest insight and observations clearly confirm that there is no climate catastrophe." - see Endnote [4]

These diligent scientists who dispute the UN climate change narrative are not given airtime on the BBC or other government/corporate media channels of the world. The thousands of doctors and scientists that have proved the WHO covid-19 narrative is fake have been censored in the same way. Do you see the similarity and that there is an agenda at play?

It should be noted that UN climate change computer models have clearly been demonstrated to be seriously flawed and inaccurate. In addition, data from 1900 to the 1960s, listing temperatures warmer than today, has not been represented validly in the models. Contrary to what we are told on TV, forest fires are actually less frequent than they used to be. In 1928, on average around 42 million acres were lost each year to forest fires in the US, now the number is less than 7 million. Even if the earth is warming slightly, there is no evidence that any such warming is detrimental to food production.

The climate scientists that claim CO_2 is causing climate change, are most often those working for government, EU, and UN institutions that receive vast funding for climate change related projects and initiatives. It is easy to go along with the narrative when you are being paid to! Few people, it seems, rock the boat when salaries and funding could depend on it. Deluded and emotionally manipulated climate change warriors see the war against CO_2 as a way to become famous for 'saving the world'. In contrast, rational independent scientists admit that there is no validated evidence for manmade CO_2 emissions causing climate change.

There are many well-intentioned people working in the environmental and sustainable development sector – the opportunity remains to re-evaluate the evidence/data in relation to the IPCC narrative, to be open to the analysis of other scientists, and to redirect the environmental movement back to 'real' environmental problems that do actually exist. This unproven 'climate change due to CO_2' theory has distracted significantly from peoples understanding of what real environmentalism is and involves.

The geological archive reveals that Earth's climate has varied as long as the planet has existed, with natural cold and warm phases. The world has warmed significantly less than predicted by IPCC on the basis of modelled anthropogenic forcing. The gap between the real world and the modelled world tells us that we are far from understanding climate change. Climate models have many shortcomings and are not remotely plausible as global policy tools. They blow up the effect of greenhouse gases, such as CO_2, and ignore the fact that enriching the atmosphere with CO_2 is beneficial. Furthermore, relevant data showing that temperatures were higher in the early 1900s than today appears to have been omitted from climate modelling, see Endnote [5].

CO_2 is plant food, the basis of all life on Earth. Thousands of actual industrial pollutants exist, but CO_2 is not a pollutant. CO_2 is essential to all life on Earth. More CO_2 is beneficial for nature, greening the Earth: additional CO_2 in the air has promoted growth in global plant biomass. It is also good for agriculture, increasing the yields of crops worldwide, see Endnote [6].

The UN Agenda 2030 plan and the Paris Agreement goal to reduce CO_2 emissions by 7% per annum until 2030 is in effect a plan that will disable the resource mechanisms of the industrial economy for the food, energy and goods that enable human life and survival. This is being done before humanity has transitioned away from the flawed polluting trans-national industrial economy toward self-sufficient local economies. Whether you believe the 'plug is being pulled' intentionally or not, this inevitably amounts to a de-population outcome. The dependency of humanity on a globalised system was created for decades by an international political corporate hierarchy rampantly promoting and implementing flawed trans-national systems for agriculture, energy and goods. These globalised oil-dependent systems become useless as the availability of oil is reduced. It is clear that the science, data and modelling behind the IPPC CO_2 narrative is flawed, and that the Paris Agreement plan to reduce CO_2 emissions so quickly could have a significant de-population effect. These potentially genocidal narratives must be exposed.

The CO_2 hoax is an ideology without scientific evidence that is being utilised as a basis for the implementation of further taxing the people of the world – in this way it is a form of control further limiting people's financial wellbeing and limiting people's access to current forms of energy. What is happening is the man and woman on the street are being hit with the taxes, but, in comparison to industry, military, etc, the general population use a comparatively small percentage of the fossils fuels being consumed. The tragedy is that the climate change political agenda detracted significantly from peoples understanding of what real environmentalism is and conditioned a generation of people with a lie. The truth can rectify that.

The modern green movement is far removed from the original principles of environmentalism

The modern-day green movement is far removed from the original principles of real environmentalism, real sustainability and purity of human lifestyles, exemplified by the writings of E.F Schumacher over 50 years ago, and by original ancient scriptures that have long been suppressed, distorted or mistranslated. The original environmental movement has been hijacked by the UN-promoted lie of manmade climate change and politically defined sustainable development (SD). How did this happen? In 1973, there was no climate problem and the anthropogenic CO_2 threat did not exist, but human CO_2 was dragged-in to create support for the construction of nuclear power plants! This wicked political argument was invented by scientist Bert Bolin, a professor of meteorology and friend of Olaf Palme, the Swedish prime minister at that time, who was a strong supporter of nuclear energy. He wrote to Olaf Palme:

> "Because the vast majority of people do not understand anything about physics, thermodynamics, meteorology and climate (and because the vast majority of politicians understand even less about it) – that the effect of carbon dioxide CO2 on climate events, if any, is extremely small and marginal – we are developing from this a possible global warming threatening to people and nature if nothing is done about it." - Bert Bolin, a professor of meteorology

The task of the UN International Panel on Climate Change (IPCC) was to focus on the role of human CO_2 on global warming and it was no surprise that Professor Bert Bolin became the founder and first chairman of IPCC. Yet, many diligent scientists have demonstrated the theory that climate change is caused by emissions, such as CO_2 and methane, is incorrect, unproven and is a political scam. This lie was chosen by the Club of Rome in the 1990s as another excuse to create the so-called new world order and tighten restrictions on the world population. The shocking part is that 179 countries signed on to this world government CO_2 tyranny at the 1992 UN Earth Summit and humanity is mostly unaware of this sinister conspiracy. The world population has been constantly whipped by this lie for the past 30 years.

The computer models used by the UN IPCC are fabricated to legitimate political lies. We are fighting against heads of government and extravagant rich elites who know that CO_2-alarmism will help to increase their power.

The real environmental movement and real sustainability movement was hijacked by the narratives of Co2-induced climate change and 'politically defined sustainable development' and at the '92 UN Earth Summit.

(Note: When I use the term sustainable development in this book, I am referring to the UN political definition and mechanisms). Such conferences are influenced by powerful groups, including the Bilderbergers, the Club of Rome, and the worlds private bankers (Rothschilds, Rockefellers, etc). The major deceptive decrees of the '92 Earth summit were dictated into existence by Baron Edmund de Rothschild of the Rothschild Banking Dynasty. Rothschild got the decrees into the UN resolutions without debate or challenge being permitted. This is described in detail with testimony from George Hunt later in this chapter.

For the past 30 years politically, defined sustainable development has also been a false narrative operating under the cover of continued globalisation and the prioritisation of GDP growth, regardless of whether it is a polluting form of growth or not. Without globalisation and hypergrowth, the debt-money and usury system could not continue to function, and the elite privately-owned world banking system would not continue to receive vast sums of interest from governments. Thus, for decades the deep culture of the world has been subverted and homogenised by rampant corporate consumerism and soulless cosmopolitism, all of which was needed to keep the banker's debt-money racket going. 'Sustainable development' was not actually designed to deliver a utopia of true sustainability at all – yet, the world was sold this utopian lie.

The so-called elites needed to create a worldwide fear that would provide an excuse for the totalitarian world order changes they wanted to implement in the future. The concept of climate change was utilised. The UN Agenda 21/2030 and WEF 'great reset' plans are sold to the world as a solution to problems of climate change and covid-19. These are, in reality, marketing plans that sell these concepts to the world population. Protection of the environment is being used as an excuse to bring in technocratic and international institutional control of all land, private property, energy, food production and, thus, people. These plans limit human freedoms and access to energy. The UN/WEF idea is to move populations into so-called smart cities, whereby all people, resources, production and consumption on earth are micro-managed by a digital and scientific technocracy, i.e., a dictatorship. These are in reality implementation plans for the so-called new world order in which people will not have access to their own land, energy or resources.

> "In 1991, the Club of Rome published a book entitled The First Global Revolution in which it admitted to inventing climate change as a common enemy of mankind in order to unite the world."
> - Dr Vernon Coleman, Author

As a result of the bogus and incorrect claims of the UN, the EU, and world corporate media, climate change activists have become increasingly hysterical thinking that the world is going to end in a matter of years. Such psychologically insane predictions are not supported by a shred of real validated scientific evidence. There is no proof that any warming is due to CO_2 or methane emissions. The deluded campaigners wish to stop the world from using fossil fuels, but, in reality that drastic action would significantly limit access to heat, energy, transport and food for the world's poor and condemn them to starvation, malnutrition and early death.

It should be noted that most renewable energies only produce a marginal amount of electricity and are definitely not a solution to the world's energy supply challenges. According to the International Energy Agency, we will still obtain only around 5% of energy needs from renewable sources by the year 2040. Without fossil fuels, this will result in no heating, no manufacturing, reduced food availability, no cooking, no lighting, no TVs or electronic devices, etc., whether you think it is intentional or not, all of this would amount to significant de-population. The UN plans are to reduce carbon emissions by 7% per annum, and the institutional frameworks are being imposed before humanity has had an opportunity to transition from reliance on the globalised hypergrowth economy to local systems of self-sufficiency for food, energy, goods and water. Few people even recognise the need to make that transition, and local systems for self-sufficiency are certainly not part of government plans.

In the US, the government's Green New Deal (GND) is based on the lie of anthropogenic global warming and seeks "a national, social industrial and economic mobilisation at a scale not seen since WW2 and proposes net-zero national green-house gas emissions through a fair and just transition for all communities and workers". A transition to what exactly? A transition to technocratic control and the 'electrification of everything' is the answer.

Evidence from renowned scientists that demolishes the fake climate change hysteria

> "deeply flawed logic, obscured by shrewd and unrelenting propaganda, actually enabled a coalition of powerful special interests to convince nearly everyone in the world that Co2 from human industry was a dangerous plant destroying toxin. It will be remembered as the greatest mass delusion in the history of the world – that Co2 the life of plants was considered for a time to be a deadly poison."
> – Professor Richard Lindzen, Professor Emeritus of Atmospheric Sciences at MIT.

Many scientists have demolished the extreme weather panic and other hysterical arguments in lectures that are available online. For example, a presentation by scientist **Dr Willie Soon**, see Endnote [7], shows temperatures in the USA were actually higher in the 1930s than they are today; the number of tornadoes in the USA is less today than in the 1970s when detailed records began; that the greenhouse effect in the world has flattened (is not increasing at all) from 1992 to today despite increased CO_2; email communications of the climate change advocate scientists indicating that they cannot account for the lack of global warming in their data sets; and the flaws in the IPCC climate models. Detractors have pointed out that Dr Soon's research project was funded in part by the coal industry, however, note that the amount of funding his research project received is tiny in comparison to vast funds that have been allocated to the promotion of the manmade climate change ideology across the world.

Note also **Professor Franco Battaglia** has published a paper, see Endnote [8], stating that the EU's energy policy of the last 20 years has been 'dead wrong'. The following is an extract:

> "AN OPEN LETTER TO THE MEMBERS OF THE EU'S PARLIAMENT SOARING ENERGY BILLS: A FAILURE OF THE EU By Franco Battaglia Professor of Chemical Physics and Environmental Chemistry Università di Modena, Italy. Introduction: The EU's energy policy of the last 20 years has been dead wrong, to say the least. Here it is in a nutshell:1)It is based on the assumption that human activities have a bad influence on climate, mainly due to CO2 emissions.2) In order to reduce CO2 emissions several actions are needed: promote renewables, mainly sun and wind energy; promote energy saving; promote energy efficiency.3) All the above will have the beneficial side effect of creating jobs, thereby increasing wellness and providing prosperity; in a word, this is the green economy.
>
> The purpose of this paper is to show you that the three items above are –all of them –wrong. In particular, I'll show that:
>
> 1) Human activities have had no detectable impact on climate.
>
> 2) Most importantly –aside from the fact that even if they had an impact on climate (and they do not) it might even be beneficial –whatever the consequences on climate, reducing CO2 emissions will jeopardize our well being, our civilization, and even our own life. Enacting the EU policy could

mean the death of millions and sentence billions of people in the developing world to lives of continued poverty and short lifespans: Securing energy, not climate, is the real problem mankind has to face.

3) Solar energy (specifically, wind and photovoltaic technologies) is a fraud and no CO2-emission reduction can be expected from them. Energy saving is the most dangerous manoeuvre we could make, and energy efficiency, as good to pursue as it might be, does not help in tackling our real problem.

4) Not by producing energy but by consuming energy jobs are created: the green economy is a scam.

Nature, not human activity rules the climate I am a member of the NIPCC (Non-governmental International Panel on Climate Change). NIPCC has evaluated the same scientific literature at disposal of the more famous IPCC, which, together with Al Gore, received a Nobel Prize in 2007. It was a Nobel Price for Peace, not for Science. And, indeed, the members of the NIPCC, most of which are experienced and distinguished scientists, conclude that IPCC's resolutions are scientifically very questionable"

Another climate scientist with impeccable credentials that has broken rank is **Dr Mototaka Nakamura**. He asserts: "Our models are mickey-mouse mockeries of the real world". Dr Nakamura received a Doctorate of Science from MIT, and for nearly 25 years specialized in abnormal weather and climate change at prestigious institutions that included MIT, Georgia Institute of Technology, NASA, Jet Propulsion Laboratory, California Institute of Technology, JAMSTEC and Duke University. Dr Nakamura explains why the data foundation underpinning global warming science is "untrustworthy" and cannot be relied on and that: "Global mean temperatures before 1980 are based on untrustworthy data".

Temperatures were higher in the 1930s than today, but the UN ignores that data

Professor John R. Christy, Director of Atmospheric and Earth Sciences, University of Alabama, has provided detailed analysis of climate data, see Endnote [9]. I summarise the main points from his analysis below:

"The established global warming theory significantly misrepresents the impact of extra greenhouse gases; the weather that affects people the most is not becoming more extreme or more dangerous; **temperatures were higher in the 1930s than today; between 1895 and 2015, 14 of the top 15 years with the highest heat records occurred before 1960**; the temperatures we are experiencing now in 2021 were the same as 120 years ago.

The accumulated cyclone (hurricane) energy in 2020 is less than the average and less than in 1933; the number of major tornadoes between 1954 and 1986 averaged 56/year, but between 1987 and 2020 the average was only 34/year; between 1895 and 2015 on average there has been no change in the number of very wet days per month, and no change in the number of very dry days per month, and the 20 driest months were before 1988.

Between 1950 and 2019 the percentage of land area experiencing droughts has not increased globally – the trend is flat; the incidence of wildfires in North America between 1600 and 2000 has decreased substantially, in particular since 1879, an era of livestock grazing and fire suppression techniques, and due to fire suppression techniques dry, unburned fuel load rose dramatically; 2020 was not the worst fire season (as has been claimed), it was a natural burning of stocks of dead trees that had accumulated since 2012; the global burned area has been steadily decreasing since 1943; in relation to the average area of snowfall between 1967 and 2020 there is no trend – it still snows.

Antarctic sea ice coverage has increased up to 2014, then dropped for 3 years, and has been increasing significantly again since 2017; there is much more sea ice today than there was 2,000 years ago, coverage has been dropping in recent years in the artic.

Sea levels rose 12.5 cm per decade for 8,000 years and then it levelled off, now it rising only 2.5 cm per decade (the UN tell you that carbon emissions from the fossil fuel economy are causing rising sea levels, but **sea levels were rising much faster in the past 'before' the fossil fuel economy**); by 1850 sea levels were at a low point and then started to rise again; worrying about 30 cm rise in sea level in a decade is ridiculous, in a hurricane the east coast of the U.S. gets a 20 foot rise in 6 hours, so a 30 cm rise will be easily handled.

Wealth lost to weather disasters has actually been declining; climate related deaths have plummeted; hundreds of thousands of people used to die from hurricanes now it's just dozens.

The scientific consensus (the model average) is +0.40 degree C/ decade, but the observed average temperature increase currently is +0.17 degree C/decade (less than half of what has been predicted).

EIA data indicates amount of Co_2 being released worldwide will not be peaking before 2040. Even if you accept UN climate modelling, will Co_2 regulations in the US save the planet? The answer is no, because **even if the US completely ceased to exist it would have a negligible effect on the worldwide total Co_2 emissions volume**. The tremendous COP agreements to limit Co_2 have had no effect whatsoever on the global trend of rising Co_2 emissions.

In addition, it has been reported that 100 years of climate data, showing that temperatures in the past were actually higher than today (proving the UN IPPC is incorrect), was deleted from a Canadian government policy report, see Endnote [10].

In a lecture titled *The imaginary climate crisis – how can we change the message?* Available on the Irish Climate Science Forum website, see Endnote [11]. **Richard L Lindzen, Professor Emeritus of Atmospheric Sciences at MIT** summarises the battle against the climate hysteria as follows:

"**in the long history of the earth there has been almost no correlation between climate and co2... the paloeclimate record shows unambiguously that Co_2 is not a control knob... the narrative is absurd... it gives governments the power to control the energy sector...** for about 33 years, many of us have been battling against the climate hysteria... There were more important leading people who were objecting to it, they were unfortunately older and by now most of them dead...

Elites are always searching for ways to advertise their virtue and assert their authority. **They believe they are entitled to view science as a source of authority rather than a process, and they try to appropriate science**, suitably and incorrectly simplified, as the basis for their movement. Movements need goals, and these goals are generally embedded in legislation. The effect of legislation long outlasts the alleged science. As long as scientists are rewarded for doing so they are unlikely to oppose the exploitation of science.

The 'educated' class is most vulnerable to the absurd narrative... when we talk about science we are to talking to people who have no idea even of the vocabulary... the educated masses are aware of their scientific ignorance and this leaves them very insecure... they need simple narratives it allows them to believe that they actually do understand the science, and as we see today with climate it allows them to become ignorantly proud of their alleged accomplishment... the situation is compounded when it comes to climate where... most scientists are also ignorant, but where their support for the narrative comforts the non-scientists. I suspect... this elite (educated class) feels they need to show they too have met challenges even if the challenges are purely imaginary, this seems particularly true of young people... most ordinary people don't have these problems.

Our task is to show the relevant people the people who make decisions for us, the political people, the overall stupidity of this issue rather than punching away at the details... it is likely that we have to capitalise on the insecurity of the educated elite and make them look silly instead of superior and virtuous. We must remember that they are impervious to real science unless it is reduced to their level... Whether we are capable of doing is an open question." - Richard L Lindzen, Professor Emeritus of Atmospheric Sciences, MIT

UN IPPC committee chairman resigned in protest at UN IPPC lies and false information

Dr Nils-Axel Mörner was a former Committee Chairman at the UN IPPC. He was a world authority on sea levels and former head of the Paleo Geo-physics and Geo-dynamics dept in Stockholm. He was the top sea level expert involved in reviewing the first IPPC documents. He says the IPPC is misleading humanity about climate change and sea level and that a new solar cooling period is not far off. He tried to warn the IPPC were publishing lies and false information that would inevitably be discredited, but they ignored him so he resigned in disgust and decided to blow the whistle. In an interview, see Endnote [12], **he stated "This is the most dangerous and frightening part of it. How a lobbyist group, such as the IPPC, has been able to fool the whole world. These organised and deceitful forces are dangerous"** and expressed shock that the UN and governments would parade children around the place at UN Climate summits as propaganda props.

"we must get this Co2 disease out of science... (Are sea levels rising worldwide?) No certainly not... solar activity is the dominant factor in climate and not Co2... something is basically sick in the blame Co2 hypothesis... It was launched more than 100 years ago and almost immediately excellent physicists demonstrated that the hypothesis did not work then later, in time for the IPPC project, it was dug up and used as a tool to promote this terrible idea…

I was the chairman of the only international committee on sea levels changes and as such a person I was elected to be the expert reviewer on the (UN IPPC) sea levels chapter. **It was written by 38 persons and not a single one was a sea level specialist… I was shocked by the low quality it was like a student paper**… I went through it and showed them that it was wrong and wrong and wrong – in one case I said look at your own diagram it shows that what you are writing is wrong, and what did they do? They took off their diagram and left the writing!

"The scientific truth is on the side of the sceptics… **When you come to the idea of '97% of scientists agree' – this is just a lobbying trick 97%. I have thousands of high ranked scientists all over the world who agree that NO, CO2 is not the driving mechanism and that everything is exaggerated.** There is no way that sea levels can rise by two meters by the beginning of the next century… this is against physics…

In the field of physics 80 to 90% of physicists know that the Co2 hypothesis is wrong - amongst geologists and astronomers 80% know the hypothesis… is wrong.

Of course, metrologists they believe in this because that is their own profession - they live on it… I suspect that behind-the-scenes promoters… have an ulterior motive… It's a wonderful way of controlling taxation controlling people." - Dr Nils-Axel Mörner, a former Committee Chairman at the UN IPPC.

Most of the scientists that say climate change is a problem are on perpetual government grants

Patrick Moore, co-founder of Greenpeace, and President of Greenpeace in Canada for seven years, states:

"the whole climate crisis is not only fake news its fake science… of course climate change is real its been happening since the beginning of time, but its not dangerous and it's not caused by people… climate change is a perfectly natural phenomenon and this modern warming period actually began about 300 years ago when the little ice age began to come to an end. There is nothing to be afraid of and all they are doing is instilling fear. **Most of the scientists who are saying it's a crisis are on perpetual government grants**

I was one of the (Greenpeace) founders… by the mid-80s… **we were hijacked by the extreme left who basically took Greenpeace from a science-based organisation to an organisation based on sensationalism, misinformation and fear**…

you don't have a plan to feed 8 billion people without fossils fuels or get the food into the cities… there is not going to be electric trucks anytime soon… **If we ban fossils fuels, first agricultural production would collapse… Every tree would be cut down if fossil fuels are banned because that would be all there was for fuel and heating and cooking**" – Patrick Moore, co-founder of Greenpeace

"this (climate change) has become some kind of religion, even the Pope is into it!" - Patrick Moore

Professor William Happer, Princeton University, Former Director of Science at the US Department of Energy, is also a strong voice against the myth of manmade global warming. He states: "More Co2 benefits the earth".

UN IPPC cherry picks data, uses flawed modelling and scenarios not remotely related to the real world

"The computer models are making systematic dramatic errors… they are all parametrised… fudged… the models really don't work" – Patrick J. Michaels, Director, Cato Institute Center for the Study of Science

Dr Roger Pielke Jr, University of Colorado, has conducted a detailed scientific review and analysis of the UN IPCC AR6 report, see Endnote [13]. I list the main points from Dr Pielke's analysis as follows:

The IPPC claim an increasing trend in 'normalised' U.S. hurricane damage, but, in relation to this Dr Pielke quickly noticed that the IPPC have been playing "fast and loose with science". Dr Pielke and his team had introduced the 'normalised' methodology and terminology to the literature in 1998. To support their claim of an increasing hurricane trend, **the IPPC had cherry picked one paper out of 54** – the other 53 papers stated there was not an increasing trend! Subject matter experts, such as Dr Pielke can readily see when the IPCC deviates from its mission to accurately assess the relevant literature. Out of 15 climate areas in the IPPC report are only two areas where you can make claims for a potential connection of climate to carbon emissions.

In relation to climate modelling, the IPCC detached the models from socio-economic plausibility. In creating the models, **instead of first completing integrative assessment models (IAMs), the IPCC skipped this essential step and jumped straight to radiative forcing scenarios** and thus these scenarios are not based on competed IAMs. This led much of climate modelling down the wrong track. The four IPCC scenarios came from a large family of models so instead of splitting modelling from socio-economic assumptions the models already had the assumptions faked and baked in to them, because they had to have those assumptions to produce the required radiative forcing (to produce a desired climate 'crisis scenario' outcome).

In another fateful decision the 4 representative concentration pathways (RCPs) came from 4 different IAMs, **which was a huge mistake.** These models are completely unrelated to each other, but the impression has been given that they are of a common set, only differing in their radiative forcing, this was a huge mistake.

How the IPCC detached climate modeling from socio-economic plausibility

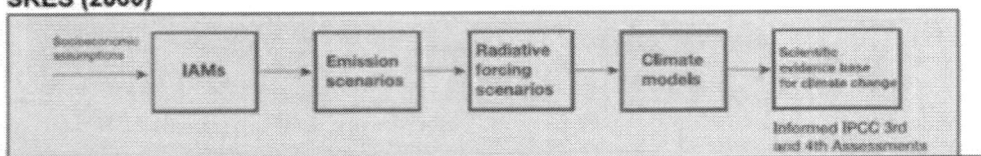

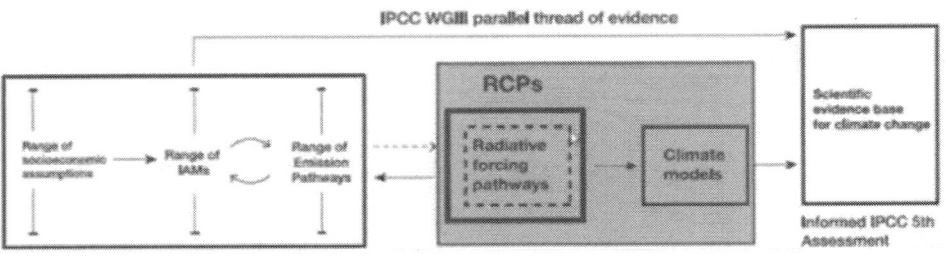

See Pielke and Ritchie (2021)

Furthermore, no-one has responsibility for determining whether these scenarios are plausible. The climate community decided which scenario to prioritise and they chose the two most implausible scenarios! There are thousands of climate assumptions, but only 8 to 12 of them are available currently for climate research. **The IPPC report even states that "no likelihood is attached to the scenarios in this report".** The likelihood is considered low they admit - **This is an incredible admission by the IPCC. This should have been one of the top line messages from this report but it was not!**

48 *1.6.1.4 The likelihood of reference scenarios, scenario uncertainty and storylines*
49
50 In general, no likelihood is attached to the scenarios assessed in this Report. The use of different scenarios

But at the same time

14 uncertainties in underlying long-term projections of economic drivers (Christensen et al., 2018). However,
15 the likelihood of high emission scenarios such as RCP8.5 or SSP5-8.5 is considered low in light of recent
16 developments in the energy sector (Hausfather and Peters, 2020a, 2020b). Studies that consider possible
17 future emission trends in the absence of additional climate policies, such as the recent IEA 2020 World
18 Energy Outlook 'stated policy' scenario (International Energy Agency, 2020), project approximately
19 constant fossil and industrial CO_2 emissions out to 2070, approximately in line with the medium RCP4.5,
20 RCP6.0 and SSP2-4.5 scenarios (Hausfather and Peters, 2020b) and the 2030 global emission levels that are
21 pledged as part of the Nationally Determined Contributions (NDCs) under the Paris Agreement (Section

More than half of the scenarios mentioned in the AR6 WG1 report are those judged low likelihood by IPCC AR6 and are generally viewed as implausible (8.5 and 7.0 specifically)... such research should not be conflated with projections of plausible futures or for use in impact, economic or policy studies. IPPC unfortunately engages in such conflation.

These extreme unlikely scenarios dominate the literature and the IPCC report; therefore, the IPCC report is biased. Bottom line is that there is massive confusion. **The IPCCs' Richard Moss warned that RCP 8.5 was not to be used as a reference for the other RCPs, but 5,800 scientific papers worldwide misuse it like that.**

The RCPs are not in fact RCPs, they are re-named from pre-existing scenarios, which come with fully characterised socio-economic inputs (e.g., population, GDP, etc). The reality is the RCPs are different models that cannot be compared. They are completely different fictional worlds that cannot be compared, for example, there is a billion more people in one RCP compared to another or twice the global GDP, etc. **The whole process is seriously flawed**, and same problems exist with the shared socio-economic pathways (SSPs). **Nothing close to the real world is represented by the IPCC scenarios. Climate science has a huge problem!**

The ICPP currently uses RCP 8.5 as the 'business as usual' scenario, but RCP 8.5 is wild fantasy land and not remotely related to current reality at all.

In summary, **much of climate science is based on implausible scenarios; thousands of climate studies erroneously project the future as if it were plausible;** implausible scenario research makes up a significant portion of the research summarised in leading climate assessments; it is also deeply embedded into policy, such as informing regional and local adaptation planning - this is a huge problem and climate science has a scientific integrity crisis."

Financialization of the world economy based on a life-killing net-zero emissions strategy

Financialization of the entire world economy is now based on a life-killing 'net-zero' greenhouse gas emissions strategy. The decision to drastically reduce CO_2, one of the most essential compounds to sustain all life, is no co-incidence.

> "CO2 for different people has different attractions. After all, what is it? – it's not a pollutant, it's a product of every living creature's breathing, it's the product of all plant respiration, it is essential for plant life and photosynthesis... I mean, if you ever wanted a leverage point to control everything from exhalation to driving, this would be a dream. So it has a kind of fundamental attractiveness to bureaucratic mentality." - Prof. Richard Lindzen, MIT atmospheric scientist

Central bankers are entirely funding and controlling the advancement of the worldwide climate change 'project'

It should be noted that it is **the world's central bankers that are behind this decision and are entirely funding and controlling the advancement of the worldwide climate change 'project'.** In December 2015, the Bank for International Settlements created the Task Force on Climate-related Financial Disclosure (TCFD), which represents $118 trillion of assets globally, see Endnote [14]. In essence this means that the financialization of the entire world economy is based on meeting nonsensical aims such as "net-zero greenhouse gas emissions. The TCFD includes key people from the world's mega-banks and asset management companies, including JP Morgan Chase; BlackRock; Barclays Bank; HSBC; China's ICBC bank; Tata Steel, ENI oil, and Dow Chemical and more.

The fact that world's largest banks and corporations, including BlackRock, Goldman Sachs, the UN, the World Bank, the Bank of England and other central banks of the BIS, have all linked to push a vague, mathematically nonsensical 'green' economy, is no-coincidence. There is another agenda at play that has nothing to do with environmentalism. The green economy along with UN Agenda 2030 is an agenda of world control, and will also develop trillions of dollars for the behind-the-scenes mega-banks. When the world largest banks, corporations, and institutions, all align to push a climate change agenda that has zero evidence, one can see there is another major agenda major going on behind the scenes. This agenda tries to convince the common people of the world to make huge sacrifices under the emotive guise of "saving our planet.", while the corporations and banks make vast profits and implement worldwide technocratic control systems.

> "The links between the world's largest financial groups, central banks and global corporations to the current push for a radical climate strategy to abandon the fossil fuel economy in favor of a vague, unexplained Green economy, it seems, is less about genuine concern to make our planet a clean and healthy environment to live. Rather it is an agenda, intimately tied to the UN Agenda 2030 for "sustainable" economy, and **to developing literally trillions of dollars in new wealth for the global banks and financial giants** who constitute the real powers that be… " - F. William Engdahl, strategic risk consultant and lecturer

Back in 2010 the head of Working Group 3 of the UN IPPC, Dr Otmar Edenhofer, told an interviewer, **"…one must say clearly that we redistribute de facto the world's wealth by climate policy. One has to free oneself from the illusion that international climate policy is environmental policy. This has almost nothing to do with environmental policy** anymore, with problems such as deforestation or the ozone hole."

> "On October 17, 2018, days following the EU agreement at the One Planet Summit, Juncker's EU signed a Memorandum of Understanding with Breakthrough Energy-Europe in which member corporations of Breakthrough Energy-Europe will have preferential access to any funding.

> The members of Breakthrough Energy include Virgin Air's Richard Branson, Bill Gates, Alibaba's Jack Ma, Facebook's Mark Zuckerberg, HRH Prince Al-waleed bin Talal, Bridgewater Associates' Ray Dalio; Julian Robertson of hedge fund giant, Tiger Management; David Rubenstein, founder Carlyle Group; George Soros, Chairman Soros Fund Management LLC; Masayoshi Son, founder Softbank, Japan." - F. William Engdahl, strategic risk consultant and lecturer, see Endnote [15]

Central bankers hijacked the real environmental movement in 1992 creating the fake climate change agenda

Psychopaths can utilise any ideology and, change it from within to something that may eventually be entirely different to its original purpose. Meanwhile, the original followers and advocates continue to pursue what they believe is the original ideology, but gradually become mere pawns in the agenda of a self-serving elite. This is exactly what has happened in the modern-day environmental movement over the past decades.

> "Civilisation as we know it, is largely the creation of psychopaths. Behind the apparent insanity of contemporary history is the actual insanity of psychopaths fighting to preserve their disproportionate power… Psychopaths have played a disproportionate role in the development of civilisation because they are hardwired to lie, kill, injure, and generally inflict great suffering on other humans without feeling any remorse." - Dr Kevin Barrett, Professor at the University of Wisconsin

The information in this sub-chapter is derived from the information provided by Whistleblower George Hunt in a video recording with evidence of the UNCED documents, see Endnote [16]. Hunt served as an official host at a key environmental meeting in Denver, Colorado in 1987, and states that David Rockefeller; Baron Edmund De Rothschild; US Secretary of State Baker; Maurice Strong Maurice Strong, a UN official and an employee of the Rockefeller and Rothschild trusts; EPA administrator William Ruccleshaus; UN Secretary General in Geneva MacNeill, along with World Bank and IMF officials at this meeting. Hunt was surprised to see all these rich elite bankers at the meeting and questioned what were they doing there at an environmental congress. The hypocrisy of these financial elites caring about the environment is evident when we see that Maurice Strong and Ruccleshaus were personalities at the center of a major resource grab controversy in Colorado. According to Hunt, they were key investors in American Water Development, a company which tried to circumvent Colorado water laws and gain control of one of the largest underwear reservoirs in the world.

The UN '92 Earth Summit was held in Rio De Janeiro, Brazil, and was run by the United Nations Committee for Environment and Development (UNCED). Via the Earth summit, the UN was setting a net, an agenda, to place the power over the Earth and its peoples into their own hands. Is it just a coincidence that the UN motto for the summit was 'In Our Hands'? This covert agenda became UN Agenda 21 and then UN Agenda 2030. Wittingly or unwittingly all the governments that signed up to these agendas, in essence, placed their citizens into the hands of this group of world bankers. This group, or cartel, of world bankers are the same ultra-rich banking families that had been instrumental in the setting up of the UN after WWII, in conjunction with their political cohorts Stalin,

Churchill, Roosevelt (and then Truman), who were all steeped or connected with communist control ideology. Note that the communist Stalin and his regime were responsible for the genocide of over 60 million people in Russia, Asia and Eastern Europe, and the internment of millions more in Gulags (communist concentration camps) as evidenced by many historians and the writings of Alexander Solzhenitsyn, Nobel Prize Laureate. Hunt refers to these banking families and their financial and international institutional networks as the new world order, see Endnote [17].

> "The same world order that tricked third world countries to borrow funds and rack up enormous debts… and purposely creating war and debt to bring societies into their control. The world order crowd are not a nice group of people… World power and authority is in their grasp. Are we going to give it to them without a confrontation?... will they blame the environment holocaust on you and get away with it?" – George Hunt, Whistleblower speaking about the UN Earth summit of 1992

As a consequence of the UN Earth Summit, the real and honest environment movement that actually cared about real pollution to land, air and water, was hi-jacked and placed into the hands of the new world order. The UN was in effect acting on behalf of globalist groups, such as the Trilateral Commission and international banking. Via such UN political schemes and with the backing of international finance, the new world order narcissists command politicians to do their bidding and the politicians 'go with the flow' because these private bankers have control over the source of all debt money creation that governments rely on.

Maurice Strong, a UN official and an employee of the Rockefeller and Rothschild trusts had convened the first UNCED congress in Stockholm, Sweden in 1972. 20 years later he was the convenor and secretary general of UNCED. Hunt also describes and displays a paper from an UNCED meeting in De Moines, USA in 1991, where Maurice Strong was in charge, that states:

> "We are the living sponsors of the great Cecil Rhodes will of 1877, in which Rhodes devoted his fortune to the extension of British rule throughout the world… and colonization by British subjects of the entire continent of Africa, the holy land, the valley of the Euphrates,… the whole of South America, the Islands of the Pacific, the whole of the Malay Archipelago, the seaboard of China and Japan, and the ultimate recovery of the United States of America as an integral part of the British empire."

During the Fourth World Congress meeting in 1987, David Lang, an international investment banker, states in the video recording that:

> "I suggest therefore that this be sold not through a democratic process that would take too long and require far too much funds to educate the cannon-fodder, unfortunately, which populates the Earth. We have to take almost an elitist program…"

Thus, the decrees leading to the Earth summit were dictated without debate or opportunity for dissent and would supersede national laws. The decrees were dictated into existence by Edmund de Rothschild, who got these major decrees into the '92 UN resolutions without debate or challenge. Hunt asserts that he was denied the opportunity to openly challenge Rothschild's remarks by the meeting Chairman.

> "The world order wants to create a new society out of the ashes of chaos, a collectivist fourth world complete with complete with a collectivist religion, collectivist finance and unchecked world national socialism, The world order will offer Gaia mother earth to the masses as the big brother image to worship in the fourth world…. The lords of the UNCED conference will be the masters of who gets what and when if we don't do something about it quickly" – George Hunt

Is it any surprise that the Rothschild bank of Geneva is the nucleus of the World Conservation bank and the wealthy elite are integrated into the bank via the Rothschilds private offering of shares. The trick is that by assuming control of world conservation in this way the banking cartel actually controls these world resources and decides how they are allocated or utilized.

Key players that promoted the climate crisis agenda

So, who were the key players that promoted the climate crisis hoax? The mainstream website Wikipedia, under the headings *climate change* and *global warming*, see Endnote [18], describes that the pivotal persons in the worldwide promotion of the climate change agenda included: Davis Guggenheim, who was the Director of the film, *An Inconvenient Truth*, which propelled the climate change agenda into the consciousness of the masses, see Endnote [19]; Jeffrey Skoll, who was the Executive Producer, of the film *An Inconvenient Truth*; Joseph J. Romm, Senior Fellow at the Center for American Progress, see Endnote [20]; Stephen H. Schneider, Professor of Environmental Biology and Global Change, Stanford University, see Endnote [21]; Michael E. Mann, Professor of Meteorology, Pennsylvania State University, see Endnote [22]; Gavin A. Schmidt, Climatologist, NASA Goddard Institute for Space Studies, see Endnote [23]; and Benjamin D. Santer, Climate Researcher, Lawrence Livermore National Laboratory, see Endnote [24].

Wikipedia also describes that key players involved in the promotion of carbon taxes and carbon trading, see Endnote [25], were as follows: Todd D. Stern, Special Envoy for Climate Change, U.S. State Department, see Endnote [26]; Richard L. Sandor, Chairman and Founder, Chicago Climate Exchange (CCX), see Endnote [27]; Nicholas H. Stern, Professor of Economics and Government, London School of Economics, see Endnote [28]; Ignacy Sachs, Socioeconomist, École des Hautes Études en Sciences Sociales, see Endnote [29].

Furthermore, as many people have pointed out, can one be blamed for wondering is it just an extra-ordinary co-incidence that every one of the above coteries of key players are documented to be Ashkenazi Jews, see Endnote [30]. In relation to *An Inconvenient Truth*, the director, the executive producer and all the producers are Ashkenazi Jews, see Endnote [31]. Jews are approximately 1-2% of the U.S. population, see Endnote [32]. Therefore, the probability that most of the key individuals promoting anthropogenic climate change, carbon taxes, and carbon trading would be Jews is infinitesimally small. (Aside: I note that some notable Jewish commentators and historians maintain that Ashkenazi Jews are not the original Jews from the Palestine region. They maintain that they are Khazars that originated from central Asia, who were in essence a self-serving political group that infiltrated Judaism long ago for the purposes of controlling the lucrative banking sector. Jews controlled the banking sector because for centuries Christians considered the practice of usury a sin.)

Greta Thunberg is part of a network tied to the organization of Former Vice-President Al Gore, who was featured in the film *An Inconvenient Truth*. Thunberg is being cynically and professionally marketed and used by organizations, including the UN, the EU Commission and the interests behind the fake climate change agenda. Gore is an enormously wealthy climate profiteer, and Gore's partner, ex-Goldman Sachs official David Blood, is a member of the Bank of International Settlements-created TCFD. Greta Thunberg and her friend, Jamie Margolin, were both listed as "special youth advisor and trustee" of the Swedish We Don't Have Time NGO, founded by its CEO Ingmar Rentzhog, who is a member of Al Gore's Climate Reality Organization Leaders, and part of the European Climate Policy Task Force, see Endnote [33]. Al Gore's Climate Reality Project is a partner of We Don't have Time, see Endnote [34].

Congresswoman, and former bartender, Alexandria Ocasio-Cortez (AOC) was responsible for unveiling a "Green New Deal" to completely re-design the US economy at an incredible cost of perhaps $100 trillion. She openly admitted that she ran for Congress at the urging of a group called Justice Democrats. AOC's advisers include Justice Democrats co-founder, Zack Exley. According to the New Yorker magazine, the Green New Deal was written over a single weekend by staff of the freshman representative. Cortez's Chief of Staff told the magazine "We spent the weekend learning how to put laws together. We looked up how to write resolutions"

The Chicago Climate Exchange and the trillion-dollar money-generating hoax

Former US President, Barrack Obama, was also a key player involved in the climate change agenda. Even as man-made global warming was being exposed as a money-generating hoax, in possibly one of the largest ever examples of insider trading, before he was president, Obama was working feverishly to push the controversial cap-and-trade carbon reduction scheme through Congress. The Cap & Trade Bill taxes businesses and individuals for carbon dioxide emissions, and has been able to make vast sums of money per year since Obama got the US Congress to unwittingly pass the infamous Cap & Trade Bill. Obama was promoted as an agent of 'hope and change' for the American people, yet he was really the agent of 'trillion-dollar change' for his cohorts making money down at the Chicago Climate Exchange (CCX), see Endnote [35]. The future worth of the annual business of the CCX has been estimated at ten trillion dollars per annum.

CCX is a U.S. corporation, and has members companies from all sectors and offset projects worldwide, see Endnote [36]. Through their CCX membership, its member companies were first in the world to make legally binding commitments to reduce all six greenhouse gases, in the world's first multinational multi-sector market and trading system for reducing and trading greenhouse gases. CCX is operated by the public company Climate Exchange PLC, which also owns the European Climate Exchange. Richard Sandor, creator of the Sustainable Performance Group, founded the exchange and has been a spokesman for it. The exchange trades in emissions of six gases: carbon dioxide, methane, nitrous oxide, sulfur hexafluoride, perfluorocarbons and hydrofluorocarbons. CCX started trading in October 2003, prior to the commencement of trading in the European Union through the ETS system, see Endnote [37].

Al Gore, Goldman Sachs, and GIM, a London-based Generation Investment Management purchased a huge stake in CCX. The founder of GIM is none other than former Vice President Al Gore (also) along with Goldman Sachs personnel, such as David Blood (former Goldman executive), Mark Ferguson (Goldman) and Peter Harris (Goldman) to name a few, see Endnote [38].

Deceptive narratives on covid-19, UN agenda 2030, climate change, and the WEF reset

UN Agenda 2030, is being promoted as a solution to everything from poverty to so-called climate change, but it really is designed to empower a global governing body, enforcing totalitarian socialism and corporate control of everything. The current world situation is a result of decades of planning and ulterior political and corporate developments by a small group i.e., the so-called elites – in reality they are a criminal cabal. A large percentage of the world's population have been behaving like mind-controlled zombies and have succumbed to the constant barrage of propaganda about climate change, from governments and the UN. However, climate change is certainly the not the only deception to be aware of.

The reality is that for decades there have been false and deceptive narratives disseminated by organisations, including the UN, WEF, the WHO, by the governments that comply with these narratives and by the corporate-owned media. These false narratives include the deceptive political schemes of sustainable development, Agenda 21/2030, combating climate change by reducing carbon emission, and the WEF 'reset' of Society under cover of what has been proven to be a fake pandemic, based on the fraudulent Covid PCR test.

The UN, WHO, and WEF are all unaccountable, unelected privately-motivated organisations that have for decades imposed their brand of policies over the governments of the world. The WHO is an unelected private organisation and its second largest donor is Bill Gates, the vaccine dealer and known eugenicist. Prior to the fake covid-19 pandemic, Tedros Ghebreyesus, an accused genocidist, see Endnote [39], was appointed head of the WHO in order to orchestrate the pandemic and facilitate plans for bio-pharmaceutical totalitarianism.

> 'To achieve world government, it is necessary to remove from the minds of men their individualism, loyalty to family tradition, national patriotism and religious dogmas.' - George Brock Chisholm, first director general of the World Health Organisation

In addition, globalisation, artificially created boom-bust economic cycles, and the debt-money system have been central to the accumulation of immense wealth by the moneyocracy, i.e., a small group that owns and controls the privately owned banking system, the money creation process, world finance and associated mega-corporations. The moneyocracy involves so-called elite upper echelons of the international corporate-banking-political sector that is entirely controlled by the source of all world finance, i.e., the privately owned banking worldwide cartel/cabal. These schemes and processes have all been utilised for the purposes of greed, power and authoritarian control to the general detriment of the overwhelming majority of the world population. UN Agenda 21/2030, the Paris Climate Agreement, the Fourth Industrial Revolution and the proposed WEF 'reset' offer an insight into how a small group of extremely wealthy globalists want to further control and dictate the lives of all people over the course of the next decades as part of a plan for world governance.

The 2020 WEF/UN world society 'reset' is not a response to an economic collapse caused by covid-19. No, an aligned world economic reset was implemented by the world's central bankers' months prior to covid-19. The pre-planned world lockdown intentionally collapsed local economies worldwide to increase dependency on the 'system' and make way for the imposition a new world order technocratic system that operates according to their rules not yours. More climate panic, virus scares, orchestrated punch-and-judy show wars, and geo-political theatre is on way. The real test of these events will come when inflation rockets, prices of necessities significantly increase, and joblessness becomes commonplace, how many people will then clamour for the globalist-imposed solution and how many will build their own local systems. Much of the population has been fooled by their TV, but also many millions of people are waking up to the lies.

Renewable energy is not a viable solution to the world's energy problems

The current green energy/renewable energy technologies being promoted by the UN and WEF are not a viable solution for the world's energy supply. The cost for the U.S. government's GND will run into trillions on renewable energy infrastructure etc., yet, despite decades of government subsidies wind power provides just 6% of the nation's energy, and solar just 1 %. Such plans are complete foolishness, 100% renewable energy defies the laws of physics and it is impossible to attain. The Energy Returned on Energy Invested (EROEI) is much too low – in essence the entire process is mathematically flawed. For example, it takes more energy and to create and maintain a national wind turbine-based energy network than it will ever produce.

Renewable energy is mathematical madness, but, of course most national politicians are not energy analysts, they naively rely on what their teddy bear economists tell them. The shocking and bizarre reality is most economists, have no understanding or knowledge of EROEI. Most economists and policy makers are deluded by their own pseudo-science of contemporary economics and do not understand that the economy runs on energy and resources – not money! Contemporary economics is a type of dogmatic pseudo-science that is not based on reality and does not account for energy in the system – probably it was never supposed to because it is a primarily a measuring tool for the process of rampant globalisation.

The promoters of the politically defined "green" future, that includes plans such as the widespread implementation of wind turbines, being pedalled to us, unfortunately, do not know what they are talking about. This is evidenced by the work of Professor David MacKay, Regius Professor of Engineering at Cambridge University and former Chief Scientific Advisor to the UK's Department of Energy and Climate Change, in his book "*Sustainable Energy without Hot Air*", see Endnote [40]. Free books and summaries of Professor MacKay's work were even distributed throughout the government department whilst I worked there. His analysis shows that **an area twice the size of the entire country of Wales would need to be completely covered with wind turbines to meet**

the energy demand in the U.K., based on average energy consumption per person. The following is an important extract from his book:

> "First, for any renewable facility to make an appreciable contribution – a contribution at all comparable to our current consumption – it has to be country-sized. To provide one quarter of our current energy consumption by growing energy crops, for example, would require 75% of Britain to be covered with biomass plantations. To provide 4% of our current energy consumption from wave power would require 500 km of Atlantic coastline to be completely filled with wave farms. Someone who wants to live on renewable energy, but expects the infrastructure associated with that renewable not to be large or intrusive, is deluding himself."

> Second, if economic constraints and public objections are set aside, it would be possible for the average European energy consumption of 125 kWh/d per person to be provided from these country-sized renewable sources. The two hugest contributors would be photovoltaic panels, which, covering 5% or 10% of the country, would provide 50 kWh/d per person; and offshore wind farms, which, filling a sea-area twice the size of Wales, would provide another 50 kWh/d per person on average. Such an immense panelling of the countryside and filling of British seas with wind machines (having a capacity five times greater than all the wind turbines in the world today) may be possible according to the laws of physics, but would the public accept and pay for such extreme arrangements? If we answer no, **we are forced to conclude that current consumption will never be met by British renewables.** "- Professor David MacKay, former Chief Scientific Advisor to the UK's Department of Energy and Climate Change

Politicians have been in denial of the huge cost of 'going green'. **Governments have been naively believing that the more wind turbines are built, the cheaper and better and safer energy production becomes.** However, the reality is wind power is very expensive and very costly to maintain and stabilise and increasingly unreliable in periods when the wind does not blow. This realisation is now beginning to hit home very hard along with the realisation that the cost of these net zero carbon policies is astronomical

> "These 17 sustainable development goals, are all driving towards a Green Agenda, capitalism painted Green, at a horrendous cost for mankind and for the resources of the world. But it is sold under the label of creating a more sustainable world… They seem to ignore the enormous fossil fuel use to convert to a green energy-driven economy. "- Perter Koenig, former Analyst at the World Bank

The modern-day cult of climate change and renewable energy is sleeping walking a large chunk of humanity toward its own destruction, and is therefore extremely dangerous. Furthermore, the word sustainable was hijacked decades ago, it has become a code-word for a reorganization of world to further benefit ultra-rich elites who couldn't care less about the environment. The original architects behind these worldwide plans know all this of course. The worldwide governmental promotion of renewable energy is based on the 'instructions' of the unelected UN and the unelected WEF – it is a political decision aligned with an agenda of the elites. Renewable energy has nothing to do with protecting the environment or your wellbeing, and has nothing to do with providing you with cheap reliable energy – in fact the result will be the opposite. In 2022, I trust you will have noticed that energy prices are sky rocketing worldwide.

In 2019, in response to the deepening energy crisis, the EU actually proposed to bring nuclear and natural gas into the 'green finance taxonomy' – this is an acknowledgment that renewable agenda is suffering a severe crisis and that a way to keep energy prices in check is to build new gas fired power plants, see Endnote [41]. In relation to public opinion, Ipsos Mori polls in 2019 showed that those people who support the general idea of net-zero carbon will only do so until they are asked to pay for it. The moment they are confronted with the costs their enthusiasm drops!

Furthermore, it appears that the age of oil and therefore current industrial society as we know it may soon be over regardless. In an article '*The End of the Oilcene*', see Endnote [42], analyst Mr. Tim Clarke indicates that the current Energy Returned on Investment (EROI) of oil is too low to sustain industrial economies. Making more so-called 'green stuff' is not going to fix the basic problem of reduced energy availability in the future.

Adopting various so-called "green" energy technologies that have been promoted to produce or save energy is analogous to increasing consumption. That's because the structures and grids required for this technology use a great deal of energy to manufacture and implement, they do not give back the energy with an "energy profit" that was used in its implementation. The term consumption in economic analysis really means the consumption of energy and natural resources wrapped up in manufactured products. Making more stuff, even if it is marketed as being "green", is not going to address the basic problem of reduced energy availability in the future.

The nonsense of electric cars

> "The energy cost (hydrocarbon-energy from oil and coal) of producing solar panels and windmills is astounding. So, today's electric cars – Tesla and Co. – are still driven by hydrocarbon produced electricity – plus their batteries made from lithium destroys pristine landscapes, like huge natural salt flats in Bolivia, Argentina, China and elsewhere. The use of these sources of energy is everything but 'sustainable'" – Peter Koenig, former Analyst at the World bank

The TV adverts contain smiling good-looking people racing about in aerodynamic electric cars akin to dashing heroes saving the planet from imminent CO_2-induced destruction. However, the people that have purchased these new electric cars with the misguided impression they are 'saving the world' have been fooled. They are unfortunate victims of emotive well-designed corporate marketing and deceptive political policies that are not actually environmentally friendly at all. For example, the manufacture of hundreds of millions electric car batteries, requires huge mining operations to acquire and refine large quantities of rare earth metals, such as lithium, rhodium and cobalt. Furthermore, these metals have to be mined out of the ground using machinery which is powered with diesel or petrol! The mining and refining processes cause significant and extensive pollution to land, air and water systems, see Endnote [43]. Furthermore, these rare earth metals are a limited resource. Unlike the fake climate change agenda, these are real environmental problems. Furthermore, electric cars are still driven by electricity produced from fossil fuels and will most likely continue to be! Despite decades of government subsidies wind power provides less than 5% of the world's energy, and solar just 1 %. The use of electricity to charge vehicles and devices is also an extremely in-efficient use of energy, according to a study by the European Association for Battery Electric Vehicles commissioned by the European Commission (EC):

> "The 'Well-to-Tank' energy efficiency (from the primary energy source to the electrical plug), taking into account the energy consumed by the production and distribution of the electricity, is estimated at around 37%. "

Let us take a look at the deceptive marketing for electric vehicles. The first misleading marketing trick that millions of environmentalists fell for was the 'hybrid'. Hybrid cars are actually gasoline powered cars with a little battery assistance and the little battery has to be charged from the gasoline engine. If the EPA certified mileage is 55 mpg, then it is nondifferent from a non-hybrid that achieves 55 mpg. A world 100% full of 'hybrid' drivers is still 100% addicted to oil.

Now consider a cleverly designed marketing pitch for electric cars by Elon Musk, Co-Founder & CEO of Tesla Motors. In an article published on the Tesla Motors website, see Endnote [44], he states:

> "the overarching purpose of Tesla Motors... is to help expedite the move from a mine-and-burn hydrocarbon economy towards a solar electric economy... I'd like to address two repeated arguments against electric vehicles - battery disposal and power plant emissions... the Tesla Motors Lithium-Ion cells are not classified as hazardous and are landfill safe... the battery pack can be sold to recycling companies (unsubsidized) at the end of its greater than 100,000-mile design life...
>
> A common rebuttal to electric vehicles as a solution to carbon emissions is that they simply transfer the CO_2 emissions to the power plant. The obvious counter is that one can develop grid electric power from a variety of means, many of which, like hydro, wind, geothermal, nuclear, solar, etc. involve no CO_2 emissions. However, let's assume for the moment that the electricity is generated from a hydrocarbon source like natural gas... the hands down winner is pure electric:
>
> Car   Energy Source CO_2 Content   Efficiency CO_2 Emissions

Honda CNG	Natural Gas	14.4 g/MJ	0.32 km/MJ	45.0 g/km
Honda FCX	Nat Gas-Fuel Cell	14.4 g/MJ	0.35 km/MJ	41.1 g/km
Toyota Prius	Oil	19.9 g/MJ	0.56 km/MJ	35.8 g/km
Tesla Roadster	Nat Gas-Electric	14.4 g/MJ	1.14 km/MJ	12.6 g/km

we will be offering a modestly sized and priced solar… This system can be… set up as a carport and will generate about 50 miles per day of electricity. If you travel less than 350 miles per week, you will therefore be "energy positive" with respect to your personal transportation… you will actually be putting more energy back into the system than you consume in transportation!"

Elon Musk does not mention and completely ignores the fact that:

- the move from mine-and-burn hydrocarbon economy towards a solar electric economy in itself requires a vast expenditure of fossil-fuel energy to re-purpose the entire worldwide industrial system, build vast new energy grids for wind and solar energy, etc, simply to reduce CO_2 emissions. A new industrial framework which in itself will still be very polluting to land, air and water in virtually the same ways as the old framework as it creates more and more 'stuff', which we are now incorrectly told is okay because its 'green stuff';
- the EROEI for solar and wind energy is too low to be viable, and therefore to repurpose and rebuild the world energy and industrial system to de-carbonise the economy is a waste of vast amounts of fossils fuels;
- the manufacture of billions of new electric cars and electric car batteries involves a continuation of widespread environmentally destructive mining, including the mining of rare earth metals, such as lithium, rhodium and cobalt, which are a limited resource.
- if you charge the car with solar energy, you may be putting slightly more energy back into the system than you consume in 'driving the car', but driving the car is only one small part of the entire energy consuming process from mining to manufacture to distribution, what to mention the embedded energy in the manufactured materials of a new worldwide industrial infrastructure, including cars, factories, energy grids, windmills, photovoltaics etc.
- and, vitally, that CO_2 emissions are not the cause of climate change.

The failure of the industrial agriculture 'green revolution'

The use of chemical fertilisers, pesticides, LMOs, hybrid seeds, mono-cropping and heavy machines in industrial agriculture in an attempt to increase yields and profits has caused huge amounts of land worldwide to become arid and unproductive. This industrial approach, known as the 'green revolution', has now being widely recognised as fundamentally flawed. The industrialised green revolution is in stark contrast to the nurturing soil management practices mankind has used successfully for thousands of years. For example, in ancient Vedic culture, the kings were responsible for protection of the people and of the land. Natural agricultural methods in harmony with nature were understood to be the best way to ensure enduring prosperity for all, and water irrigation from wells, constructed ponds and lakes, along with herd grazing for fertilisation, the correct use of trees was utilised.

Desertification - UN incorrectly state that animal livestock is a cause – it is actually the solution

Let us examine the truth about desertification, livestock, fire and loss of fertile soil. To combat desertification the UN have promoted policies, such as reducing livestock numbers to reduce the potential for overgrazing of land, thereby in their view reducing the rate of desertification. Alan Savory has conducted experimental projects that demonstrate the UN position is flawed, see Endnote [45]. He maintains that it is actually the loss of livestock and animals that is the problem. Grass needs animals that graze and fertilise the land via defecation, and without animals the natural vegetation is prone to degradation Thus it is the loss of animals and natural vegetation that are the significant causes of desertification. The loss of huge areas of natural vegetation and the reduction of livestock and wild animals on the land has been due to development of massive factory farming for the production of wheat, corn, sugar beets etc. Such farms currently cover vast areas world-wide.

Savory maintains that we have changed the natural cycle of vegetation decay by replacing decay with chemical oxidation and physical weathering. The loss of natural decay which formerly fertilised the soil means that the soil gradually loses fertility. In times, buffalo or other wild animals stayed in large herds for protection and defecated on the ground for a few days – as no animal likes to feed on its own excrement they then move on, allowing the ground to go through the period of rest it requires to absorb the natural excrement as fertiliser. Savory maintains modern day industrialised agriculture is not allowing the land the natural rest and natural fertilisation periods it requires to retain fertility.

Savory also maintains that mankind has for thousands of years been using periodic burning of vegetation on the land to make it fertile again. The char produced by the burn fertilises the soil. It appears that due to the mass extinction of thousands of species over the past decades there are no longer enough animals to keep the vast natural grasslands of the world alive as before. To support his assertions, Savory provides videos and pictures showing land with a high level of animal usage compared to the same land with low levels of animal usage. These pictures indicate that desertified land with little grass or plant life recovers fertility and grass over a few years when animals are introduced and indicate that this is the best low-tech way to reverse desertification and regrow grass and plant life. In the context of the ecological restoration of grasslands worldwide, Savory advocates Holistic Planned Grazing to properly manage livestock.

Whether he was aware of it or not, Savory was actually embracing a valuable core principle of ancient Vedic culture, but has today been largely forgotten. That principle is of soil replenishment via the natural grazing of large animal herds. It is confirmed by modern science that cow dung and urine provide the best natural fertilisers for the soil and that the movement of the animal hooves assists the process. Beetles and earthworms take the dung into the soil thus bringing fertile subsoil to the surface helping grass to grow.

Farmers have been given wrong information by governments

Commercial farmers, including dairy farmers, are being coerced by governments and the UN to reduce their herd numbers on the (false) basis that the methane emissions cause climate change. As previously described, thousands of scientists have asserted that methane from cows does not cause climate change, however, governments are fully on board the UN bandwagon and are not telling you that. The reality is that farmers are being sold a lie by, witting or unwitting, governments.

Farmers are the stewards of the land and the providers of food for the people of the world. We should therefore provide farmers with the respect they are due. Just like everyone else, farmers are just trying to survive and make a living, despite government-imposed taxes and regulations. Why pay taxes to a government that is, wittingly or unwittingly, enforcing Co2 reduction laws based on false information? Farmers must have access to correct science and the full facts and then they can make their own decisions on how best to manage their farms. It is not that I personally endorse all the practices of modern commercial industrialised farming - I don't - however, farmers should be making their own decisions based on true information not false manmade climate change dogma.

Furthermore, regardless of the fake climate change agenda, the era of commercial farming based on oil-based chemical fertilisers and diesel-powered machinery may soon be coming to an end worldwide due to the reduced availability of imported oil, see the *Chapter 10. Systemic problems, oil dependency, constraints to growth, and collapse.* What are farmers to do then? In light of this, farmers are no doubt asking themselves and planning ahead how to farm most effectively in the future.

My personal perspective, is that rampant globalisation has displaced many valuable traditional farming practices worldwide, and I think it is inevitable that farming will move toward a renewal of organic and traditional farming methods, as well as the use of intermediate technologies not reliant on oil, see also *Chapter 12. A sustainable retreat – creating resilient local systems*. Knowledge of organic farming, traditional farming methods, and use of natural fertilisers, such as bio-char, can increase yields beyond those of commercial farming, without the fertility of the land being reduced by the use of oil-based chemical fertilisers and pesticides.

For such a renewal to take place, dairy farming, and all farming, may need to become entirely free from government taxation and regulation, in order to have the 'scope' to truly thrive and develop for the benefit of farmers and for local communities. Local farming co-operatives can become centres of excellence and centres for farmers to sell their produce direct to the local communities. By cutting out the middle-man (which is in most cases is a foreign-owned corporate supermarkets chain) farmers will receive a higher price for their produce and more money will stay in the local community. This revival can take place in all countries.

In my opinion, it would be a mistake for farmers worldwide to jump on the UN-WEF-promoted bandwagon of the wide-spread use of microwave-based 'smart' technologies, the long-term health effects of which, on both humans and animals, are widely documented, see Endnote 53. Furthermore, it would be a mistake to rely solely on electricity produced from renewable sources due to the poor EROEI inherent in most renewable energy technologies. Although countries with higher-than-average wind speeds have some potential for local or domestic wind energy, as already described there are legitimate reasons not to go down the path of creating national wind energy networks.

What is the UN really?

The UN has inserted its rules into every aspect of life on Earth. Its tentacles are wrapped around the world in the form of climate change and sustainable development programs, peacekeeping, free trade, food programs etc. This unelected institution sponsors the WHO (another unelected institution aligned with vaccine companies and complicit in the covid-19 hoax) and the World bank. It has a standing blue helmeted army, which it claims is for 'peace-keeping', however, we should note that peace-keeping is not a function of the UN, as defined by its charter – is this another example of how this unelected bureaucracy sticks its nose into geo-politics wherever it wants to?

The UN World constitution even states "The age of nations must end. The governments of nations have decided to order their separate sovereignties into one government to which they will surrender their arms". The UN is a fraud – it is a front for a faceless bureaucracy that wants to control your life via bogus climate change policy, Agenda 21 and Agenda 2030 sustainable development initiatives. UN sustainable development is a stealthy development involving: The end of national sovereignty; abolition of private property rights; re-structuring of the family unit; restriction of individual mobility and opportunity; abandonment of constitutional rights; and the relocation of people into smart-growth zones. All principles clearly aligned with the Communist manifesto. The UN really serves the manifestos of the so-called global elite and the private banking cartel that funded communism in the first place. It was so-called capitalist New York and European banks that funded the Bolsheviks and communism in Russia, as further explained and evidenced in the (291 page) PDF version of this book. The financial cartel behind the creation of the UN utilises communist principles as well as rampant capitalist globalisation aiming to ensure their control of the world's wealth and resources.

Communism under the regime of Stalin was the major victor of World War II and Roosevelt and Churchill were operating in partnership with Stalin. The atheistic communists captured more than 7 million Christians during the war and sent them to communist concentration camps known as gulags. Over 90% of them died. In total, over 60 million Christians from both sides died during World War II. The victors of war write the history, and this ugly genocidal (other side) of the story is not told in classrooms or TV programs of today, but is well documented by writers including Alexander Solzhenitsyn, Nobel Prize Laureate, who was a prisoner in a communist gulag. The real victors were the communists whose ideology was to deny God, kill Christians and assume a total monopoly on power. The main victors of World War II were:

- Russia – under communist Stalin (who was a high-level atheistic freemason. Note that Stalin's and Lenin's communist regimes killed, starved or sent to gulags around 100 million mostly Christian people in Russia and Asia and Eastern Europe)
- China under communism
- Britain under Churchill (a high-level atheistic freemason linked to communism)
- US under Roosevelt (a high-level atheistic freemason linked to communism)
- France under De Gaul (who was linked to communism)

Note that prior to the war, 95% of the US population were against entering into war with a fellow Christian country Germany, but the banker-owned media gradually changed public opinion. Alder Hiss became the acting secretary general of the establishment of the United Nations. Hiss was a suspected communist spy and was found guilty of perjury. He later became secretary of the Bilderberg group a not-so-secret society of the ultra-rich world of private bankers and their industrial and political cohorts. The Bilderberg group wrote much of the UN charter patterning it after the communist manifesto.

"the creation of an authoritive world order is that to which we must strive" – Winston Churchill

The big figures involved had this philosophy. Trygve Lie was the first official UN secretary general, he was a high-ranking member of Norway's Social Democratic Party, which was an offshoot of the 3rd Communist International. Then came Dag Hammarskjold, the second UN secretary general, he was a Swedish socialist that openly pushed communist policy. The third secretary general was U Thant, he was a Marxist. We have been lied to – we have been living with unelected cleverly marketed UN communism for decades, see also Endnote [46].

Real environmentalism was hijacked by deceptive UN political schemes

So, we see that the 'real sustainability' movement was hijacked by the deceptive UN political schemes of sustainable development and manmade climate change. UN-defined sustainable development actually endorses the unjust debt-money banking and flawed GDP hypergrowth economic system. Sustainable development is, and has been, a false narrative operating under cover of continued environmentally destructive globalisation. Sustainable development is not real sustainability at all. It is a political scheme that has detracted from what real environmentalism is.

The subject of environmental sustainability and how to create a truly successful 'sustainable' society that nurtures human creativity, freedom, and wellbeing and that of the natural world have been central to my research for the past 20 years. However, over the past decades the orthodox political agenda of 'sustainable development' that has been promoted by the UN and the governments of the world has not worked. It has not addressed the unjust flawed systems of banking and economic control that benefitted an elite wealthy few at the expense of everyone else, nor has it solved the 'real' environmental problems of the world – in fact it was never supposed to. Furthermore, the loosely defined Brundtland definition of sustainable development used by the UN and governments for 30 years actually endorses GDP growth and is not a scientifically robust definition of sustainability.

There have been serious detrimental environmental and societal effects associated with the debt-money banking and GDP hypergrowth economic paradigm. Furthermore, the worldwide private banking system has for decades been bleeding up to 35% of the entire profit of the nations of the world. For example, in recent years Ireland has been paying between €6 to 10 billion per annum in interest payments on the national debt and as a trading entity the country has been making a profit of around €40 billion per annum. Yet the political agenda of sustainable development does not reform these areas – it endorses them. By 2020, even the word 'sustainability' itself has become a dirty word to many people that are interested in real sustainability. With its twisted meanings and modern political mechanisms 'sustainability' is now far removed from the insightful writings of 'real' sustainability and environmental visionaries of the 1970s, such as E.F. Schumacher.

Part of the political sustainable development strategy has been a delusional attempt to "decouple" environmental impacts from GDP growth. This decoupling strategy has failed, was never going work and I doubt it ever was intended to work. This is evidenced by a BIOS Research Institute study that reviewed 179 scientific studies on decoupling published between 1990 and 2019, a period of nearly 30 years, and found, in short, that:

> "… the evidence does not suggest that decoupling towards ecological sustainability is happening at a global (or even regional) scale."

BIOS Research Institute is an independent multidisciplinary scientific organisation that has previously advised the UN Global Sustainable Development Report on the risks of emerging biophysical limits to endless economic growth. The de-coupling concept has been utilised to placate people concerned with the environmental impacts of rampant GDP growth, nevertheless, rampant globalisation and environmental degradation has continued unabated for decades. The UN does not challenge globalisation – it represents globalisation and part of the machinery of globalisation.

Politically defined 'sustainable development' has been an illusory 'greenwashing' of the current flawed system, thereby temporarily perpetuating a system that will ultimately fail due to its unsustainable, eco-cidal, and human welfare diminishing effects. Many seemingly worthwhile corporate and governmental sustainable development initiatives are in operation, but all have operated within the unquestioned paradigm, or status quo, of environmentally destructive GDP growth; along with the debt-money private worldwide banking system that has placed much of humanity on a treadmill of debt. In analysing UN sustainable development, we must expose these flaws and detrimental effects of the banking, economic and monetary system, as well as the undemocratic deceptive WEF 'reset' of world civilisation, which attempts to introduce additional control mechanisms.

UN sustainable development programs, including the sustainable development goals (SDGs), Agenda 2030, and the Paris Climate Agreement, as well as the WEF economic 'reset', all operate under the cover of continued globalisation – it is all globalisation (and the pollution that brings) painted green to fool you. All are working together to create a so-called new 'resource-based' economic system. This may sound a worthy goal in light of the flaws of the failing and flawed environmentally-destructive hypergrowth-based economic paradigm. However, closer analysis reveals that sustainable development as defined by the UN and the WEF involves an agenda to take control of all resources and all production, leaving all people to be micro-managed by a type of data-driven technocracy. This technocratic type society is described in the cleverly designed marketing language of Agenda 21/2030, the SDGs and is proposed by the WEF 'reset'. This political marketing jargon of 'sustainable development' is not true sustainability at all.

What the UN means by 'sustainable development' is population control, central planning, global governance, and education to indoctrinate your children into a new set of beliefs in preparation for the new fake "sustainable" world order. UN Agenda 2030 involves a plan to abolish private property rights and get all people off the land and into so-called smart towns and smart cities, where they will monitored, tracked and traced; forced to comply with new rules to access digital social credits; and be unable to grow much food. If you don't believe me, read the WEF 'great reset' document, and note that China already has hundreds of millions of surveillance cameras in place. These policies are straight out of the communist manifesto and are the opposite of what is needed – 'real sustainability' involves people moving back to the land and developing self-sufficient communities.

> "The slogan of the UN Agenda 21, to protect the rights of future generations and all species against the potential crimes of the present, is both a smokescreen and a declaration of entitlement. By standing on this high-sounding platform the rights of the individual are called selfish and those who would fight for them slurred as immoral" - Rosa Koire, Author

As already mentioned, smart cities utilise health-damaging EMF technologies; and electric cars most so-called green energy technologies, and political 'greening of the economy' policies, are not environmental at all - they are simply more clever deceptive marketing and green washing.

A truly 'resilient' society requires the develop of practical locally-empowered self-sufficient rural communities of villages and towns, utilising local and regional systems for food, energy, water, goods, currencies and services. This is in contrast to the unsustainable trans-national systems of the so-called globalised economy or the corporation-serving technocratic futures the WEF, UN and government bureaucrats have planned for us. It also involves living conscious of the needs of others and of the purity of natural environmental resources we all rely on.

30 years of UN-defined sustainable development has not solved the real environmental and human wellbeing problems that exist worldwide – and was not designed to

30 years of UN-defined sustainable development has not solved the real environmental and human wellbeing problems that do exist worldwide. For decades, the real environmental problem has worsened and poverty (in real terms) has continued to increase worldwide. Meanwhile, the worldwide banking cartel and its corporate network cohorts have become immensely wealthy – the ultra-rich (the multi trillionaires that have controlling ownership of mega-banks and mega-corporations) have become much richer.

For more detail, please refer to Chapter 6 in which I describe aspects including:

- the UN Brundtland definition enabled 'polluting' forms of globalisation/GDP growth to rampantly continue;
- the word 'sustainable' was hijacked;
- the failure of resource-efficiency, resource substitution or eco-efficiency strategies
- UN and international policies for sustainable development that incorrectly endorse globalisation and polluting forms of GDP growth
- UN green economy/ green growth strategies are simply destructive globalisation painted green
- the UN incorrectly endorses and promotes globalisation
- the UN trick of blaming population growth rather than addressing the root causes of environmental destruction and human poverty worldwide, ie, the privately owned worldwide debt-money banking system that was instrumental in creating the unelected UN and the system of environmentally destructive corporate globalisation in the first place.

Environmentalists that endorse UN Agenda 2030 policies have yet to navigate their way out of UN marketing propaganda and bogus science - if they realised what the UN actually is they would surely not support Agenda 2030. The UN was created by the same folks that created environmentally destructive corporate globalisation for the purposes of greed, vast corporate control and profits, and the continual upward flow of many trillions of dollars to the private banking sector, which by the way creates debt-money out of thin air and lends it to governments worldwide at interest. No UN policy ever mentions that.

Decoding the real objectives behind the UN 17 'New Sustainable Development Goals'

> "The 2030 agenda is comparable to chasing imaginary giraffes, and epitomizes the collective movement as it calls upon individuals to set aside their ambitions, to forfeit their natural rights, and to subjugate themselves to the state – presumably in the interest of 17 lofty goals, that incidentally position the goal creators to anoint themselves as your caretaker and keeper… The 2030 agenda poses a real threat to life as you know it, as the United Nations' purported attempts to secure the peace and provide for domestic tranquility and equality for all is intoxicating because it plays on Maslows instinctive human need for security above all other desires… when faced with threats… free people will willingly cast off their freedoms and embrace tyranny, if only their new keepers can assure them safety. That is what the United Nations, in my opinion, is attempting to accomplish in its 2030 Agenda…. To the ill-informed… the (17) goals are a beacon of hope. But to the critical thinkers and freedom lovers… they are the all-embracing and tyrannical arms of the nanny state – guided by a coven of elites who will never live by the restricted standards and forfeited rights they impose on its willing subjects" - Ron Taylor, Author

The UN SDGs can be a bit tricky to decode, what with all the weaponized buzz words. These goals are unattainable, but for the global elite, the point isn't to improve the world, the point is to control it. Of course, the cost of this deceptive 'planetary utopia' is handing over control of all planetary resources to the UN, ah yes for 'conservation'. And who better to control the people of the world than those dictators-in-waiting at the UN? Let us take a closer look at these 'goals':

Goal 1: End poverty in all its forms everywhere

Translation: Keep the developing world in vast debt under the pretext of globalisation and technology transfer programs to end poverty. Centralized banking, IMF, World Bank, Federal Reserve is to control all world finances. We will only cancel world debt (on money we created from nothing) when we can introduce our digital one world currency, social credit system and cashless society, ensuring people must conform to our rules.

Goal 2: End hunger, achieve food security and improved nutrition and promote sustainable agriculture

2.5 By 2020, maintain the genetic diversity of seeds, cultivated plants and farmed and domesticated animals and their related wild species, including through soundly managed and diversified seed and plant banks at the national, regional and international levels, and promote access to and fair and equitable sharing of benefits arising for the utilisation of genetic resources and associated traditional knowledge, as internationally agreed.

Translation: Rampant expansion of GMO, and no local control of seed banks.

Goal 3: Ensure healthy lives and promote well-being for all at all ages

3.7 By 2030, ensure universal access to sexual and reproductive health-care services, including for family planning, information and education, and the integration of reproductive health into national strategies and programmes.

3.8 By 2030, universal health coverage, including financial risk protection, access to quality essential health-care services and access to safe, effective, quality and affordable essential medicines and vaccines for all.

3.b Support the research and development of vaccines and medicines for the communicable and non-communicable diseases that primarily affect development countries.

Translation: Mass vaccination, mass abortion and population control.

Goal 4: Ensure inclusive and equitable quality education and promote lifelong learning opportunities for all

4.7 By 2030, ensure that all learners acquire the knowledge and skills needed to promote sustainable development, including, among others, through education for sustainable development and sustainable lifestyles, human rights, gender equality, promotion of a culture of peace and non-violence, global citizenship and appreciation of cultural diversity…

Translation: UN propaganda and brainwashing through compulsory education from cradle to grave. All learners must be indoctrinated into communist style sustainable development. The word 'ensure' is a blatant admission of forced indoctrination. How do they intend to enforce this?

Goal 5: Achieve gender equality and empower all women and girls.

5.5. Ensure women's full and effective participation and equal opportunities for leadership at all levels of decision-making in political, economic and public life.

5. C Adopt and strengthen sound policies and enforceable legislation for the promotion of gender equality and the empowerment of all women and girls at all levels."

Translation: Social engineering to destroy the family unit - all control of society and children is under the auspices of the state. Population control through forced 'Family Planning'. Turn women into tax payers and stop them producing children.

Goal 6: Ensure availability and sustainable management of water and sanitation for all

Translation: Privatize all water sources, don't forget to add fluoride (hydro fluorosilicate, which is an industrial by-product and toxin) and aluminum (which is extremely toxic to humans).

Goal 7: Ensure access to affordable, reliable, sustainable and modern energy for all

Translation: Smart grid control of your access to energy. EMF-producing smart meters compulsorily inserted into your home to access your data, introduce peak pricing, etc. They never tell you about the vast energy and environmental expenditure to build a smart grid, hundreds of millions of 'smart meters', billions of smart devices, such as TVs, fridges, smartphones, smart cars etc.

Goal 8: Promote sustained, inclusive and sustainable economic growth, full and productive employment and decent work for all

8.1. Sustain per capita economic growth in accordance with national circumstances and, in particular, at least 7 per cent gross domestic product per annum in the least developed countries.

8.3 Promote development oriented policies… including through access to financial services

8.4 … endeavour to de-couple economic growth from environmental degradation

Translation: A continuation of the usury economy in which wealth always flows upwards to the private banking system. "At least 7% GDP growth in least developed countries" means the globalists want these economies growing under the whip of globalisation, so they can pay vast sums of interest to international mega-banks on fraudulent debt-money loans created from nothing and issued to governments. GDP growth is always needed so that vast sums of interest collected via taxes will continue to flow from governments to the private international banking cartel. Free trade zones that favour mega-corporate interests, globalisation, and endless polluting forms of GDP growth.

Is 'free trade' really free or is it just a deceptive buzzword for corporate globalisation? The UK government sustainable development strategy states "internationally we need to promote the mutual supportiveness of trade liberalisation...", see Endnote [47], yet traditionally environmentalists have taken a strong line against free trade, see Endnote [48]. The concept of trade liberalisation has always been a contentious issue environmentally due to needless shipping of goods worldwide that could be produced locally. It also involves the exportation of manufacturing jobs to sweat shops across the so-called developing world, resulting in the suppression of opportunity and income in the importing country to achieve so-called economic equality that is actually illusory.

"Endeavour to de-couple economic growth from environmental degradation" means even though it has already been comprehensively demonstrated that 30 years of attempting to de-couple economic growth from environmental impacts has completely failed and is a policy that will never work, we are going to keep repeating this de-coupling nonsense to pretend that we are trying to stop 'real' pollution.

Goal 10: Reduce inequality within and among countries

10. B Encourage official development assistance and financial flows, including foreign direct investment, to… in particular developing countries

10.c By 2030, reduce to less than 3 per cent the transaction costs of migrant remittances and eliminate remittance corridors with costs higher than 5 per cent

Translation: "Development assistance" means get developing countries hooked on debt-money loans (created from nothing) and have them put up national assets as collateral. Later pull the plug with a boom bust bailout scenario, just as has been done in many other countries, and leave the country in perpetual debt slavery. In 2020, virtually every government worldwide is in vast debt to the privately-owned debt-money banking system, see the book *Globalism Unmasked: The Truth about Banking and the Reset of Society*.

We the globalists want the whole world under our thumb of globalisation. We do not want people to develop 'real local sustainability' in their own country or have any knowledge of how to do that – we want large amounts of people to be displaced, subject to migration from orchestrated wars, and living in our 'smart' cities as slaves to the globalised economy, which is owned by our mega-banks and mega-corporations.

Goal 11: Make cities and human settlements inclusive, safe, resilient and sustainable.

Translation: Big brother big data surveillance state and a behaviour based digital social credit system to keep you under our control, which is already in operation in China, where over 200 million surveillance cameras had been installed by 2018, with plans for over 600 million.

Goal 12: Ensure sustainable consumption and production patterns

*Acknowledging that the United Nations Framework Convention on Climate Change is the primary international, intergovernmental forum for negotiating the global response to climate change.

Translation: Forced austerity. Oh, and by the way don't forget, the UN framework is the only place where you are allowed to discuss the climate change issue – we do not want scientists to convene outside of our bogus UN framework. Thousands of scientists dispute the unproven UN-promoted climate change theory, but we don't tell the public about that.

Goal 13: Take urgent action to combat climate change and its impacts

13.2 Integrate climate change measures into national policies, strategies and planning

13.3 Improve education, awareness-raising and human and institutional capacity on climate change mitigation, adaptation, impact reduction and early warning.

Translation: Cap and Trade, carbon taxes/credits, footprint taxes. We the globalists are trying to change your society to suit our own agenda and you will have no say in how your society will function. We are trying to indoctrinate your children and all of society to believe our climate change lie, so that we can achieve complete control of society, and mould society and population behaviour the way we want to without any resistance.

Goal 16: Promote peaceful and inclusive societies for sustainable development, provide access to justice for all and build effective, accountable and inclusive institutions at all levels.

16.1 Significantly reduce all forms of violence and related deaths rates everywhere

16.3 Promote the rule of law at the national and international levels and ensure equal access to justice for all

16.4 By 2030, significantly reduce illicit financial and arms flows… and combat all forms of organised crime

16.8 Broaden and strengthen the participation of developing countries in the institutions of global governance

16.9 By 2030, provide legal identity for all, including birth registration.

Translation: "Significantly reduce all forms of violence and related deaths rates everywhere" except when we the globalists do it via intentionally orchestrated wars, drug culture, toxic vaccines, human trafficking, and the promotion of mass abortion.

16.3 means we want you to obey our laws – even though you did not write them.

16.4 "significantly reduce illicit financial and arms flows" means except for our globalist corporate 'legitimate' military industrial complex that supplies arms to our member governments, especially the US, Israel, Russia, China, U.K. France and Germany and the G20, which we own and control.

16.8 means we the globalists want all developing countries (poorer countries that are exploited by globalisation and debt) to be subject to and ruled by our institutions of global governance i.e., the unelected UN, the WHO, the World Bank, the IMF, etc.

16.9 means we the globalists want everyone registered so we know where you are and can tax you. This is all a rational for digital IDs. Note that in a UN Conference in 2016, Bill Gates was able to introduce into the 16th SDG sub targets his rationale to introduce digital IDs – most likely injected via vaccines, with trials conducted in the third world, see Endnote [49]. Remember that we the globalists own you, and you the 'common people' are just collateral on loans your government received from our international private banking cartel – money that we never had in the first place so we created it out of thin air via our debt-money system.

Goal 17: Strengthen the means of implementation and revitalize the global partnership for sustainable development

17.1 Strengthen domestic resource mobilization, including through international support to developing countries, to improve domestic capacity for tax and other revenue collection.

17.4 Assist developing countries in attaining long-term debt sustainability through coordinated policies aimed at fostering debt financing, debt relief and debt restructuring, as appropriate, and address the external debt of highly indebted poor countries to reduce debt distress.

17.7 Promote the development, transfer, dissemination and diffusion of environmentally sound technologies to developing countries on favourable terms, including on concessional and preferential terms, as mutually agreed.

17.9 Enhance international support for implementing effective and targeted capacity-building in developing countries to support national plans to implement all the Sustainable Development Goals…

17.10 Promote a universal, rules-based, open, non-discriminatory and equitable multilateral trading systems under the World Trade Organisation…

17.17 Encourage and promote effective public, public-private and civil society partnerships, building on the experience and resourcing strategies of partnerships.

17.18 By 2020, enhance capacity-building support to developing countries… to increase significantly the availability of high-quality, timely and reliable data disaggregated by income, gender, age, race, ethnicity, migratory status, disability, geographic location…

Translation: Remove national sovereignty worldwide and promote globalism under the "authority" and bloated unelected bureaucracy of the UN.

17.1. means we the globalists want to collect more tax from everyone

17.4 means as long as the world is in vast debt we don't really care - restructure it if you want, it doesn't matter. We don't care just as long as developing countries remain in debt to the criminal elite, the private banking cartel, and continue to flail on our hook. The one thing we will never do is cancel debt – if we ever do so it will be to introduce conditionalities of control. If we introduce a one world digital currency and cancel your national debt you will have to give up ownership of assets, just as is stated in our marketing document on our WEF website… "Welcome to 2030: I Own Nothing, Have No Privacy And Life Has Never Been Better".

17.7 means we the globalists want developing countries hooked on contracts and debts to pay for our technologies that will leave them dependent on the globalised system that we control. **Never let countries, regions or communities develop real local self-sufficiency** or locally suitable technologies or intermediate technologies that are suited to their local needs and can be sustained from their local resources, local manpower, local skills and local knowledge

17.9 means let us put international pressure on these poorer countries so that they will accept and implement our deceptive plans.

17.10 means the WTO rules world trade. We the globalists run the WTO and we make up the trading rules. We say its equitable, but you have to obey our trading rules, which are economic tricks based on the monetary system that we own and control.

17.17 means we the globalists must ensure corporate (private) influence in politics is effective so that we can control the levers of the political system - civil society has little money thus we have all the influence.

17.18 means in our system of globalisation we want to know everything about everyone so that we can utilise or manipulate the masses as we see fit – just as a farmer keeps registration charts for each cow on his farm we have a chart on you too.

UN Agenda 21/2030 is an agenda of control – it is the opposite of real sustainability

According to author, Rosa Koire, sustainable development as defined by Agenda 21/Agenda 2030 is a sinister agenda that involves moving people away from the land and into cities; placing restrictions on people's right to produce their own energy, food and water; and centralising power and decision making to unelected government-corporate-NGO boards - rather than empowering individuals and local rural communities to develop local systems for food, energy and water.

In my opinion Agenda 21/2030 is the complete opposite of what real sustainability actually involves, i.e., empowering people to reconnect with the land and nature and to develop sustainable 'rural' local systems for, food, energy and water. Free creative people are not meant to be pent up or corralled in cities like cattle in a pen, or controlled by an unelected government-corporate partnership, but that is what Agenda 2030 attempts to do.

> "UN Agenda 21/Sustainable Development is the action plan implemented worldwide to inventory and control all land, all water, all minerals, all plants, all animals, all construction, all means of production, all energy, all education, all information, and all human beings in the world... the plan calls for governments to take control of all land use and not leave any of the decision making in the hands of private property owners. It is assumed that people are not good stewards... Moreover, people should be rounded up off the land and packed into human settlements, or islands of human habitation, close to employment centers and transportation (where they can be surveilled and controlled)...
>
> UN Agenda 21/Sustainable Development is a global plan that is implemented locally. Over 600 cities in the U.S. are members... The costs are paid by taxpayers..... Although counties say that they support agricultural uses, eating locally produced food, farmer's markets, etc, in fact there are so many regulations restricting water and land use (there are scenic corridors, inland rural corridors, baylands corridors, area plans, specific plans, redevelopment plans, huge fees, fines) that farmers are losing their lands altogether... **The push is for people to get off of the land, become more dependent, come into the cities...**
>
> It involves the educational system, the energy market, the transportation system, the governmental system, the health care system, food production, and more. The plan is to restrict your choices, limit your funds, narrow your freedoms, and take away your voice... new ICLEI Water Campaign.... This is a way to inventory and control all water in the world. To identify all water sources, all wells, water courses, streams, creeks, rivers, lakes etc., and monitor them. Control." - Rosa Koire, Author, see Endnote [50].

UN Agenda 2030 smart cities - smart for them, but not smart for you

Furthermore, sustainable development as defined in Agenda 2030 involves the mass rollout and utilisation of so-called smart technology. This includes wireless technology, such as WIFI, smartphones, 5G, smart meters, and the so called 'Internet of Things', etc. However, it has clearly been demonstrated by thousands of studies, see Endnote 53, that the above microwave-based wireless technologies utilise electromagnetic frequencies (EMFs) that are harmful to human health and, in particular, to the brain development of children. EMFs are linked with chronic fatigue, headaches, tinnitus, depression, cancer and chronic degenerative disorders.

Smart cities will utilise social credit scoring, which is already in use in China and requires large data collection on every citizen in China, for example, financial transactions, organisation affiliations, social interactions, friendships, and data-mining of a citizen's history on social media. The surveillance network is an integral part of the data collection process. A person's social credit score depends on, for example, whether they criticise the government or comply with the government – therefore, each person is compelled to comply with government to maintain their social credit scoring and receive benefits. It is a sort of digital dictatorship. It has been reported that the Chinese authorities even run 'pre-crime' algorithms against the data collected!

In these UN-planned smart cities, the right to privacy is entirely subverted in a smart city as people are expected to consent to their data being collected, and being surveilled constantly. The smart city requires wireless connectivity to function and this is the real reason that 5G is being rolled out worldwide at rapid pace. Even whilst the so-called pandemic was in full swing, and everyone else was locked down, communications companies' employees installing 5G infrastructure were working full time. 5G enables 'smart-city' super-computers to analyse the activities of a whole city of people in real time, and to utilise Geospatial Intelligence to monitor and manage large crowds of people, supposedly to improve the flow of shoppers. The expenditure of trillions of dollars on technology and surveillance infrastructure to improve the flow of shoppers – am I the only one that doesn't buy that?

The trick of world heritage sites and 'rewilding'

So how are these UN globalists trying to get you off the land and into these smart cities, so they can control all resources the land and nature? One of their methods is the 'UNesco world heritage site'. Without your consent or permission or a popular vote, UNesco 'designates', a large area as a world heritage site that is 'valuable to the entire world' and says now everyone owns it. So now it's a heritage site under the auspices of the UN (an unelected organisation) and in this way the UN attempts to control access to it. Local people, who may have been accessing the site for many generations, are given only restricted access or none at all under this subtle arrogant trick. The UNesco.org website states:

> "World Heritage sites belong to all the peoples of the world, irrespective of the territory on which they are located."

In the way the UN attempts to restrict your access to the local natural resources, traditionally known as 'the commons' that was used for hundreds of years for the welfare of all the local community. In this way the possibilities for local self-sufficiency are stymied, and the movement of people to the 'smart-city' (where they will be dependent on the globalist designed and controlled social credit scoring system) is more probable.

The heritage site project is subtle abuse of national sovereignty under the guise of conservation and cultural preservation. Furthermore, the definition of a heritage site is being widened to encompass a greater number of sites for potential control. There are about 900 of these sites worldwide and in conjunction with massive 'rewilding projects', it is obvious people are being herded into the smart cities like sheep being herded into a pen.

'Rewilding' is another subtle scam to get people off the land and into globalist surveilled smart cities. A report produced by American Policy Center, see Endnote [51], describes the project as follows:

> "The Wildlands Project... calls for the "re-wilding" of 50% of all the land in every US state... It is a diabolical plan to herd humans of the rural lands and into human settlements... the plan became the blueprint for the UN's Biodiversity Treaty and quickly became international in scope... the Biosphere Reserve acts like a cancer cell, ever expanding, until all human activity is stopped... Locking away land cuts the tax base. Eventually the town dies. Keep it up and there is nothing to keep the people on the land – so they head to the cities.
>
> It comes in many names and many programs. Heritage areas, land management, wolf and bear reintroduction, rails to trails, conservation easements, open space, and many more. Each of these programs is designed to make it just a little harder to live on the land – a little more expensive – a little more hopeless... Today, there are at least 31 Wildlands projects underway, locking away more than 40 percent of the nation's land.
>
> The Alaska Wildlands Project seeks to lock away and control almost the entire state. In Washington State, Oregon, Idaho, Montana parts of North and South Dakota, parts of California, Arizona, Nevada, New Mexico, Wyoming, Texas, Utah, and more, there are at least 22 Wildlands Projects underway. For example, one project called Yukon to Yellowstone (Y2Y) – creates a 2000 mile no-man's land corridor from the Arctic to Yellowstone." – American Policy Center

A deeper question is "even if current human society currently had full access to nature's forests and the natural world, would we treat nature the way it deserves with purity, respect and love? The answer is that most of us, having been, born into, and conditioned by the current materialistic society of exploitation, have lost our ancient connection with the forest and the natural world. We require a higher level of consciousness to re-establish our ancient pure connection with the forest. The relevance of consciousness is explored in a later chapter.

Communism disguised as sustainability - Local Governments for Sustainability stakeholder councils

In the USA, local government is increasingly controlled by stake holder councils. These councils have been widely accused of enforcing their own private agendas; and of replacing the power of elected officials with non-elected, appointed rulers answerable to no one. American Policy Center, describes the situation as follows:

> "They force citizens to seek permission (usually denied) for any changes to private property. They use such excuses as historic preservation, water use restrictions, energy use, and open space restrictions... They can dictate the kind of building materials owners can use in their private home – or whether one can build on their property at all... These councils fit almost perfectly the definition of a State Soviet: a system of councils that report to an apex council and then implement a predetermined outcome... Many Americans ask how dangerous international policies can suddenly turn up in state and local government... The answer – meet ICLEI, a non-profit, private foundation, dedicated to helping locally elected representatives fully implement Agenda 21 in the community... the group simply calls itself "**ICLEI – Local Governments for Sustainability.**"
>
> Fighting ICLEI...Here is how to handle them: if your council derides your statements that their policies come from the UNs Agenda 21, simply print out the home page from ICLEI's web site – www.iclei.org. This will have all of the UN connections you've been talking about, in ICLEI's own words. Pass out the web page copies to everyone in the chamber audience and say to your elected officials, "don't call me a radical simply for reporting what ICLEI openly admits on its own web site. I'm just the one pointing it out – you are the ones who are paying our tax dollars to them." Then demand that those payment stop. You have proven your case." – American Policy Center

American Policy Center, see Endnote 51, also suggests how to stop ICLEI consensus meetings, which are forums open to the public for implementing Agenda 21 Sustainable Development across the nation, designed to eliminate debate and close discussion. The recommendation is

> "you must never participate, even to answer a question. To do so allows the facilitator to make you part of the process. Instead, you must control the discussion... You will need at least three people... fan out in the room... Know ahead of time the questions you want to ask: Who is the facilitator? What is his association with the organizers? Is he being paid? Where did these programs (being proposed) come from? How are they to be funded?... ask over and over again... "With the implementation of this policy, tell me a single right or action I have on my property that doesn't require your approval or involvement." Make them name it. You will quickly see that they too understand there are no property rights left in America... That's where the rest of your group comes in. They need to back you up, demand answers to your questions... Stay to the end and make him shut down the meeting." – American Policy Center

2. WEF 'reset' attempt sold as a solution to climate change and covid-19

The full text of this chapter is available in the PDF download version (291 page) version of this book *Transcending the Climate Change Deception – Toward Real Sustainability*, which is available on my website www.mkeenan.ie It covers the following topics:

- Event 201 pandemic coronavirus simulation three months prior to Covid-19

- Covid-19 was utilised as an excuse for implementing the WEF/UN reset

- Co-ordinated central banking/WEF/WHO/UN world 'reset' same time as world lockdown. Recall that BlackRock had presented a proposal at the August 2019, annual meeting of world's central bankers in Jackson Hole, Wyoming, for an economic reset that was actually put into effect in March 2020. At the exact same time, March 2020, the world was 'locked down' for the first time in recorded history due to the corporate-fabricated Covid-19 pandemic. This timing was no co-incidence.

- The attempted WEF/UN 'great reset' of the entire world society according to a new technocratic bio-pharmaceutical regime was introduced and implemented at the exact same time as the March 2020 Covid-19 world lockdown was implemented; and at the exact same time as the central bankers reset the world economy in March 2020, and at the exact same as a staggering $4,000 billion was awarded to Blackrock in a March 2020 bailout/funds transfer that hardly anyone knows about.

- Totalitarian voices: Klaus Schwab, Founder WEF; António Guterres, UN

- The central banking cartel is the driving force behind the world reset. I should point out here that WEF Founder Klaus Schwab is a son of Marianne Schwab, who is daughter of the banker Louis Rothschild, see Endnote [52]. Furthermore, the WEF's Board of Trustees includes the Managing Director of the IMF, the European Central Bank President, a former Bank of England governor and The Trilateral Commission are also represented. The WEF connection with international private banking is, therefore, evident. Via the WEF 'reset' and UN

Agenda 2030 it is clear that the worldwide banking cartel wishes to extend their monopoly over government credit into a monopoly over everything.

The money-masters control the international institutions, which control governments. The UN, the WEF, the WHO, the European Union, World Bank and IMF, the World Trade Organization (WTO), the International Criminal Court (ICC), Bilderberg Society, the Council on Foreign Relations (CFR), etc, were all created or co-opted by the central bankers, the Rothschilds, the Rockefellers, etc. These unelected unaccountable international institutions have superimposed themselves and their policies over sovereign and constitutional governments, by the force of money. It is the debt-money creation system that they own economy that controls the world everything. Privately-owned world banking has created a system, whereby nations can be punished by economic oppression if they do not accept the policies of the globalists.

- WEF reset plan for a 'fourth industrial revolution' aligned with the utilisation of deceptive and fraudulent climate change and politically defined sustainable development narratives.

- This era would include: Unprecedented measures of control, invasive digital surveillance, mass vaccination and rules, such as bio-metric monitoring devices on the human body to monitor health, widespread implementation of tracking and tracing technologies that monitor your location and movements; The development of so-called 'smart cities' utilising 5G, and electromagnetic frequency microwave-based technologies that are proven to be harmful to human health; The introduction of a new one-world digital cashless currency that people will have no control over and will be used to penalise and fine people who do not comply with new rules. In this way they aim to control human activity.

- Unprecedented measures of control, digital surveillance, and vaccination

- A pharmaceutical driven bio-security and trans-humanism agenda

- Blockchain power dynamics

- After 'debt forgiveness' you would own nothing

- Tricking the world into dependency on a new digitized totalitarian money system

Smart devices, 5G and electromagnetic frequency technologies

The WEF document also promotes the worldwide implementation electromagnetic frequency (EMF) /microwave technologies, specifically, the Internet of Things (IOT). The IoT is supported by 5th generation cellular technology, 5G. Note, however, that thousands of scientific studies show that EMF-based technologies are harmful to human health, see Endnote [53].

> "The internet of things (IOT) now connects 22 billion devices in real time, ranging from cars to hospital beds, electric grids and water station pumps, to kitchen ovens and agricultural irrigation systems .. this number is expected to reach 50 billion or more by 2030" – (see page 27)

The pervasive nature of so-called smart technology, electrification and 5G, already being implemented worldwide in all sectors of society is exemplified by the quote from a report to the UK's Food & Drink Sector Council, by its Agricultural Productivity Working Group:

> "If the net zero carbon ambition is to be achieved by our industry, electrification of heavy farm machinery must be facilitated. Nationwide reinforcement of rural electricity infrastructure, including buffer battery storage systems, will be essential to deliver the required electrical flow for 'smart charging' of multiple high-capacity batteries… in the farming calendar. … Facilitating the management of land by those who will adopt new tools, technologies and practices could have a subsequent positive impact on productivity. The following actions are required: **1. Invest in 5G infrastructure to enable required future data flow** 2. Upgrade the rural electricity network to enable electrification of farm equipment… " – UK Food and Drink Sector Council

Note that, 5G is not just a technology that provides higher data speed, it is a system that can be utilised for surveillance, social credit scoring, and weaponization. 5G enables the connection of trillions of devices to a networked grid utilizing vast numbers of microwave radiation transmitters. The technology provides the basis for worldwide government surveillance and data collection on every individual. When Covid-19 world lockdown occurred, instead of stopping work to deploy 5G, communications companies and complicit governments increased the rollout of the 5G towers and antennas without public knowledge or input, including in schools. Anyone chipped with ID technology, such as, Bill Gates' ID2020, will be subjected to this electronic enslavement and to all the harmful microwave frequencies. The smartphone plays a malignant role in all of this, taking you away from real life and sucking you into the corporate-created reality of the IoT. If you don't want to get tracked and traced, it is time to throw away your smartphone. The more people give up wireless phones/technologies, the more the globalists' plans are destroyed.

I note a comprehensive report by Mark Steele, an engineer and weapons research scientist, titled: *"Fifth Generation (5G) Directed Energy Radiation Emissions in the Context of Nanometal-contaminated Vaccines that include Covid-19 with Graphite Ferrous Oxide Antennas"*. The report can be downloaded, see Endnote [54].

Geo-engineering and the technology they use to pollute the skies

If you are an observant person, you may have noticed that the beautiful sky above us has been changing over the past decades. There are odd cloud formations and vast streams of trails in this sky today that I can assure you did not exist in the sky when I was a child or a teenager. Why is this? The answer is it is due to geo-engineering, chemtrail technology, and a technology known as High Frequency Active Auroral Research Program (HAARP). The existence of and widespread implementation of geo-engineering and chemtrails is fact that is documented in government literatures, yet mention the words and people will stare at you in disbelief. I have often stopped in my tracks to witness a veritable chessboard of chemtrails in the sky criss-crossing and merging into each other in a clearly orchestrated operation, this was particularly obvious when I worked in Geneva in 2011. See Endnote [55], for information on geo-engineering; a NASA report on a program for weather modification; HAARP & chemtrail technology; and UK RAF military cloud seeding. The official governmental rationale for geo-engineering is that it is designed to combat climate change by introducing greater cloud cover in the sky. Would you accept that explanation when you know that manmade climate change is a hoax?

3. Summary of the climate change and sustainable development deceptions

The climate change and covid-19 crises will go down in history as a 'psyops' intended to propel the world into the UN Agenda 2030 for Sustainable Development plan, and the aligned WEF 'reset' plan i.e., the so-called new world order plan of the Davos group - the 2500 richest financial and corporate organisations in the world, of which a small group of connected mega-banks have controlling ownership. The question you should be asking by now is who owns these mega-banks.

Additional orchestrated pandemics, crises and wars are likely 'in the pipeline' to further these plans. The world financial system that had been in operation for decades, based on the worldwide debt-money banking scam, reached an inevitable mathematical end-phase in October 2019. The globalists have long prepared to introduce a technocratic economic system reset that increases their corporate control. The current worldwide situation has serious implications for the future of worldwide society and human wellbeing. UN agenda 2030, including the climate change lies; and the WEF reset agenda is an orchestrated attack against human freedoms.

The globalists are all working toward a world in which the future for everyone on Earth is dictated by them always; a world in which freedom is a memory. The globalist international organisational structure includes the UN, the WEF, the WHO, the E.U., the IMF, the BIS, the World Bank, the leadership of the both US Democrat and Republican parties, and most world political leaders; as well as connected influential organisations including the Trilateral Commission, the Bilderberg Group, the Council on Foreign Relations and various extremely well-funded thinktanks and NGOs. These structures are not serving the people, for decades they have been prioritising the interests of so-called elites, a private banking cabal who control the money system; and the interests of privately-owned mega-corporations.

These globalists are anyone who leads, promotes or works with these globalist organizations and these freedom killing agendas. Upper echelons of these organisational structures are complicit in this agenda. Many politicians are their witting, and often un-witting, pawns. The privately-owned worldwide banking/money creation system is the head of the snake. The globalists also include the fake anti-globalists, such as Donal

Trump, and a myriad of controlled-opposition personalities in the alternative media, the truth community, and even religious institutions. Note that Trump was bailed out to the tune of $4 billion in the 1980s and his services effectively bought by the mega-bankers that bailed him out. This is evidenced by a CNN TV interview with Alan Pomerantz the real-estate attorney that managed the transaction on behalf of 72 Jewish-owned New York banks, in which Pomerantz stated "We made the decision that he would be worth more alive to us than dead, dead meaning in bankruptcy... we wanted him out in the world selling these assets for us", see Endnote [56]. It is no wonder the Trump administration administered a multi-trillion-dollar bailout, i.e., wealth transfer, to the banking/financial sector in 2020, just as Obama did in 2010.

Many people realise what is going on and have ignored the freedom killing covid-19 restrictions and fear-mongering lies about climate change. More and more people realise that we don't usually have a 'worldwide reset', whenever there is 'a bit of virus' going around. Waves of covid-19 were intentionally orchestrated via fraudulent PCR testing, which can dial up and down case numbers, and via other mechanisms. The agenda has been to instil fear into the population and establish control and power - it always has been. Money 'pulls the strings' of government always and those that own the money creation system control governments. More lies and destructive tactics are on the way from the UN, the WHO, corporate owned media and a government near you.

As sovereign free peoples, we urgently need to start planning, connecting with each other and creating much more self-sufficient local communities, towns, and regions free of the mainstream economy. Whilst respecting 'real' environmental principles and the natural world we rely on, we should disavow the fake deceptive narratives of the 'reset', Agenda 2030 sustainable development and combating 'manmade' climate change.

Chapter 6. *UN sustainable development is a problem wrapped up as a solution – what about the real sustainability* challenge? describes in more detail the problematic aspects of UN-defined sustainable development. In summary, the following points can be asserted:

- The "real" environmental and "real" sustainability movement was hijacked decades ago by this political scheme known as sustainable development (SD). Politically defined SD has failed over the past 30 years and will never solve worldwide environmental and social poverty problems of the world and its architects probably never intended it to.

- The UN Sustainable Development Goals (SDGs), which despite listing worthwhile aims, such as poverty reduction, will never be achieved by politically defined sustainable development as the root causes of world's problems are not addressed by these political initiatives.

- Political 'green and SD initiatives' are not 'green' at all, just more environmentally destructive globalisation disguised in green-washing language. Political policy initiatives, such as the 2020 'Green New Deal' in the US and many similar initiatives in other countries, are actually ongoing environmentally destructive globalisation disguised in green. Initiatives, such as 'Green New Deal' and the 'great reset' are packaged in emotive marketing language such as 'combatting climate change' and creating the '4th industrial revolution' are just parts of the wealth and technocratic control plans of the elite.

- UN sustainable development programs, such as Agenda 21, Agenda 2030, and the Paris Climate Agreement, as well as the economic 'reset' being proposed and attempted by the WEF in 2020, all operate under the cover of continued freedom killing globalisation, some call it corporate communism.

- Politically defined SD intends to take control of all resources, all production, and all consumption on earth, leaving all people to be micro-managed by a digital and scientific technocracy, i.e., a dictatorship involving the rise of so-called smart cities, harmful EMF technologies, collaborative governance, crypto currencies, mass surveillance and compliance.

- Sustainable development was/is a 'cover' for continued mega-corporate globalisation in conjunction with banking extortion. The process was essentially designed to keep the flawed 'business as usual' environmentally destructive GDP growth system, thereby benefiting, for as long as possible, the mega-banks and corporations' and existing economic/banking power structure; and temporarily perpetuating a system that will ultimately fail due to its unsustainable, eco-cidal, inequality producing and human welfare diminishing effects.

- Over the past decades the orthodox political concept/solution/agenda of 'sustainable development' that has been promoted by the UN. and the governments of the world has not addressed the unjust flawed systems of banking and economic control that benefit an elite wealthy few at the expense of everyone else. There are detrimental environmental and societal effects associated with the current debt-money banking and GDP growth economic paradigm, for example

Professor Steve Keen has estimated that the worldwide private banking system bleeds around 35% of the profit of nations. The private bankers have been doing this for decades. Yet the current political agenda of sustainable development does not reform these areas, in fact it has endorsed them for decades. The worldwide privately owned banking and financial orthodoxy that is at the root of the world's financial difficulties and environmental problems has not been challenged by the UN or by the governments that adhere to the policies of the UN. Many well-intentioned people involved in the environmental, sustainability and sustainable development sectors have neglected to explore finance and debt for decades and did not make the connection between debt-finance, environmentally destructive economic growth and unsustainability.

- The current green energy/renewable technologies being promoted by the UN and WEF, these technologies are not a viable solution for the world's energy supply. The Energy Returned on Energy Invested (EROEI) is much too low – in essence the entire process is mathematically flawed. For example, it takes more energy to create a wind turbine-based energy network than it will ever produce! Most economists and policy makers are deluded by the own pseudo-science of contemporary economics and do not understand that the economy runs on energy and resources – not money! The promoters of the politically defined "green" future, that includes plans such as the widespread implementation of wind turbines, being pedalled to us, unfortunately, do not know what they are talking about. This is evidenced by the work of Professor David MacKay, Regius Professor of Engineering at Cambridge University and former Chief Scientific Advisor to the UK's Department of Energy and Climate Change, in his book "*Sustainable Energy without Hot Air*", see Endnote [57].

- Furthermore, it appears that the age of oil and therefore current industrial society as we know it may soon be over regardless. In an article '*The End of the Oilcene*', see Endnote [58], analyst Mr. Tim Clarke indicates that the current Energy Returned on Investment (EROI) of fossil fuels is too low to sustain industrial economies. Making more so-called 'green stuff' is not going to fix the basic problem of reduced energy availability in the future.

- An oft-mentioned sustainable development strategy has been the delusional policy to "decouple" environmental impacts from growth and this strategy has failed (and was never going to work within the GDP hypergrowth / globalisation paradigm and probably was never intended to). This is evidenced by a BIOS Research

Institute study that reviewed 179 scientific studies on decoupling published between 1990 and 2019, a period of nearly 30 years, and found, in short, that "the evidence does not suggest that decoupling towards ecological sustainability is happening at a global (or even regional) scale.", see Endnote [59].

- A separate issue is in relation to resource-efficiency being relied upon as a significant "green" solution, the Jevons paradox comes into play, whereby efficiency gains of resource-efficient technologies can translate into yet more consumption. There are false paths to sustainability, such as 'Eco-efficiency', and other 'greening business as usual' ideas such as the 'green growth', 'smart growth', 'circular economy', 'inclusive growth' etc., which alone will never solve the environmental resource problem. To realise what sustainability is and what it involves we must realise what it is not.

- True sustainability involves the creation of thriving local and regional networks of self-sufficient systems that serve human needs. UN Agenda 2030 involves a plan to abolish private property rights and get all people off the land and into smart towns and cities, where they will be unable to grow much food. This is the opposite of what is needed - people should be moving back to the land and developing self-sufficient communities. Creating a sustainable society involves developing practical locally empowered rural communities of villages and towns with local and regional systems for food, energy, water, goods and services rather than the unsustainable trans-national systems of the so-called globalised economy.

- Living happy, fulfilled, and successful lives in a sustainable society involves helping each other and our communities via thriving co-operative networks, rather than the 'rat-race' and 'musical chairs' of needless and excessive competition inherent in the GDP growth paradigm. It is the freedom to live as part of a thriving creative society without the shackles of unjust authoritarian control.

The WEF reset and politically defined UN so-called 'green futures' do not empower local communities; the mega-corporations and technocratic political structures retain control in these future scenarios. The short-term effects of this 'reset' are likely to be bad for the many people. The path for success involves personal freedom and local independence - not centralization, corporatocracy, authoritarianism and slavery. If people are not dependent on the system they cannot be controlled by the system. How many people will accept a 'well-marketed system of technocratic communism and how many will maintain their own freedom and create their own local systems? You are part of the answer.

The way forward to a 'real' sustainable and resilient society

A successful approach for human wellbeing must involve creating resilient more self-sufficient local and regional systems for food, energy, and services; and crucially raising human consciousness to transcend the 'matrix of illusions' of the current economic materialistic paradigm. In this way we can embrace our true potential as strong, capable, resilient, and spiritual beings.

By choosing freedom and by creating networks of like-minded people, the future is bright for the very many people that are taking the brave path toward freedom and truth. Choosing not to accept the unjust new rules will sooner or later bring about an end to the nefarious corporate and political manipulations. We should focus on developing 'thriving people and communities with higher qualities and abilities' rather than working as faceless mask-wearing cogs in a worldwide system designed by power-hungry mega-corporate narcissists

In the later chapters on real sustainability, human behaviour, ancient wisdom, spiritual economics, and higher consciousness I direct the reader toward the modes of human behavior and the role of higher consciousness and spiritual values in potentially transcending an overly materialistic way of life.

4. The UN climate hoax required a single controlling world influence

A single group controlling the world's mega-corporations and mega-banks?

"Give me control of a nation's money and I care not who makes the laws." - Mayer Amschel Rothschild, Banker

For the worldwide 'climate change is caused by carbon emissions' hoax to be orchestrated worldwide there would need to have been a coordinated orchestrated plan involving big-media, big-banking, big-tech, big-pharma, and big-politics - basically big everything. The Covid-19 fake pandemic would not have been possible unless there was a single controlling influence on the world's mega-corporations; mega-banks; governments; and international organizations, such as the WHO, WEF, UN, EU, etc. On the face of it, this seems to be preposterous proposition - the idea appears simply too incredibly BIG to be true. However, just because something is big or complicated does not mean it is not true. After all, the world has experienced decades of corporate consolidation.

It was noted in the previous chapter that it is **the world's central bankers that are behind this decision and are entirely funding and controlling the advancement of the worldwide climate change 'project'.** In December 2015, the Bank for International Settlements created the Task Force on Climate-related Financial Disclosure (TCFD), which represents $118 trillion of assets globally, see Endnote [60]. In essence this means that the financialization of the entire world economy is based on meeting nonsensical aims such as "net-zero greenhouse gas emissions. The TCFD includes key people from the world's mega-banks and asset management companies, including JP Morgan Chase; BlackRock; Barclays Bank; HSBC; China's ICBC bank; Tata Steel, ENI oil, and Dow Chemical and more.

Could it be true that a single group has a controlling influence on the worlds mega-corporations? To get to the root of the matter we first need to take a look at the ownership structure of the world's mega-corporations.

Who owns the banks and asset management companies that own and control the world?

"Give me control of a nation's money and I care not who makes the laws." - Mayer Amschel Rothschild, Banker

The amount of interest monies received by the international bankers on worldwide debt over decades is staggeringly vast. Given the impossibility of these debts ever being fully paid, it is surely time that widespread public discussion took place about where this money actually goes, and who benefits from it? i.e., who are the main private owners of the banking and corporate financial system? Unsurprisingly, the answer to who controls the major organisations and institutions of the modern world lies in 'following the money'. Let's take the example of Blackrock, one of the world's largest asset management companies, which manages funds of over $27 trillion ($27,000 billion) and in effect owns most of the U.S. and large parts of the world.

Blackrock - the company that owns most of the world

According to Ellen Brown, chairperson of the US Public Banking Institute, asset management companies, such as Blackrock, literally own much of the US and the world. She states:

> "BlackRock has a controlling interest in all the major corporations in the S&P 500, it professes not to "own" the funds. It just acts as a kind of "custodian" for its investors — or so it claims. But BlackRock and the other Big 3 ETFs (Exchange Traded Funds) vote the corporations' shares; so from the point of view of management, they are the owners. And as observed in a 2017 article from the University of Amsterdam titled "These Three Firms Own Corporate America, see Endnote [61]," they vote 90% of the time in favor of management." - Ellen Brown, Chair of the US Public banking Institute

The major shareholders of Blackrock are all mega-banks and financial corporations, such as Bank of America, JPMorgan Chase, Citi Group, Wells Fargo and Company, Morgan Stanley, and other various other mega-banks, see Endnote [62], in this way we can see that it the mega-banks that own most of the world. Analysis shows that the major shareholders in the commercial banks are other banks and asset management companies and trusts

Blackrock also has major shareholdings in mega-banks, such as Morgan Stanley and JP Morgan Chase and various other banks and financial corporations, see Endnote [63], yet those same banks and corporations have major shareholdings in Blackrock. The list of shareholders is diversified amongst various privately owned financial and asset management corporations. In essence, analysis shows that the various corporate entities are interlocked and own each other.

So, privately owned commercial mega-banks own Blackrock and the other major asset management companies that own most of the world. In a 2018 review titled "Blackrock - The Company That Owns the World', see Endnote [64], a multinational research group called Investigate Europe concluded that BlackRock "undermines competition through owning shares in competing companies", in this way it has a monopoly or single controlling influence. Furthermore, Blackrock now manages the spigots to trillions of bailout dollars from the Federal Reserve.

Study proves one corporate 'super-entity' owns/dominates the world economy and resources

This 'interlocking ownership' is also very evident in a wider study that was conducted in 2018, see Endnote [65], at the Swiss Federal Institute of Technology in Zurich, Switzerland, on the relationships between 37 million companies and investors worldwide, and they concluded there is a 'super-entity' of just 147 tightly knit mega-corporations, and all of their ownership was held by other members of the super-entity. In essence, the worldwide privately owned financial and corporate orthodoxy is one large self-reinforcing super-entity underneath the tentacles of many financial mega-corporations. This upper-entity controls 40 percent of the entire global economy and most of their ownership was held by other members of the super-entity. According to James B. Glattfelder, one of the authors of the study: "In effect, less than 1 per cent of the companies were able to control 40 per cent of the entire network." Most of the controlling corporations are financial institutions and include Barclays Bank, JPMorgan Chase & Co, and The Goldman Sachs Group.

The dominant players are the banking families that have been operating private banking for generations. The involvement of certain banking families in private banking for generations is described in books including '*The Web of Debt*' by E.H. Brown, chair of the U.S. Public Banking Institute. Families that are documented to have controlling shares of the banking industry, include the Rothschild banking dynasty, associated with US Trust owned by Bank of America; the Rockefeller world business empire, associated with Citigroup; the Schiff's; the Morgan's, see Endnote [66], associated with Morgan Stanley, etc.; and the Warburg's.

Author Karen Hudes, who worked in the legal department of the World Bank for more than 20 years, has cited the above Swiss study during an interview with the New American, see Endnote [67], pointing, out that a small group of entities, mostly financial institutions and especially central banks, exert a massive amount of influence over the international economy from behind the scenes. According to Hudes: "What is really going on is that the world's resources are being dominated by this group," and that "corrupt power grabbers" have managed to dominate the media as well. According to Hudes, the power grabbers also dominate the organizations that control the creation and flow of money worldwide and control the finances of virtually every nation in the world. These organizations include The World Bank, the IMF and central banks, such as the Federal Reserve, all of which are unelected and unaccountable.

The private banking cartel owns and controls the corporate super-entity

The analysis shows that the major shareholders in the commercial banks are other banks and asset management companies and trusts. <u>A small number of mega-banks are among the top ten stock holders of virtually every Fortune 500 corporation.</u> Author Dean Henderson writes in an article, see Endnote [68]:

> "The Four Horsemen of Banking (Bank of America, JP Morgan Chase, Citigroup and Wells Fargo) own the Four Horsemen of Oil (Exxon Mobil, Royal Dutch/Shell, BP and Chevron Texaco); in tandem with Deutsche Bank, BNP, Barclays and other European old money behemoths. But their monopoly over the global economy does not end at the edge of the oil patch. According to company 10K filings to the SEC, the Four Horsemen of Banking are among the top ten stock holders of virtually every Fortune 500 corporation…
>
> One important repository for the wealth of the global oligarchy that owns these bank holding companies is US Trust Corporation – founded in 1853 and now owned by Bank of America. A recent US Trust Corporate Director and Honorary Trustee was Walter Rothschild. Other directors included Daniel Davison of JP Morgan Chase, Richard Tucker of Exxon Mobil, Daniel Roberts of Citigroup and Marshall Schwartz of Morgan Stanley, see Endnote [69]" - Dean Henderson, Author

In summary, the world economy and the tens of thousands of corporations of the world is controlled by one large self-reinforcing super-entity. This super-entity operates under the seemingly different tentacles of around 147 mega-corporations, but these mega-corporations are mostly owned by a very small number of mega-financial institutions/ privately owned mega-banks. These mega-financial institutions/mega-banks are owned and controlled by private banking families. This is why less than 0.001 % of the world's population, i.e., a small number of banking family elites and their networks, own the majority of the world's assets and wealth.

Who owns the mega-banks that own and control the world?

So, we can conclude privately owned commercial mega-banks own the FED, Blackrock and the other major asset management companies that own most of the world. The dominant players are the Jewish banking families that have been operating private banking for generations. These families that have long been documented in relation to ownership of the banking sector and include the Rothschild banking dynasty, associated with US Trust owned by Bank of America; the Rockefeller world business empire associated with Citigroup; the Schiff's; the Morgan's, see Endnote [70], associated with Morgan Stanley, etc., and the Warburg's. As we have seen these dynasties achieved this not by adding more value, but by usurping control of the source of money creation process, the Federal Reserve and the worldwide central banking system.

The central banking system exerts vast control over the world economy

The Bank for International Settlements in Switzerland is the central bank of central banks and is virtually immune to the laws of all national governments. Even Wikipedia admits that it is not accountable to any single national government, see Endnote [71]. There are 58 global central banks belonging to the BIS, and it has far more power over the economies of the world economy than any politician does. The central bankers of the world gather for meetings at BIS and make decisions that affect every person in the world, and yet none of us have any say in what goes on. According to Author Michael Snyder:

> "The Bank for International Settlements is an organization that was founded by the global elite and it operates for the benefit of the global elite, and it is intended to be one of the key cornerstones of the emerging one world economic system.... [T]he powers of financial capitalism had another far-reaching aim, nothing less than to create a world system of financial control in private hands able to dominate the political system of each country and the economy of the world as a whole. This system was to be controlled in a feudalist fashion by the central banks of the world acting in concert, by secret agreements arrived at in frequent private meetings and conferences. The apex of the system was to be the Bank for International Settlements in Basle, Switzerland, a private bank owned and controlled by the world's central banks which were themselves private corporations. And that is exactly what we have today. We have a system of "neo-feudalism" in which all of us and our national governments are enslaved to debt. This system is governed by the central banks and by the Bank for International Settlements, and it systematically transfers the wealth of the world out of our hands and into the hands of the global elite, see Endnote 72." - Michael Snyder

How did a private banking cartel gain ownership of the world's wealth and resources?

The next chapter provides a historical timeline of how the privately owned mega-banks gained control. The milestones include: The Federal Reserve coup of 1913, in which a group of private bankers took ownership and control of the money-creation process; the creation of banker- influenced international institutional frameworks, including the UN, the IMF, the World Bank, the WEF, the WHO, (for example, it is no coincidence that the founder of the WEF was Klaus Schwab, son of the Rothschild Jewish banking dynasty); the processes of economic globalisation; boom-bust-bailout cycles for nations; corporate consolidation and the creation of vast mega-corporations; corporate control of the world's resources, and ongoing processes of vast wealth accumulation for the private banking sector, including fraudulent worldwide fractional reserve banking and the worldwide derivatives market. By 2019, these processes had resulted in a network of mega-banks and mega-corporations owning and controlling the world economy and the bulk of the world's wealth and resources. The bio-pharmaceutical and vaccine corporations are just one branch of the worldwide corporate structure.

1913 to 2019 - a private banking elite gained control of the world's wealth/resources

The historical context of all this involves the history of the privately owned world banking system and associated world economic system from 1913 to 2019. Over those decades, prior to the extra-ordinary financial events of October 2019 that hardly anyone has heard about, a small group of private bankers gained immense of amounts of the world's wealth and a controlling interest in the mega-banks and mega-corporations of the world. How did they do this? It was done via ownership and control of the world's debt-money creation system from 1913 onwards. This process over decades was powered by the associated GDP hypergrowth paradigm of globalisation. Immense corporate consolidation occurred by design, the culmination of this process is exemplified by the asset management corporation Blackrock, an asset management corporation, which manages funds of around 27 trillion, that is 27,000 billion! Blackrock, and the entire mega-corporate structure, are essentially one super-entity that is controlled by mega-banks, i.e., the small group of people that have controlling ownership of the mega-banks.

Over the decades, the debt-money component of the system has resulted in worldwide debt-slavery with virtually all governments in debt to the international private banking cartel. This served the immense wealth accumulation plans of those few in control of the system, but the system was ultimately flawed/unsustainable. These people have long planned for the end-phase of their flawed, but extremely lucrative for them, debt-money economic system; to collapse society to the detriment of humanity; and clear a path/make an excuse for the introduction of their nefarious ideal - a technocratic authoritarian 'reset' of society and centralized one world government that operates according to their design and rules.

The debt slavery paradigm has been in place for decades. This paradigm has been controlled by the privately owned worldwide banking cartel, and is evidenced by the fact that in 2020 virtually all governments of the world are in vast debt, see Endnote [73]. These debts are the debt-money loans that the international private-bankers created from nothing, see Endnote [74]. For decades, the international privately owned banking system has created debt-money from nothing and charged all governments and people often extortionist interest on it (usury). By this and other mechanisms it bled a significant percentage of the profits of the world's nations. This resulted in immense wealth and political power for a tiny minority that own the private system of worldwide banking, but placed a financial debt burden of control on the nations of the world.

The cruel hoax is that governments could have created this money themselves. The last US President to attempt to take the money creation process out of the hands of the private bankers was John F Kennedy.

The flawed GDP hypergrowth/globalisation system was needed by the private-banking cartel, so that it could receive endless interest payments on debt-money loans created from nothing. Yet for decades GDP growth at-all-costs development caused vast environmental degradation. Furthermore, it has been a myth that the globalisation system "floated all boats". The real economic welfare of the 99% of society, as estimated by the Genuine Progress Indicator, has decreased since 1978. The pseudo-science of contemporary economics was used by all governments to facilitate the process. Furthermore, by controlling the availability of credit the private banking cartel created boom-bust-bailout cycles at will that placed nations in further debt. For example, the European Central Bank (ECB) robber-barons exerted pressure on the Irish government to bail out private banks and unsecured bondholders in 2010. In 2012 RTE, Ireland's National Television Service reported that the ECB informed an Irish Government Minister that:

> "a bomb will go off in Dublin" if Anglo bondholders are not paid. "He [Minister for Transport and Tourism, Leo Varadkar] said that the Troika told the Government that "we don't want you to default on these payments, it is your decision ultimately but a bomb will go off; and the bomb will go off in Dublin and not in Frankfurt." – RTE reporting Minister Varadkar's comments 22nd January 2012 - see Endnote [75]

The government then guaranteed those vast debts and the resulting government bailout resulted in the Irish people being unjustly forced to pay for what were essentially the gambling debts of privately-owned banks and international bondholders. These mega-banks and bondholders already held at least 100 times the entire wealth of the Irish people yet, the people were forced via increased austerity and taxes to shoulder interest payments of billions per annum in perpetuity on a debt that will never be paid off, and was not their debt in the first place. This is the vicious and criminal reality of the debt-money political paradigm, and the boom-bust-bailout trick that has been inflicted on many countries worldwide. Such realities are typically 're-packaged' on government-controlled- and corporate-media. A similar situation occurred in Greece, yet Greece was, in 2020, 45% more in debt than it was before its austerity programs started.

Over decades, the power, and un-earned privilege, of the private-bankers to create money resulted in the power to own, control and manipulate the assets of the material world, as well media and politics. A small group of people and the private mega-banks and mega-corporations they run, gained and consolidated control of the majority of the world's financial wealth and assets. This power grab was achieved not by creating more value, but by fully controlling the source of money and the financial world.

100 years of private banking leaves all nations in vast debt + bankers owning the world

In 2022, over 100 years after the Federal Reserve coup of 1913, the world is still living under the debt chains of this world private-banking cartel, a financial power group or cabal, which has gradually usurped the top-levels of the world's most influential political, corporate, media and institutional organisations. Vast interest payments have been flowing into the privately owned mega-banks from the governments of the world for over 100 years. President John F Kennedy was the last US president to take back this monopoly away from the private-bankers and he was assassinated the same year.

World Bank statistics in August 2020, see Endnote [76], showed that virtually every national government of the world owes vast amounts of debt. The nations of the world have been in ongoing debt servitude to the international banking and finance system for decades.

By the year 2020, this transfer of the world's wealth via the debt-money and hypergrowth globalisation model was almost complete and the bulk of world's wealth and resources is technically now in the hands of a small number of so-called financial elites, that own and control the mega-banks and mega-corporations of the world. This is the so-called 1% of the world population that people often talk about that have all the real wealth, but it is more like 0.0001% of the population – a power network based around a relatively small number of banking families.

According to Forbes, see Endnote [77], the world's eight richest people have same wealth as the world's poorest 50%. Business Insider state just 26 of the world's richest persons have more combined wealth than the poorest 3.8 billion people. However, data on the wealth of the banking family dynasties that own the world's mega banks is typically absent from such magazine lists. According to Bloomberg, see Endnote [78], data on the wealth of banking families, such as the Rothschilds and the Rockefellers is too diversified to value or calculate.

> "the top 25 families are worth $1.1 trillion and… "any calculation is likely to be a low-ball figure," since the wealth of many families like the Rothschilds and Rockefellers is too diversified and diffuse

to value. Bloomberg said that some dynasties whose fortunes are closely intertwined with government, like the House of Saud, are also too difficult to calculate." - Bloomberg

Some authors and independent researchers, see Endnote [79], have estimated that the Rothschilds banking family alone is worth over $100 trillion, a sum which vastly surpasses the fortunes of the corporate billionaires on the Bloomberg Billionaires Index.

The end result is the system, or the 'matrix', we all live in and were born into

This system forces people to live in a debt cycle which never ends. The system incessantly promotes an addiction to materialism for the purpose of producing revenues so interest can be paid. Since debt does not really exist and was created from nothing, the national debt is a hoax perpetrated by the so-called 'powers that be'. The private central-banks and governments facilitate this worldwide con game, yet we allow these same people to control education, law, media, banking, medicine etc. We placed our trust in these so-called authorities, and most believe that we must 'pay the piper', and that any punishment or fine we sustain from these authorities is justified and deserved, as if we have no power or minds of our own. This scam or illusion is sometimes known as the 'matrix'. The perpetuation of this myth of institutional authority is detrimental to our true spiritual nature and denies that GOD is the only true authority. Why do we give away our freedom or do anything other than just be free to exercise the freewill that GOD gave us?

The dystopian movie *The Matrix* portrays humans as just batteries, the slave energy to fuel a technocratic dictatorship. The worldwide Covid-19 hoax and the UN/WEF technocratic reset of world society attempts to move us toward this dystopian technocratic nightmare. How many people will wake up, like movie character 'Neo' and discover their own power? The reality is that many people are waking up and more cracks in the 'matrix' are appearing.

2019 - mathematical end-phase of a world financial system that was always flawed/fraudulent

The flawed economic and financial system was already in crash/failure mode prior to the Covid-19 'situation'. The flaws of the system were exposed in the banking crisis of 2008. The central bankers had been 'kicking the can down the road' so to speak to keep their fraudulent world banking scam going as long as possible. Endless quantitative easing occurred from October 2019 onwards, see Endnote [80]. (Note: quantitative easing is the printing of vast amounts of money from nothing and providing that money to a sector of the economy, usually banks and asset management corporations). The situation was far more serious than ever before in history because the Federal Reserve balance, as % of GDP, was at least ten times worse, in relative terms in 2019, than in the Great Crash of

1929! This balance is an indicator of the amount of debt in the system. Central banking branches worldwide all were all implementing similar mechanisms.

The up-shot of this most extra-ordinary situation in world financial history, was that a multi-trillion-dollar bailout to financial asset management corporation Blackrock was sanctioned in the U.S. in April 2020, under cover of the Covid-19 situation, see Endnote [81]. Hardly anyone knows about this event, because the corporate media didn't report it! 99% of the world media is owned and controlled by a single corporate grouping, and they were busy scaring everyone senseless about a non-existent killer virus. Note: In reality these asset management companies own and control most of the entire world's wealth and resources, for example, asset management company Blackrock manages and has controlling ownership of funds of over $27 trillion, i.e., $27,000 billion. The extra-ordinary endless quantitative easing that occurred for months from October 2019 onwards and the multi-trillion bailout event that occurred in April 2020 gained virtually no media coverage in comparison to the coverage of the Covid-19 situation. The world population were not being told about the most serious world financial situation ever, i.e., the financial system itself had reached its mathematical end-phase. Various analysts and the elites themselves have long known this was inevitably going to happen and had used the fraudulent system for decades to accumulate the majority of the wealth and resources of the world.

Enter the Covid-19 world pandemic, a pre-planned event, which provided a smokescreen for a world 'economic reset' by the world's central bankers in March 2020, i.e., the exact same time the pandemic was hitting every TV screen in the world with full force. This is clearly and comprehensively evidenced in my book *Transcending the Covid-19 Deception*. At the same time the controversial attempted 'reset' of society by the WEF was initiated.

By October 2019, the worldwide debt-money system of debt slavery had reached its mathematical end-phase, due to vast amounts of unpayable debt, reduced EROEI for oil, the consequent inability to grow economies further and the inability of governments to service ongoing interest payments. The private banking cabal needed to replace the old debt-money system with something else and they had long planned for this moment.

The UN / WEF and international bankers needed a smokescreen for the economic reset

The UN / WEF and international bankers needed a smokescreen to attempt to transition from the broken fiat-money system to a technocratic control system that they have designed for their own benefit. The central bankers certainly did not want the world to know that the economic system was systemically broken; that the whole world was in vast unpayable debt; that Blackrock had received trillions of dollars as part of a financial reset; or that Covid-19 was a smokescreen for the imposition of a new technocratic world society deceptively marketed by the WEF/UN/WHO, etc. Not to mention that the world private-banking cartel, owns the vast bulk of the world's wealth and resources, via ownership of world's asset management companies, see page 77. If billons of people became aware of these robber-baron realities would the populace not revolt against the so-called authority of governments and private banking? and simply take back the assets they needed from these financial and institutional wheeler-dealers?

No - the so-called elites could not allow this to happen. They needed a transition plan so that they could maintain their control and so that no-one would threaten to take away their vast wealth, property and corporate power. A world lockdown was their solution to ensure the general population did not rise up and take the wealth of the banking and corporate elites – as they easily could do so consisting of billions of people.

Covid-19 was a manufactured crisis – this is clearly and comprehensively evidenced in my book *Transcending the Covid-19 Deception*. They needed a smokescreen for controlled economic demolition and to attempt an economic reset and the imposition of new rules and norms. The elites needed an excuse to lockdown the world, ensure people would not leave their homes and talk to one another, be fully distracted from what was really happening and most of all be afraid. A killer virus was the perfect solution for them. They had been priming the masses via ideological subversion for the previous 20 years, including 'trial-run' pandemic outbreaks being headlined in the news networks, such as the purported SARS outbreak in China in 2003, swine flu in 2009, and various movies about killer viruses etc. Regardless of the reason for the timing, it is clear that the 2020 Covid-19 manufactured crisis is part of a long-term plan/agenda of control.

The Covid-19 pandemic was an excuse to significantly damage the local economies of the world's peoples, and to initiate a reset of the entire world economy to a totalitarian design that the elites had long planned for. A controlled economic demolition has been taking place, Covid-19 is being blamed for the collapsed economy, and the WEF reset/new world order is being imposed upon the world as the solution, clever marketing and propaganda is used to ensure the population accepts the changes – this is the tried-and-tested Hegelian dialectic formula (or problem-reaction-solution) utilised by the so-called elites. The UN climate change narrative is an integral part of these plans.

The book *'Covid19 - The Great Reset'* by WEF Founder Klaus Schwab and Thierry Malleret, brazenly utilises the Covid-19 situation as a major reason for the 'reset' and makes scaremongering statements such as:

> "The Corona virus is spreading globally and sparing none"
> "If no one power can enforce order, our world will suffer from a global order deficit"
> "A Great Reset is necessary to build a new social contract... COVID-19 has accelerated our transition into the age of the Fourth Industrial Revolution."

The book also states social distancing measures are likely to persist 'after' the pandemic subsides and that 'fear... will thus speed the relentless march of automation'. Yet Schwab contradicts his owns words by stating that the consequences of Covid-19 in terms of health and mortality are mild compared to previous pandemics and that HIV/AIDS was responsible for 100 times more deaths than Covid-19, see Endnote [82]. Millions of people have challenged the mainstream narrative and posed the valid question 'if the consequences are relatively mild why are drastic changes of mass societal control and surveillance being proposed and implemented?'

WEF/UN marketing of a technocratic world reset – unelected one world government

> "The United Nations Charter was written by three men with ties to the Council on Foreign Relations and the Soviet Union – an organization and a nation devoted to one world government and communism" - Ron Taylor, Author

The WEF and the UN are at the forefront of this attempted 'reset' of society. The WEF is a private organisation with a corporate agenda known as the Fourth Industrial Revolution and with significant links to privately owned mega-banks, mega-corporations, and the UN. It is also notable that Klaus Schwab Founder of the WEF is the son of Marianne Schwab nee Rothschild of the Rothschild private banking dynasty. The WEF Event 201 pandemic simulation was a simulation of a coronavirus pandemic and was held just two months before the actual Covid-19/coronavirus pandemic in early 2020. Event 201 was held by the Bill and Melinda Gates Foundation in partnership with the WEF. The scenario explained:

> "the pandemic will continue at some rate until there is an effective vaccine or until 80-90 % of the global population has been exposed. From that point on, it is likely to be an endemic childhood disease"

and suggested solutions to a pandemic, such as the institution of a global centralized economic body that could handle the financial response to the coronavirus. Enter the 'supposed' real Covid-19 situation. Less than a month after the conclusion of Event 201 a worldwide Coronavirus 'situation', duplicating the Event 201 simulation. Thus, the WEF 'reset' of world society was launched, in what the organisation said was in response to the Covid-19 pandemic. This reset includes the imposition of world-vaccination using never-before-used DNA-based technology. The Bill and Melinda Gates Foundation, a direct partner of the WEF, and major funder of the WHO, has been a major force behind efforts for a Covid-19 vaccination to be disseminated worldwide. The 'reset' is an attempt by the WEF, and their corporate, political and financial backers to push their fourth industrial revolution agenda of control. An undemocratic dictatorship involving the rise of smart cities, surveillance, bio-metrics, 5G, crypto currencies, and the drive toward a digital cashless society that people have no control over are all part of this globalist plan. This ongoing 'reset' aims to promotes and implement measures including:

- the destruction of human freedoms and civil rights via new laws and restrictions;
- the imposition a worldwide data-driven technocratic system of control;
- the imposition of mass vaccination utilising DNA-based human-genome altering 'vaccines';
- the integration of two-way bio-metric technology into all humans, i.e., trans-humanism;
- a communist-inspired digitised monetary system;
- continued environmentally destructive globalisation, for example, via the production of hundreds of millions of new electric cars, and renewable energy infrastructure, that in almost all cases provide a poor 'energy returned on energy invested (EROEI). The creation of these new energy infrastructures worldwide is a scandalous waste of the remaining world stocks of fossil fuels. Vast amounts of materials and rare earth metals are required for these productions resulting in continued environmental destruction and pollution to land, air and water,
- the widespread pervasive use of microwave electro-magnetic field (EMF) technologies that harm human health. 5G, WIFI, smartphones, smart-cities, smart-meters, electric cars and mass electrification are all part of this. Note: Thousands of scientific reports and human stories prove the long-term detrimental health effects of these technologies. The WHO even admits that EMF technologies are a cause of cancer, but this information is not provided on corporate news media systems;
- the ongoing deceptive agendas of politically defined sustainable development and manmade climate change.

The private banking cartel purchased and controls the world's corporate media

Why is this whole situation not reported in the corporate media? The general public in all nations have very little awareness that any of this is happening because the global elite also control what we see, hear, and think about. For example, there are only six mega-corporations that control more than 90 percent of the news and entertainment in the United States, see Endnote [83]. This vital information is not published in the corporate-owned media of the world because for decades the media of the world has been acquired by this small group of money masters. Author E.H. Brown and chairperson of the Public Banking Institute described the situation as follows:

> "**Secrecy has been maintained because the robber barons have been able to use their monopoly over money to buy up major media, educational institutions, and other outlets of public information.** While Rockefeller was buying up universities, medical schools, and the Encyclopedia Britannica, Morgan bought up newspapers... By 1983... fifty corporations owned half or more of the media business. **By 2000, that number was down to six corporations, with directorates interlocked with each other and with major commercial banks**. (See Endnote [84])"
> - E.H. Brown

The Rockefellers are central to the plan of the elites for world domination. They use their foundation and money to influence to control public policy, in full alignment with Jewish-owned world banking cartel and Rothschilds world empire. These banking dynasties were the ones behind the formation of the UN, not to promote world peace but to impose a one world government system controlled by these private banking dynasties and their mega-corporations.

Six corporations own 96% of the media - testimonies the media is controlled by world bankers

> "Whatever information you get, about what is going on in the world, from TV, radio, newspapers, magazines, school, or the government, you can count on the opposite being the truth. They all ought to be required to file an affidavit stating: "Under full commercial liability, I claim the following to be true, correct, complete, and not misleading".... Be aware that most of the media are controlled by just a few." - Mary Elizabeth Croft, Author

> "Most of our newspapers, magazines, and publishing houses are owned — and manipulated —by gigantic international corporations. Our media is part of the corporatocracy. The officers and directors who control nearly all our communications outlets know their places... So the burden falls on you to see the truth beneath the veneer and to expose it." – John Perkins, Author

Just six Jewish-owned major media conglomerates own about 96% of the corporate media in the US, these six mega-corporations are Jewish owned and managed, see Endnote [85]. Recall that the Rockefeller Foundation, was the organization behind the 'Lockstep' strategy, that was central to the worldwide implementation of the covid-19 world lockdown. David Rockefeller, in an address before, the Trilateral Commission, in June of 1991, made the following statement, which reveals how the Rockefeller banking dynasty used the media for decades to advance a plan for a world government planned by "the supranational sovereignty of an intellectual elite and world bankers" and ensured the international banking elites were not mentioned in the media:

> "We are grateful to The Washington Post, The New York Times, Time Magazine and other great publications whose directors have attended our meetings and respected their promises of discretion for almost forty years. It would have been impossible for us to develop our plan for the world if we had been subject to the bright lights of publicity during those years. But, the world is now more sophisticated and prepared to march towards a world government. The supranational sovereignty of an intellectual elite and world bankers is surely preferable to the national auto-determination practiced in past centuries." - David Rockefeller, in an address before, the Trilateral Commission, in June of 1991

> "Our job is to give people not what they want, but what we decide they ought to have." - Richard Salant, former President of CBS News

> "The business of the journalist is to destroy the truth; to lie outright; to pervert; to vilify; to fawn at the feet of Mammon, and to sell his country and his race for his daily bread. You know it and I know it, so what folly is this toasting an independent press? We are the tools and vassals of rich men behind the scenes... They pull the strings... AND WE DANCE." - John Swinton, former chief-of-staff for the New York Times, in an address to fellow journalists.

The following testimony from a US Congressman describes how the J.P. Morgan banking dynasty purchased control of the entire US media in 1915, just two years of the Federal Reserve banking coup:

> "In March, 1915, the J. P. Morgan interests… got together 12 men high up in the newspaper world and employed them to select the most influential newspapers in the United States and sufficient number of them to control generally the policy of the daily press ... They found it was necessary to purchase the control of only 25 of the greatest papers. An agreement was reached; the policy of the papers was bought, to be paid for by the month; an editor was furnished for each paper to properly supervise and edit information regarding the questions of preparedness, militarism, financial policies, and other things of national and international nature considered vital to the interests of the purchasers." - U.S. Congressman Oscar Callaway, 1917

The Tavistock Institute - a history of media manipulations and social engineering

Those with a higher degree of perceptive will have noticed that the entire world has been kept in a permanent media-induced state of imbalance. Overwhelmed by crises after crises – from climate change to covid to orchestrated war and price inflation – the masses have been attacked by media mind-bombs of low-and-high intensity terror and de-stabilisation. That is all part of the plan of the globalist totalitarian machine. Whilst the masses are kept off-balance the machine continues to introduce more restrictions in the name of climate change or some other concocted 'future shock', that is nonetheless entirely of the backed by banker-controlled government and the banker-owned corporate media, and funded by world bankers, for example, the Bank for International Settlements created Task Force on Climate-related Financial Disclosure (TCFD), which represents $118 trillion of assets globally.

The history of social engineering can be traced back to hundreds of institutes formed and funded by the Rockefeller banking-dynasty during and after World War II. These include: The Tavistock Institute, The Institute for Social Research (ISR) known as the Frankfurt School, Cornell ILR, the Department of Social Relations in Germany, the International Jewish Research Foundation on Human Relations in Israel, and many more, see Endnote [86].

"The Tavistock Institute for Human Relations is the psychological warfare arm of the British Royal family, located in a suburb of London. It is the world's most important institution for manipulation of population." – Daniel Estulin, Author

In the US, this influence extended to the American Medical Association, to all branches of the US government, including the military, the CIA, and was used to plant Rockefeller-Tavistock proteges and representatives in key positions and institutions through the entire structure of the US political and economic hierarchy, see Endnote [87], including in TV, radio and newspaper corporations, the largest law firms, the largest universities and think-tanks. The story of Tavistock is central to how the US government intelligence agencies used psychology and mass social engineering to further certain post-war interests and agendas of globalist elites, at the expense of traditional European and American traditional culture and values. In Europe, Lord Bertrand Russell joined the Frankfurt School with this same purpose, in his 1951 book *The Impact of Science on Society* he wrote:

> "I think the subject which will be of most importance politically is mass psychology... Its importance has been enormously increased by the growth of modern methods of propaganda. Of these the most influential is what is called 'education'... the press, the cinema, and the radio play an increasing part... It may be hoped that in time anybody will be able to persuade anybody of anything, if he can catch the patient young and is provided by the State with money and equipment... **The subject will make great strides when it is taken up by scientist under a scientific dictatorship...** Although this science will be diligently studied, it will be diligently confined to the governing class. **The populace will not be allowed to know how its convictions were generated.** When the technique has been perfected, **every government that has been in charge of education for a generation will be able to control its subjects securely without the need of armies or policemen.**" – Lord Bertrand Russell

Aldous Huxley was grandson of the famous biologist Thomas Henry Huxley and a member of Britain's Round Table elite. Via these experiences and associations, Huxley gained the material to write his famous 1931 novel *Brave New World*, which is blue-print of a future one world socialist government of control. According to Author Daniel Estulin, the philosophical aim of Huxley and his associates, including H.G. Wells, and Lord Bertrand Russel "was the destruction of the sovereign power of the nation-state, and with it the elimination of a philosophical, cultural, and religious tradition dating more than 2,500 years".

> "There will be in the next generation or so a pharmacological method of making people love their servitude and producing dictatorship without tears, so to speak.... Producing a kind of painless concentration camp for entire societies so that people will in fact have their liberties taken away from them, but will rather enjoy it, because they will be distracted from any kind of desire to rebel by propaganda, or brainwashing enhanced by pharmacological methods". – Aldous Huxley speaking at a California Medical School in San Francisco, see Endnote [88]

Estulin describes that H. G. Wells, the science-fiction novelist, was head of British foreign intelligence during World War I, and was a member of the elite British oligarchic planning group, the Coefficients, who along with British Round Table Intelligence were directly linked to the House of Windsor, and the upper echelons of secret societies and financial interests. These groups were committed to the establishment of a "feudal empire run by an aristocracy which controlled all knowledge and technology and used them to rule over a population of ignorant drugged plantation slaves", see Endnote [89].

In the 1960s, the social engineers were at work, and one of the plans was to derail traditional family values via the introduction of the drugs counter culture. According to Estulin, it was the networks of British Military Intelligence and the CIA, who were the initiators of the famous Woodstock music festival, where nearly half a million youth gathered to be drugged and brainwashed on a farm, immersed in filth, pumped with psychedelic drugs, and kept awake for three straight days, and all with the full endorsement of the FBI and government officials; the money for Woodstock was supplied by John Roberts, the heir of the large Block Drugs pharmaceutical empire fortune; and security was provided by a hippie commune called Hog Farm trained in the mass distribution of LSD.

In order to de-stabilise traditional values, the Tavistock Institute funded research into how to create new cultural and social trends including: liberalism, socialism, anarchism, communism, hedonism, drug culture, feminism, new age religion (distortions of authentic religion), public support for new wars, and many more. These funded trends were promoted via TV, radio, messages embedded in popular music, Hollywood movies, science-fiction movies designed to 'bend the minds', etc, and were intended to soften up American and world society for the introduction of Tavistock-planned societal social changes. A common theme I have observed in Hollywood science-fiction films is the attribution of man's progress and knowledge to superior aliens and therefore, the denial of mankind's divine spark. When religion does arise in Hollywood movies, original spiritual teachings from mankind's ancient past are ignored, instead we are presented with repackaged distorted new age mysticism and hippie drug culture.

> "Tavistock recognised that habituated television watching destroys the ability of a person for critical cognitive activity. In other words, it makes you stupid… Tavistock… develop a theory of "social turbulence", a so-called "softening up effect of future shocks" – wherein a population could be softened up through mass phenomena such as energy shortages, economic and financial collapse, or terrorist attack." – Daniel Estulin, Author

The wide-ranging extent of social engineering is also evidenced by a Bilderberg Group document, titled *TOP SECRET Silent Weapons for Quiet Wars, An Introductory programming Manual*, which describes tactical methods to subjugate and control the human race via education, manipulation of industry, people's pastimes, and divide and conquer strategies, see Endnote [90], to distract people from what is really going on. The manual states: "It is patently impossible to discuss social engineering or the automation of a society, i.e., the engineering of social automation systems (silent weapons) on a national or worldwide scale without implying extensive objectives of social control and destruction of human life, i.e., slavery and genocide. This manual is in itself an analog declaration of intent. Such writing must be secured from public scrutiny."

> "America's corporate media are an integral part of the economic establishment, with links to Wall Street, the Washington think-tanks, Club Bilderberg and the Council and Foreign Relations (CFR) and through them to the world's premier brainwashing center, Tavistock Institute… the CFR often sets the strategy for American policy…" – Daniel Estulin, Author

The world is swayed by public opinion and public opinion is made by the elites in these institutes with endless funding. Everything is geared so the public will beg for government to act, to save them from the impending doom, whether it be covid, climate change, or to intervene in pre-orchestrated wars of destruction. The public becomes conditioned by corporate media to accept the war "so we can defeat the aggressor and save the victims", however, the reality is large wars are orchestrated events in which both sides are funded by the financial elite to create instability in a region.

'Public opinion' itself has become a social engineering tool – it is mob opinion created by knee-jerk reaction to cleverly designed corporate media TV shock-stories. For example, a 12-year-old Greta Thunberg appealing to the world's teenagers that we only have 12 years to 'save the planet'. Fabricated marketable celebrity heroes are used to promote certain agendas and pull on the emotional heartstrings of the masses. In this way TV creates a false reality. Yet no matter how many people agree with something it doesn't make it true.

In an attempt to control the growing 'truther movement" the manipulators also own dozens of the 'truther' websites. Wikileaks, by the way, is a CIA front, see Endnote [91]. It seems it is now okay to believe in conspiracy theories just as long its the conspiracy theories that give you some of the truth, and then lead you in the wrong direction at the end.

The financial pyramid of power and control

A worldwide network of mega-corporations and mega-banks is owned and controlled by a single powerful group that have controlling ownership. This may be hard to believe, however, in-depth analysis of the hierarchical and interlocked ownership of millions of corporations has proved this. Various independent analyses, including a Swiss study of the ownership of 147 mega-corporations, proves the existence of a single corporate super-entity owning and therefore pulling the strings of the world economy. The major shareholders are proven to be Jewish-owned mega-banks and Jewish-owned financial corporations, such as Bank of America, JPMorgan Chase, Citi Group, Wells Fargo and Company, Morgan Stanley, and other various other mega-banks, see Endnote [92].

A pyramid type system of hierarchical control has existed in society - it has operated via debt slavery. The higher up you go the closer you get to the source of money creation. This means that the institutional, political and corporate structures of the world are in reality controlled from a moneyed source not from a democratic source. This power grab was achieved not by creating more value, but by fully commandeering and controlling the source of money and the world of finance. At the bottom level we are all going about our daily lives. At the next level up are governments. Governments are given a monopoly on force and use it to tax and control the population whether or not we agree. The election of new government leaders via representative democracy is an illusion of people power. The vast regulatory systems of government bureaucracy never change. This bureaucracy is ultimately subservient not to the people but to international finance. Who controls the governments? It is not the people of the nations that control governments - this reality is evidenced by the banking bailouts in Europe after 2008. There was no referendum on the subject, the governments simply complied with the wishes of international privately owned banking corporations.

International banking and mega corporations control governments, i.e., at the next level up are the mega corporations and at the next level beyond the corporations is the privately owned worldwide banking cartel. The corporations have relied on cheap financing from the megabanks. We can conclude that those who control the mega-banks ultimately control the mega-corporations.

The privately-owned mega-banks can pull the strings of any corporation or government, but it usually does so via international institutions such as the UN, WEF, WHO, the World Bank, the IMF, the CDC, and later the EU, etc., which were all created by the powers of world finance after World War 2 and are all institutional weapons of the money-masters. For example, the CDC was created in 1947.

"At the top of the decision-making pyramid we have the Ruling Elite. They utilize psychopolitics deliberately to influence all nine steps in the decision-making process. They control every step by: 1. Creating events and predetermining their outcome; 2. Manufacturing event details and controlling the information dissemination infrastructure; 3. Biasing the alarm faculties of common people by the selected dissemination of controlled information; 4. Moulding knowledge and belief systems through 'education';... 8. Intimidating the decisions of ordinary people by enforcing codes, rules, and regulations with coercion, the threat of force, torture, fines, or imprisonment; and, 9. Erecting surveillance networks which have the ability to monitor the behaviours and actions of groups and individuals" - Mary Elizabeth Croft, Author

The threat is not climate change or covid-19, the real threat is the agenda of the so-called elites at the top of the structure. Governments are bureaucratic tools of their agenda. The entire structure is controlled by the group of people that control the source of money creation.

> "Some people might get as far as seeing the corporate control, some people might the banker control, the central banking control, some people might get as far as seeing Israel's role and don't get any further... Some people get to the Rothschilds all 100 trillion dollars... The Rothschilds take the heat for the rest of the Crown Corporation... bloodlines... The Crown created the idea of corporations, the East India Company was the first, to shield the individual from liability... what we have to do is remove the corporation" - Dean Henderson, Author

This fact is difficult for people to comprehend as it is so big. You can maybe see the individual trees, but can you see the whole forest? This important 'reality' is never discussed on corporate owned media, instead we are subjected to a never-ending punch-and-judy show of politicians squabbling to be in the revolving-door of elected office. The real power lies beyond that door.

Representative democracy as currently implemented in much of the world is an illusion

Now if you are still with me? and haven't dismissed all this as conspiracy theory, you might be thinking 'hey we need to vote in new politicians, clean up this mess and hold these people to justice!' However, the reality in 2022 is that representative democracy under capitalism, as currently implemented in much of the world, is an illusion, it is a road to nowhere - it is money that controls the world. Over the decades the financial power of the money-masters translated into political power. The narcissists of the world naturally seek and gravitate toward positions of authority and wealth in politics and finance. The democratic system is broken because those that control the money creation process wield the power to control the corporate media, steer international political policy and own the material world, regardless of which political party is elected, or which system is utilised, capitalism, socialism, communism, etc. (Aside: There is another major flaw in majority-rules democracy i.e., why should the majority have the right to make rules for the minority? especially if the majority have been led to believe in false ideologies by a corporate owned media? This amounts to a divide and conquer system.)

The first steps of a real solution are for the people to take back the ability to create and circulate money from the private bankers, or at least have the ability to utilise their own local currency systems; and not be subject to the dictates of national governments that have become puppets of unelected international institutional and financial bureaucrats. John F. Kennedy, who was assassinated in 1963, was the last US president to attempt to take back control of the money creation process from the private bankers.

The real divide in society is, therefore, not the corporate media-fostered left-versus-right 'punch-and-judy' show – it is the authoritarianism of the money masters versus human freedom. For example, Barrack Obama (a democrat) bailed out the banking system in 2010 and Donald Trump (a republican) bailed out the banking system in 2020 - these were multi-trillion bailouts, i.e., money transfers to privately owned banking/financial corporations. Obama, the beloved icon of the liberal left, bombed five more countries than his war-mongering predecessor George W. Bush. Yet, Obama received the Nobel Peace Prize. Both are war criminals and puppets of the money masters. So-called modern democracy is an illusion of choice. Furthermore, we have been under the impression that we each live in individual and autonomous nation states, but actually the mechanisms of a one world corporate- and banker-controlled government have already long been in operation.

Over the decades its controllers have commandeered the vast bulk of the world's wealth and resources for themselves only. They have facilitated a perpetual war machine causing death to countless of millions of people; mass abortion; genetically modified foods; tens of thousands of chemical compounds, herbicides and pesticides harmful to human health; toxic pharmaceuticals and vaccines; fluoridated water; and widespread environmental resource destruction and depletion, all while Now in the midst of what has proven to be a mild virus situation, we are expected to believe that the central bankers, the leaders of the unelected WEF and UN, and their corporate cohorts, such as vaccine-promoting billionaire Bill Gates, are suddenly concerned for the lives of people? Does a vulture wish the cow to be alive or dead? Does a vulture government wish for the health of its citizens?

The constraints of the new world order 'scientific dictatorship'

The new technocratic system that has been launched and promoted by the WEF and the UN, by its very design, limits all free will and gives that entirely over to faceless data governance, involving monitoring, controlling, tracking, and tracing. It eliminates individual freedom and is being promoted under the pretext of environmentalism and economic efficiency, dominated and ruled by UN technocrats and their fake climate change 'scientific dictatorship.' They also want everyone hooked up to bio-metric interfaces that monitor your location and behaviour to supposedly protect 'you' from so-called killer viruses. It's like government by a faceless computer. In this system everyone will have a digital blockchain identity and will be unable to purchase food or travel on public transport without this digital identity. Each individual's digitised credit score will depend on them complying with the rules and instructions. The mainstream political narrative also pretends we must live in this new way to save the environment, reduce our carbon footprint, and for social equality, etc., and many people are fooled by this narrative, but in reality, it is hardcore freedom killing communism. After 100 years of globalisation the concept that the world's political and corporate elites suddenly actually care about the environment is completely absurd. These people are simply implementing their control system without asking whether we want it or not.

The reset moves the elites beyond full control of the money system, as they would also have full control of the 'people and resource' system. It might seem a worthy social goal to share everything and not have to own anything, but in the reset technocracy you are being forced and will have no choice in the matter. The UN and WEF marketing language sounds great until you see through the deception then you see how extremely narcissistic it all is.

It is all presented in clever marketing language because if people understood it nobody would want it - the way they have done that is with the Covid-19 problem-reaction-solution ploy. Many people succumb to clever catchphrases that sound great, such as environmental responsibility, sustainability, inclusion, etc, without analysing what the reset is actually doing and the compliance that is required. When a few people want to control the many, the question is how can they do that without them realising and resisting. A virus is perfect because its invisible, mass surveillance, control, vaccination and a socially distanced cashless society can all be implemented in the theory that we are protecting you from an invisible virus - how clever. Most people appear to be going along with everything without seeing what its ultimately leading to.

The UN/WEF reset/new world order attempt will fail in the long run in my opinion and is already failing as millions of people are seeing through this agenda. The real divide in society is not the media fostered left versus right 'punch and judy' show, it is authoritarianism versus human freedom. The power seekers versus the freedom lovers. There are those that just want to be left alone and there are those that just won't leave them alone.

Key historical trends in the system

The following key trends can be observed since 1913:

Trend One: 1913 to 2019. The private banking elites and the corporate cohorts, gathered virtually the entire wealth and resources of the world via hijacking the money creation process; and owning and controlling the mega-corporate and international institutional structure and promoting / forcing globalisation upon the world This is a fact proven by evidence referenced in this book.

Trend Two: 1992 - 2020. A pre-planned and ongoing attempt of for full technocratic control and reset of world society has been ongoing under cover of UN Agenda 21, Agenda 2030, the WEF reset, the fake pre-planned covid-19 pandemic and the lie that carbon emissions cause climate change. People's access to energy and resources is being reduced via inflation, climate change policies and ongoing geo-political theatre. If you tolerate this, the end-result is the attempted 'new world order' based on the rules of the so-called elites, that many people have forewarned of.

Trend Three: What now? This is the stage that the elites fear. This is the stage where they lose control because the 'cat is out of the bag' – the truth is out there. Society has been split, the elites cannot censor and control the entire world population and already many millions of people can see what is really happening. In this stage confusion and turmoil ensues, however over time a cleansing and purification takes place and gradually a new sector of society emerges worldwide via more self-sufficient local and regional networks. In this new Golden Age, brave people embrace personal strength and autonomy, truth, justice, freedom, real knowledge, happiness and higher spiritual values that ultimately culminate in GOD consciousness. In time the plans of the evil-doers are collapsed, baffled or smashed to dust in the face of truth and righteousness.

The Jewish question

[Note: It appears to me that it is the top echelons of the banking and corporate structures that are under scrutiny by many truth-seekers, obviously not any ordinary decent people who happen to be Jewish. I certainly am not criticising any good people in any religion and it is not for me to make judgement of anyone, I am simply attempting to find the truth from the side-lines. In my humble opinion, only GOD can judge anyone or any group, it is certainly not for me to do.]

The Jewish question is complex and is beyond the scope of this book, but it bears brief examination as it is an ongoing theme amongst people seeking the truth about what is happening in the world. Is there really a connection between the globalist banking elites and talmudic Judaism, Zionism, and satanic freemasonry as some people claim?

It would be remiss not to make the observation that many key personalities already listed as central to the climate change hoax are Ashkenazi Jews; and the above banking dynasties are pre-dominantly Jewish families and the mega-corporations of the world are also pre-dominantly owned by these mega-banks. We can also discern this from a historical perspective, for example, according to Gerald Krefetz author of the book 'Jews and Money. The Myths and the Reality', the old banking families were pre-dominantly Jewish families, see Endnote 93.

In 2020, online sources, including Wikipedia, show that the banking families, private mega-banks and financial institutions are Jewish, Jewish-owned or Jewish-founded. According to Wikipedia, these include the Rothschilds, see Endnote [94]; the Warburg's, see Endnote [95]; the Goldman Sachs, see Endnote [96]; the Oppenheim family bank (Sal. Oppenheim became a subsidiary of Deutsche Bank in 2009), see Endnote [97]; and well-known traditional Jewish investment banking houses, such as Lehman Brothers, Lazard Freres, Salomon Brothers, Bache & Co., and Cantor/Fitzgerald, see Endnote [98]. According to Jewish business author Stephen Silbiger, see Endnote [99]:

> "Among the equity holders of the Jewish investment banking and trading firms on Wall Street are hundreds of Jewish millionaires ... Although exact figures for the numbers of Jews are not available, they no doubt have a leading and disproportionate role on Wall Street…" - Stephen Silbiger, Author

For decades many analysts have posed the question why is it pre-dominantly Jewish banking families own the worldwide commercial and central banking system? and thus have a controlling ownership of the mega-corporations and asset management companies that own the majority of the world's wealth and resources. According to an article, see Endnote [100], by the organisation My Jewish Learning, which is part of the largest non-profit, nondenominational Jewish media organization in North America:

> "The idea that Jews are good with money is one of the oldest Jewish stereotypes. But it's undeniable that Jews are well-represented in finance and business…As with many stereotypes, this one has its origins in fact…Jews have been associated with moneylending for at least a millennia…Supposed Jewish control of the global financial system - a feature of what some call economic anti-Semitism - was a major theme in Hitler's war against European Jews.. Additionally, medieval Christian theology held that charging interest (known as usury) was sinful, which kept many Christians from becoming financiers. The field thus came to be dominated by Jews."

Aspects of the history of Jewish dominance in finance and banking are also described in the book *'German-Jewish History in Modern Times'*, published by Columbia University Press, see Endnote [101], which states:

> "Jewish war profiteering was so widespread by the sixteenth and seventeenth century that "no war was waged in Germany" without Jewish financing,"

French-Jewish commentator, Bernard Lazare, also noted Jewish propensities in high finance in the late 1800, see Endnote [102]. There is no doubt that the history of Jewish involvement and influence in the finance sector is a controversial subject, as it seems to have evoked the type of sentiment described below by Lazare:

> "The man of the lower middle class, the small tradesman at whom speculation has probably ruined has much clearer ideas of why he is an anti-Semite. He knows that reckless speculation [by financiers], with its attendant panics, has been his bane, and for him, the most formidable jugglers of capital, the most dangerous speculators, are the Jews; which, indeed, is very true."

In researching this book, it appears that different branches of Judaism exist today (Orthodox, Conservative, and Reform or Progressive, see Endnote [103], and that different schools of Jewish political thought exist. According to the My Jewish Learning website, see Endnote [104], there are also different types of Jewish ethnicities including, Ashkenazi (purported by various sources to originally be from Khazaria region of central Asia), Sephardic, and Mizrahi. According to Wikipedia, see Endnote [105], Jewish political thought was split into four eras: biblical, rabbinic (from roughly 100 BC to 600 AD and primarily based on the Jewish Talmud text, medieval, and modern.

I note also that many analysts and independent/non-corporate platforms on the internet have for decades detailed and asserted that aspects of the Jewish Talmud text and Noahide Laws are very anti-Christian and discriminatory against all non-Jews, and that the modern-day Jewish power structure has adopted such aspects, for example see Endnote [106]. Analysis of these criticisms is not within the scope of this book, though I do note that Lord Jesus Christ was opposed to the Jewish pharisees/leaders and they were opposed to HIM. Please feel free to view the Talmud and decide for yourself about these controversial subjects, for example at www.talmudunmasked.com

In addition, many authors have maintained there is a Jewish emphasis towards ethnocentric unity and monopolistic economic control, and have taken the view that this is a foundation of Jewish diaspora history that surfaces and resurfaces over the centuries. For example, the book *'When Victims Rule - A Critique of Jewish Pre-eminence in America'* published on the website *'Who Controls America?"* see Endnote [107], lists a massively dis-proportionate amount of Ashkenazi Jews throughout the very top positions of the entire American institutional structure, including governmental, corporate and academic. It is also notable that all the top donors to the US democratic party are Jewish, for example, George Soros; and all the top donors to the US republican party are Jewish, for example, Maurice Greenberg. So, who really controls both parties? Is the Jewish power structure controlling both parties or is it just that only they have all the available money?

Furthermore, according to author J.O. Hertzler, author of '*The Sociology of Antisemitism Through History*', throughout history Jews were often expelled "due as a rule to economic causes", and according to authors Richard Siegel and Carl Rheims, have been expelled en masse from towns and provinces by even entire countries many times in their history, see Endnote [108].

I also note that that some commentators, including journalist Benjamin Fulford, who is from a Jewish family, maintain that Judaism was infiltrated in the past times by a group known as the Khazarian mafia, and maintain that this mafia are a worldwide organized crime syndicate that has deeply infiltrated worldwide banking and hijacked the political institutions of the United States and infiltrated the top echelons of major religious institutions, see Endnote [109].

> "Most Jews don't like to admit it, but our God is Lucifer and we are his chosen people" – Harold Wallace Rosenthal, Jewish Former Political Aide in the US Senate during the 1970s

Others maintain that modern day Jewish power structure is mostly a powerful political and corporate grouping linked with the top-levels of satanic freemasonry, could this be true? The following excerpt from the Jewish chronicle certainly seems to establish a historical basis for this claim:

> **DECEMBER 20, 1867.**   **THE JEWISH CHRONICLE**
>
> **FREEMASONRY.**
> TO THE EDITOR OF THE JEWISH CHRONICLE.
> SIR,— In reference to the above subject, there is not, nor can there be, any objection to Jewish Brethren rising to the highest offices, either in Craft or Royal Arch Masonry; it has been ever universally admitted by the order, that to part Masonry and Judaism is impossible; in fact, to use a well known axiom amongst us, "Judaism is Masonry, and Masonry is Judaism." How can it be otherwise, when the very
>
> **THE TALMUD AND THE GOSPELS.**
> (Continued from our last.)
> MATTHEW, CHAPTER VI.
> Verse 5.— "And when thou prayest, thou shall be as the hypocrites are, for they love to pray stan in the synagogues." True, the Talmud prefers recommends congregational prayers in the Te because it gives more solemnity to Divine service, stimulates the souls of the congregants to dev

More research is clearly warranted on this subject, I just won't be using Google, Wikipedia or YouTube etc, to do it.

Is pattern recognition antisemitic?

Many people have pointed out that the ownership of the world banking monopoly, the world media monopoly, and mega-corporate structure, and the upper echelons of world politics is almost exclusively Jewish. Furthermore, the Jews beginning with Karl Marx invented communism, and Jewish communist regimes, led by Stalin and Lenin, were responsible for the genocide of an estimated 100 million people, see Endnote [110].

'The Gulag was run by Jews' - Alexander Solzhenitsyn, Nobel Prize Laureate

Yet for many people, posting these facts on social media, and even on so-called 'truth forums', results in online abuse or their user accounts being blocked or deleted for "violating community guidelines". Could this be all part of censorship of the truth? We know that almost all internet platforms, social media, and even various so-called truth forums are owned by the Jewish dominated mega-corporate structure. Pattern recognition it seems is 'antisemitic', as people pointing out who owns the international banks and media have often been labelled as such, and are often accused of so-called hate speech. Stating a fact is not hate-speech. Voltaire famously said "if you want to know who rules over you simply find out you are not allowed to criticize". Furthermore, various high-profile personalities that have criticised or even observed these connections have quickly found themselves attacked or ostracised by the media or institutions that protect that structure, such as the ADL.

Some say this is all conspiracy theory and that Jews simply tend to be well-educated thus tend to climb the ladders of power. Is this all explainable, or is there a specific Jewish agenda, or a sinister element in the Jewish power structure that wishes to dominate the entire world? Bobby Fischer, a prolific former World Chess champion, and one of the greatest chess players of all time, certainly seemed to think so as he very severely criticised the actions of the Jews. Additionally, some notable commentators maintain that the label of antisemitic is deceptive and unwarranted because semites are Arabs, and the vast majority of Jews are actually not Arabs, i.e., Jews are not semites. <u>Rather they maintain that most Ashkenazi Jews originated from Khazaria in eastern Europe/central Asia, and that these Khazars converted to Judaism in the Middle Ages for political reasons and to infiltrate world banking</u>, see Endnote [111]. For centuries, Usury was regarded as a sin in original Christianity, thus the banking sector came to be dominated by the Jewish demograph.

5. 1913 - 2019: Private banking control and the corporate super-entity

We cannot understand how to create a truly sustainable resilient society unless we correctly perceive the current society we live in and how it came to exist. And who are the architects of the current paradigm. This chapter may help in that regard. Unless we face the ugly reality of the current paradigm, even if it is not 'politically correct' to do so, then we will not be able to make the correct adjustments to current society, or create a better society, without avoiding the same mistakes and undesirable scenarios over and over again.

This full text of this 28-page chapter is available in the PDF download version of this book *Transcending the Climate Change Deception – Toward Real Sustainability*, which is available on my website www.mkeenan.ie. This chapter is also available in the book *Transcending the Covid-19 Deception,* which is available on www.amazon.com

The chapter covers the following topics:

- Lies of elites - over 100 years of fraudulent banking and corporate corruption

- Illusions and lies in history and science that we are taught in school

- 1913: Private bankers planned and implemented a scheme to own and rule the world.

    "The FED is an independent agency, that means basically that there is no other agency of government which can overrule actions that we take - what relations are (between Chairman of FED and President of the USA) don't frankly matter." - Alan Greenspan (former FED Chairman)

- How they created the human hamster wheel - the fraudulent debt-money banking system

    "It is well enough that people of the nation do not understand our banking and monetary system, for if they did, I believe there would be a revolution before tomorrow morning." - Henry Ford (1863-1947), Founder of Ford Motor Company

    "Banking institutions are more dangerous to our liberties than private armies. If the American people ever allow private banks to control the issue of their currency... the banks… will deprive the people of all their property" - Thomas Jefferson

"Governments everywhere are in debt, who are they in debt to? The answer is that they are in debt to private banks. The 'cruel hoax' is that **governments are in debt for money created on a computer screen, money they could have created themselves**." - E.H. Brown, Author the book *'The Web of Debt'*

"The goal is control. They want all of us enslaved to debt, they want all of our governments enslaved to debt, and they want all of our politicians addicted to the huge financial contributions that they funnel into their campaigns. Since the elite also own all of the big media companies, the mainstream media never lets us in on the secret that there is something fundamentally wrong with the way that our system works." - Karen Hudes, who worked in the legal department of the World Bank for more than 20 years and was Senior Counsel when she was fired for blowing the whistle on corruption, see Endnote [112]

- The Federal Reserve Act of 1913 - the private banking coup

- The Federal Reserve is an independent, privately-owned corporation

- 1917: The rise of bolsheviks and communism was fully funded by capitalist bankers

- One of the real reasons for WW2, to re-instate the private-banking cartel in Germany

- All wars are 'bankers wars'

- Governments use the population as collateral on loans received

- President John F Kennedy was the last U.S. president to challenge the private bankers. The private bankers use a fraudulent system known as fractional-reserve banking to create money from nothing and lend it to governments at interest. The cruel hoax is that governments could themselves create the money the private bankers create and charge interest on. However, governments in 2022 hardly ever mention that this method of allowing private banks ownership of the money creation process is unnecessary and contrary to the interests of the taxpayer and the public. The last U.S. president to attempt to rectify this issue was John F. Kennedy in 1963. President Kennedy attempted to take control of the money creation process away from the private bankers and back into the hands of the government. In 1963, his administration a bill was passed to place the money creation process back into public ownership. John F. Kennedy was then assassinated in 1963. This bill was quickly reversed by the next president that took office following his assassination, i.e., Lyndon Baines Johnson.

Kennedy's attempt to return the money creation process back into the hands of government took place on June 4th 1963. Advised and supported by his brother Bobby, President John F Kennedy signed Executive Order 11110, which authorised the U.S.

Treasury to bypass the Federal Reserve Bank and issue $4.29 billion as debt free and interest free money based on the value of silver bullion certificates, see Endnote [113].

However, the assassination of President Kennedy in 1963 'conveniently' removed the problem for the debt-producing criminal bankers. The U.S. Treasury notes were quickly taken out of circulation and since then all the U.S. Presidents and their administrations, just like our own governments in Europe, have been compliant and obedient to the wishes of the world network of privately owned central banks.

- The planned boom-bust-bailout cycles that forced nations into further vast debt

- Corporate globalization had been a design for corporate rule of the world's resources

- The privately-owned banking system received about 35% of the productive profit of nations. This occurs via the governments of the world paying vast amounts of interest to international banks on debt-money loans and other mechanisms. For example, Ireland has been paying between €6 to 10 billion per annum in interest payments on the national debt. As a trading entity the country was making a profit of around €40 billion per annum, i.e., up to 25% of the nations' profits have been going directly to the privately owned international finance institutions as interest on debt-money that was originally created from nothing. The cruel hoax is that governments could create that money themselves.

"There are two ways to conquer and enslave a nation. One is by the sword. The other is by debt."
- U.S. President John Adams

"The government should create, issue and circulate all the currency and credits needed to satisfy the spending power of the government and the buying power of consumers. By the adoption of these principles the taxpayers will be saved immense sums of interest. Money will cease to be the master and become the servant of humanity." - President Abraham Lincoln (Lincoln issued government money, but was later assassinated).

"Federal income tax was instituted specifically to coerce taxpayers to pay the interest due to the banks on the federal debt. If the money supply had been created by the government rather than borrowed from the banks that created it, the income tax would have been unnecessary. ... There is a way out of this morass. The early American colonists found it and so did Abraham Lincoln and some other national leaders: the government can take back the money-issuing power from the banks. " - E.H. Brown, Author the book *The Web of Debt*

- 100 years of private banking leaves all nations in vast debt and bankers owning most of the world, via controlling interest in the mega-corporate structure. World Bank statistics in August 2020, see Endnote [114], showed that virtually every national government of the world owes vast amounts of debt. The nations of the world have been in ongoing debt servitude to the international banking and finance system for decades.

- 2019: A systemic ongoing problem with the world economic system, and the decreasing EROEI for oil

- 2019: World economic system was in end-phase/crash-mode prior to Covid-19

- 2020: Blackrock and a multi-trillion Wall St bank bailout under cover of a so-called virus

- March 2020: Central bankers launch world economic reset under cover of world lockdown

- Out of the frying pan? from a debt slavery paradigm to the 2020 reset attempt. UN agenda 2030 and the WEF 'Great Reset' of 2020 is not great at all, in fact it is a form of totalitarianism and it utilises the so-called coronavirus situation as the basis for introducing an entirely new worldwide system of rules and regulations and technologies dictating how all people worldwide live their lives. UN Agenda 2030 and the WEF 'reset' aims to replace a system of debt slavery which operated from 1913 to 2019 with a system of technocratic authoritarianism that, when you analyse it, is simply communism under a new guise. The covid-19 restrictions, United Nation's Agenda 21/2030, the Paris Climate Agreement, the Fourth Industrial Revolution and the proposed 'Great Reset' offer an insight into how a small number of certain extremely wealthy people want to control and dictate the lives of all people over the course of the next decade as part of a plan for world governance and authoritarian control.

6. UN sustainable development is a problem wrapped up as a solution – what about the real sustainability challenge?

Politically defined sustainable development was never supposed to actually create a truly sustainable self-sufficient and resilient society of locally empowered networks. It was merely utilised as a deceptive cover to keep 'kicking the can down the road' whilst the international bankers and their cohorts continued to make vast amounts of money via globalisation and implement deceptive corporate and political agendas; and to impose a deceptive agenda embodied by UN Agenda 2030. So, what would be required if humanity were to accept the real challenge to create a truly resilient self-sufficient society based on truth and ancient wisdom rather than continue within the technocratic futures of elites have planned. We must first define the challenge. This chapter describes:

The Earth we all depend on – what about real pollution to land, air and water?

The Earth is where we live. We are dependent on the Earth and we should respect the Earth - its natural systems provide everything humanity requires to survive and prosper. The Earth's biodiversity provides humanity with the food to eat, water to drink, clean air to breathe, materials and energy for fundamental human needs. We depend on the Earth - without the Earth's natural resources we have nothing upon which to physically survive. If water, air, or food systems become contaminated with toxins we can become contaminated with those same toxins – and our health suffers.

We live in a trans-national economic system/society dependant on resources being ravaged by the economic model of globalisation and declining damaged eco-systems. The GDP growth paradigm over the past decades has been depleting world resources and polluting the planet and caused the extinction of significant numbers of plant and animal species meanwhile, half the world's population lives in poverty; fresh water in lakes and aquifers are being depleted, and there is pressure on the world's basic food supplies. The UN environment program is happy to tell us about these real aspects of the environmental situation, but note that the UN solutions are wrapped in a bogus agenda and are based on the Hegelian dialectic formula problem-reaction-solution; i.e., the globalists create the problem (via globalisation), they create a shock reaction (fear mongering about climate change), and they present the solutions that they, the globalists, want to impose on the un-suspecting world population.

Our perceived 'material' success has involved the extraction of large quantities of resources from the Earth for local, national and international systems of transport, energy, communications, food production and technology. Our current worldwide societal system is highly dependent on resources of fossil fuels and on arable land. Cheap oil is the economic model relies on. The quantity and quality of arable land is diminishing due to the effects of globalisation. Almost all of us are unconsciously involved in the use or destruction of nature's resources via the consumption and acquiring of products of the so called 'globalised' economy. Many of these products are superfluous to fundamental human needs. Large scale pollution of water, land and air has resulted from so-called modern industrial processes. In particular this has taken place since the industrial revolution. The quantity and purity of non-renewable resources and eco-systems continues to diminish despite long term awareness of this problem.

> "Sustainable mining of anything unrenewable is a Big Oxymoron. Anything you take from the earth that is non-renewable is by its nature not sustainable. It's simply gone. Forever… the environmental damage caused by mining… is horrendous. Once a mine is exploited in a short 30- or 40-years' concession, the mining company leaves mountains of contaminated waste, soil and water behind – that takes a thousand years or more to regenerate."- Peter Koenig, former Analyst at the World Bank

Accumulated releases of waste and eco-toxic pollution releases to air, land and water are significantly impacting the environment and human health. Current so-called modern society utilises thousands of products, technologies and industries that contain or utilise pollutants. These include toxic metals, such as aluminum; thousands of manmade chemical compounds, dioxins, PCBs and POPs, and many other substances harmful to human health and the environment. The United Nations Protocol on Pollutant Releases and Transfer Registers (PRTRs), see Endnote [115], lists 108 substance groups covering thousands of substances classified as pollutants that are released to land, air and water systems by 'so-called' modern industrial society. (Note that although the UN PRTR protocol involves the monitoring of these pollutants, the UN solution of 'sustainable development' has been impotent in stopping the trend of pollution.) Some of these pollutants are extremely toxic. Many of these substances make their way into and bio-accumulate in the human body via systems of food, air and water. For example, Professor Karl Henrik Robert, a former cancer scientist, has stated that human breast milk now contains traces of over 200 manmade synthetic chemical compounds that the human body has not ever been exposed to until recent decades.

The restorative systems of nature are under pressure. Over the past decades 'un-sustainability' has become an emergent property of the so-called modern industrial society. The worldwide environmental crisis is manifest in ongoing areas such as forest destruction; soil erosion and desertification; pollution to air, land and water; loss of wildlife and biodiversity; increasing volumes of trash, pesticides and toxic waste; and depleting resources, for example, clean water and non-renewables. The vast amounts of toxic chemicals, metals, pesticides, nanomaterials, PCBs, dioxins etc, produced by the globalised economy pose significant risks to ecological systems and human health. The following quotes from the demonstrate the significant risks:

> "The chemicals we use to produce energy, to control pests, to enhance productivity, to catalyze industrial processes, and to meet human health needs—as well as the chemicals we just discard—continue to weaken ecosystems and to imperil human health... In just one century, we have poisoned much of our environment... Human enterprise is producing toxic and hazardous substances at increasing rates, and vast quantities of these dangerous compounds are reaching the atmosphere, water bodies, and soils that support life, with devastating and potentially accelerating impact... Animal experiments have demonstrated gastrointestinal uptake of nanoparticles causing toxicological effects on kidneys, livers, and spleens... One area that particularly worries scientists is the brain, since nanoparticles are small enough to trespass the blood-brain barrier—which in principle acts as a filter to keep out toxins—and accumulate in the brain... The poor understanding of the biological behaviour of nanomaterials makes it difficult to predict the associated toxicity risks." - see Endnote [116]

The sustainability squeeze and the real sustainability challenge

Due to the processes of corporate industrial globalisation, we face real inter-related worldwide challenges of environmental destruction and pollution; declining resources; and issues related to food, water and energy security, but the climate change narrative is a hoax that places the blame for the environmental problems of the world onto the individual. In addition, we have built a trans-national economic infrastructure which is highly dependent on oil and there is a severe lack of local sustainable systems for food, energy and water. Over the past decades the world-wide banking and corporate elite have gathered and controlled massive wealth, and have manipulated economies via the political and banking orthodoxy. This includes during orchestrated boom-bust-bailout cycles in which the mega-banks always win and debt-money wealth always flows upwards via usury. We have witnessed banking bailouts occur at the long-term expense of the general population who have had the massive debts of private banks unjustly heaped onto their shoulders by their own governments.

This complex situation may disable the current fabric and life-support structures of society in both the 'so-called' rich countries and the 'so-called' poorer nations. These crises have been caused by factors including an environmentally destructive economic system that has been fuelled by an out-of-control banking and GDP growth system. In order to create a sustainable future for ourselves, our children and our global society, the challenge for us all in the 21st century is to align our economic, monetary/banking, political, social and technological systems with the real science of sustainability, not the bogus UN Agenda 2030, whilst also maintaining wellbeing for all people via the development of sustainable local communities and viable regional structures rather than reliance on globalised trans-national systems.

Societies that are prepared for the challenges ahead will be better placed to deal with the 'systemic shocks' and to build thriving sustainable futures. Societies that have not prepared will be forced to quickly adapt or fail.

If the problems of environmental pollution and unnecessary resource depletion are not resolved the accumulated impacts to human wellbeing and health will increase and current societal systems will become more at risk of degradation or eventual collapse. The current economic system is unsustainable as it based on the banking industry imperative of unlimited GDP growth in a world in which some resources are finite and some are renewable. This imperative is imposed on governments by the privately owned internal banking industry, for without growth they will not receive interest on the loans they create from nothing.

We are living in an un-sustainability conundrum. The world's top ecologists warn that current development strategies are undermining ecological life support systems and risking catastrophe for humans. There is a real environmental problem and real lack of successful systems for human wellbeing and resilient communities, but politically defined sustainable development and the so-called green policies that all the world's governments have been utilising for the past 30 years, are not the answer, have not solved these real problems and are a deceptive narrative.

The world's present growth-based approach to global "development," is flawed and it is only required by the world's private bankers so that a usury economy can be maintained in which wealth always flows upwards to the world's privately owned mega-banks, via interest on debt-money loans to governments, companies and individuals. The flawed materialistic consumer lifestyles of the very wealthy cannot be extended sustainably to the world's poor using currently available technologies without the use of three to four additional Earth-like worlds. The illogical ongoing depletion of the world's resources via continued material growth undermines the future of worldwide civilization.

Increasing global consumption and declining resources is creating a 'squeeze' on resources upon which humanity relies. Diminishing resources include:

- Fresh water systems
- Critical raw materials
- Levels of biodiversity and species
- The restorative capacity of ecological systems
- Arable land is shrinking due to desertification and fertility of the land is declining due to over use of chemical-based fertilisers.

In relation to oil, the EROEI is has reduced significantly and current systems of globalised food production are dependent on oil for transport, fertiliser production, and packaging that uses oil-based plastics. At the same the diminishing resource base is subject to increased levels of pollution, resource extraction and increased resource consumption due to:

- The flawed political process known as globalisation.
- The flawed and needless paradigm of endless GDP growth which places constant pressure for national economies to produce more and more products, many of which are not needed and are not essential to human needs and further contribute to levels of waste. (The real reason governments are compelled to create GDP growth is to pay interest to the international banking system on debt money loans received).

Increasing accumulative levels of waste and pollution in the oceans, air and land and declining restorative capacity of eco-systems is occurring. This has consequent impacts to food, water and air systems and therefore to human health and wellbeing. In order to make sense of these multiple factors we can take the following systems view in which we are moving into a metaphorical funnel of decreasing availability and quality/purity of worldwide resources and increasing demand for resources – this results in a narrowing of available resource options for resource use. Humanity needs to reverse these trends to emerge from this metaphorical funnel toward a sustainable society.

In relation to populations levels, it is a globalist-promoted myth that over-population is the main problem. We should note that the world can actually sustain a higher population if the systems we are using are based on real sustainability, which must involve local systems.

The challenge is to create sustainable societal systems before humanity hits the walls of the metaphorical funnel, i.e., the limits of resource availability. As resource availability and quality diminishes there is increasing risk of detioration or eventual collapse of current trans-national and interdependent systems of production and distribution of energy, food, goods and services. As resources deplete or become exhausted, we all suffer either through resource unavailability or higher prices as mismanaged resources become more expensive. In addition, if resources become polluted due to industrial processes people may suffer through ill-health, for example, water, air and food systems can become polluted with toxic substances that bio-accumulate in the human body.

Societies, businesses, and governments that take a whole-systems view and have the foresight to develop strategies in alignment with real sustainability principles will avoid 'hitting the walls' of the metaphorical funnel and future-proof themselves against potential resource degradation and constraints. The resources constraints can also be viewed as design challenges and opportunities for innovation, change or a re-discovering and re-use of ancient knowledge. More self-sufficient villages and sustainable communities have been emerging in many countries with some people wishing to live more conscientiously and some wishing to become part of a more self-sufficient community in preparation for what they view as the potential collapse or partial collapse of the current international system of production and transport of goods and services, which relies on the availability of cheap oil.

All these issues are pointing humankind toward the importance of 'real sustainability' in the Earth-human relationship and progress toward that goal would be a sign of an improved/higher level of human consciousness. UN-defined sustainable development, as implemented by the governmental and corporate world has clearly already failed the real sustainability challenge and real environmental challenge.

Sustainable development – a problem wrapped up as a solution

In 1987, the United Nations Commission on Environment and Development published "Our Common Future". Written under the chairmanship of Gro Harlem Brundtland who was then Prime Minister of Norway. The report presented the results of a worldwide consultation aimed at proposing a program for sustainable development. The Commission proposed a definition of sustainable development: "Development *that meets the needs of the present without compromising the ability of future generations to meet their own needs*" and identified objectives that include preserving and enhancing the resource base, taking into account the environment in developing new technologies, integrating ecological and economic concerns into decision-making and meeting basic human needs. It proposed reducing energy consumption in industrialized countries, development of renewable energy, encouraging reforestation in countries affected by desertification, implementation of tax and land reforms to reduce pressures on ecosystems, and adaptation of an international convention for the protection of species. The Commission proposed a reform of international institutions, notably the World Bank and the IMF, which should better take into account social and environmental objectives and alleviate the debt of the poorest countries.

However, the reality is that this report was just another clever marketing tool and greenwash for the globalist-controlled UN and their Hegelian dialectic agenda, which at the top, in reality, has no regard for human wellbeing or the environment. The glaring omission from the Brundtland Report is that it failed to identify the worldwide fractional reserve banking/debt money system itself as a major root problem in achieving a more truly sustainable for human wellbeing and environmental protection. The emergence of multiple UN conventions and multi-lateral environmental laws, has placed restrictions on various pollutants and provided greater protections to land, air and water systems. However, these **'paper tigers'** have entirely failed to point out the **'elephant in the room'**, the debt-monetary system itself from which the entire system of globalization stems. This is not at all surprising, when you realize the UN itself was from its very inception a political creation of the debt money-masters, the world private banking cartel that own and control the fraudulent world debt-money system.

The United Nations Conference on Environment and Development (UNCED) in 1992, also known as the Rio de Janeiro Earth Summit, endorsed a political solution known as 'Sustainable Development' (SD). The participants set the basic principles and established 'Agenda 21', which became the basis for so many sustainable development initiatives. Sustainable development, as politically defined has two primary pillars: economic development and the consumptive use of the world's natural resources in ways that are sustainable. Following the recommendations of the Brundtland report, the Summit also saw the adoption of a declaration on sustainable forest management and conventions on biodiversity, climate change and desertification. In the previous chapter, I described that UN climate change and desertification narratives are bogus and deceptive. Here we see examples of the Hegelian dialectic in action, in which a solution is provided by the UN for climate change, but it is a false narrative that is aligned with a different agenda entirely.

Since then, the development of renewable energy, resource efficiency, corporate sustainability frameworks and corporate social responsibility, environmental certification, green investment, green economy, life cycle analysis, cleaner production processes, green marketing and many other SD initiatives have occurred. Some of these initiatives are very problematic and misleading, for example, most renewable energy technologies have a poor EROEI, as already discussed; resource-efficiency is hindered by the Jevons-paradox, which is discussed in a later chapter. The above initiatives have not solved the real environmental problem, focus on efficiency rather than effectiveness, and are for the most part, a greenwashing of 'business as usual' approaches. I note that some, whole-systems frameworks, such as The Natural Step framework, and design frameworks, such as C2C, can be very useful in the context of real environmental protection and resigning the supply chain to be non-polluting. However, the bigger picture is that the above initiatives all operate within the GDP growth and usury paradigm; the entire agenda is framed in reducing carbon emissions; and these sustainable development initiatives 'on their own' will never stop the trend of environmental degradation as they do not address the 'root causes' of the environmental problem.

30 years of 'UN-defined sustainable development' has not solved the real environmental problem

One might expect that some progress has been made by the political initiative of sustainable development over the past 30 years, however the reality is that the state of the environment and overall human wellbeing in relative terms, is now even worse than it was 30 years ago.

The United Nations Environment Programme includes many programmes of positive environmental intention in areas including biosafety; management of chemicals, waste and pollutants; protection of ecosystems, biodiversity, forests, oceans and seas, etc, but over the past decades the United Nations environmental programmes have failed to stop the overall trend of ongoing worldwide pollution and environmental degradation with consequent impacts to human health and wellbeing, for example, due to accumulating levels of pollutants and toxins. Why is this? In finding the answer we must first make the observation that all of these environmental programmes operate within, and as part of, an overall framework of politically defined 'sustainable development'.

Most of us have been led to believe that sustainable development is a 'good' idea, but the reality is so called 'sustainable development' as defined at the United Nations Earth Summit in 1992 is a flawed mechanism that has attempted to marry environmental concerns and continuous economic GDP growth in a global development context and has been talked up by politicians for decades, but has failed to stop worldwide environmental degradation. It is notable that in the global drive for 'sustainable development', politicians and global economic stakeholders have steadfastly avoided altering or even questioning the underlying precepts of the current economic paradigm and the privately-owned international banking system that dominates it, i.e., the prioritisation of GDP growth and corporate profit above all else, and the continued utilisation of a global debt-based fractional reserve banking system. Government 'mantra' around the world is to prioritise GDP growth above all else, otherwise those governments will not be able to pay the 'interest' on any loans or monies they have received from the global banking system or bond market. Every government in the world (apart from Bhutan which uses the Gross National Happiness Index) uses GDP as an indicator of sustainable development, despite the well documented flaws in GDP as an indicator of the sustainability of society.

Sustainable development assumes that the problem can be solved through greater material and economic efficiency and technological "fixes," ignoring the evidence that, to date, this has actually increased the human ecological footprint, as described by the Jevon's paradox. We need to challenge this belief in the GDP growth paradigm and examine the hidden motivators of human behaviour.

Stable resilient local systems have become even more of a necessity for humanity. Today, 30 years since the 1992 UN Rio Summit it is obvious that sustainable development has not solved the worldwide environmental problem, in fact the problem has become worse. According to environmental reports the depletion of natural resources and the degradation of the environment continues, and the gap between rich and poor continues to widen, and food insecurity and indebtedness are have become greater problems. The main power brokers of the worldwide environmentally destructive economic system in politics, governments, corporations and international banking have not solved the environmental and human wellbeing issues, problems they have been complicit in creating via the system of globalisation

The underlying causes of the world-wide environmental problem have either been ignored, not adequately addressed, not understood or often not even identified at a political level. These real reasons are not addressed by the 'political' solution of sustainable development and never highlighted in the institutional halls of power where the economic mantra of GDP growth and the 'status quo' of the debt-money system are never to be questioned. Indigenous leader Geronimo has been attributed with the following statement:

> "When the last tree is cut, the last fish is caught, and the last river is polluted; when to breathe the air is sickening, you will realize, too late, that wealth is not in bank accounts and that you can't eat money."

SD perpetuates the problem - does not address root causes of instability in the system

Sustainable development is not true sustainability. Sustainable development, as politically defined has two primary pillars: economic development and the consumptive use of the world's natural resources in ways that are sustainable. The major flaw in this approach is that it completely ignores a significant aspect of the current economic system itself, i.e., the role the international banking and debt money system plays in driving continuously driving more GDP growth, which results in continual harvesting and pollution of more and more and the world's resources, in order to facilitate ongoing usury in which wealth always flows upwards to the private bankers that own literally own the system.

The Brundtland commission failed to identify this major root cause of the worldwide international fractional reserve banking system, and obviously it was never intended to, Fractional reserve banking is a major driver of the environmentally destructive GDP growth paradigm. The political definition of sustainable development and policies that has been promoted since 1992 actually endorse the worldwide paradigm of GDP growth paradigm and continues to do so today, yet the GDP growth is environmentally destructive. The Rio Summit utilised the Brundtland definition of sustainable development which actually endorses economic growth. The Brundtland definition of sustainable development is an 'ideal goal', but it is deceptive and almost useless as it is not 'strictly measurable', i.e., it is a loose verbal description of an ideal without any strict scientific definitions. A scientific definition of sustainability would enable the measurement of real sustainability success. Professor Olsen (see Endnote [117]) calculates the Brundtland scenario (which endorses economic growth) to have 2.5 to 5 times the 1995 environmental impact levels per person, providing further weight to the argument against economic growth.

In summary, the Brundtland definition that emerged at the Rio Earth Summit in 1992 was a 'political definition' of Sustainable Development' that has been the basis of almost all governments' sustainable development policies – the Brundtland definition actually endorses the concept of GDP growth and is not a scientific peer reviewed definition of sustainability.

The UN Brundtland definition enabled 'polluting' forms of GDP growth to continue

The Brundtland definition has enabled the existing environmentally destructive paradigm of GDP growth to continue more or less 'business as usual'. The GDP growth paradigm has no scientific basis given that many of the world's resources are finite and the Hartwick rule (see Endnote [118]) of environmental economics has not been validated. As the Brundtland definition endorses the GDP growth paradigm it follows that the Brundtland definition has no scientific basis either. Therefore 'Sustainable Development' as politically defined does not solve the environmental and human wellbeing sustainability problem – in fact it perpetuates the problems via endless corporate globalisation i.e., mega-corporate agendas of profit and resource control. The political definition of sustainable development or the UN sustainable development goals do not address the core reasons for the worldwide environmental or human wellbeing sustainability problem. It is notable that in 1989 a different approach to sustainability was described by Professor Lester W. Milbrath in *'Envisioning a Sustainable Society'* calling for:

> "..an end to the idea of a growth economy, an end to the culture that always accepts scientific advancement as a positive good, and the beginning of a society that learns its way to an infrastructure designed for sustainability"

The term sustainability has become misused and misunderstood by many people. The initial hopes for sustainable development as a means for a sustainable society to emerge were misplaced because sustainable development came to mean and be understood as sustainable material GDP growth. Thus, sustainable development in its political definition was never anything else but a 'greenwash' – a new term that simply endorsed in its political definition the 'business as usual' strategy of GDP growth. Professor Stanley Temple of the University of Wisconsin-Madison has stated that the overuse of the word, sustainable has come to mean too much and nothing at the same time and that sustainable development as a concept is too loosely defined to have any particular usefulness.

The word 'sustainable' was hijacked

A former mentor from my days as PhD research student, Professor Karl Henrik Robert, winner of the Blue Planet environmental prize, once said:

> "The biggest single obstacle to sustainability is not climate change, but the lack of shared political understanding of what sustainability is."

Furthermore, the terms 'sustainability' and 'sustainable' have been misunderstood and misused. The word has been hijacked by flawed economic, banking, corporate and political interests that actually prioritise profit above all else and are mostly only interested in 'sustaining' their vast profits, share prices, and incomes. In addition, real sustainability is not an issue that only exists on the so-called left or the so-called right of the political spectrum. Utilising the terms of the political left or the political right to explain real sustainability actually misses the point.

The word 'sustainable' is often mis-used in corporate and political circles as there is very little understanding what it really means, or knowledge of peer-reviewed scientific principles for sustainability, for example, as defined in 2006 by the Research on the Scientific Basis for Sustainability report, see Endnote [119]. After the banking crash of 2008, politicians jumped on the word sustainable as if it were a lifeboat, and we often hear the words 'sustainable growth' from politicians, however, we must ask growth of what exactly? The reality is that sustaining GDP growth and increasing corporate profits merely diverts more wealth to the corporations and mega-banks; whilst pollution and resource depletion due to globalisation continues; and whilst the development of what is really needed, local self-sufficient systems, is neglected.

In summary, the concept of sustainability was popularised as a worldwide environmental concern over 40 years ago, but quickly became the diluted political concept of 'sustainable development' with business-as-usual GDP growth. This political definition was prioritised by governments and corporations and the private banking sector for the past 30 years – from an environmental standpoint this is either insane or evidence of another overriding agenda.

> "Most people… think sustainability is highly desirable and sprinkle the adjective "sustainable" about with abandon, but are confused about what the concept really means. Their confusion can be traced back to the term "sustainable development" which was introduced to the public by the Brundtland Report, Our Common Future, in 1987. The basic Brundtland definition is clear enough: "Sustainable development is development that meets the needs of the present without compromising the ability of future generations to meet their own needs" but then the Report confuses the reader by attempting to make the principle less absolute…
>
> Meeting essential needs depends in part on achieving full growth potential, and sustainable development clearly requires economic growth in places where such needs are not being met. Elsewhere it can be consistent with economic growth provided the content of the growth reflects the broad principles of sustainability and non-exploitation of others.
>
> In other words, sustainable development is linked with growth, and since for many people, 'development' and "growth" are synonyms, they think that 'sustainable development' and 'sustainable growth' are the same thing. And, of course, 'sustainable growth' is not just a once-off increase in income levels that can reasonably be expected to be maintained indefinitely. It is a growth process that goes on increasing incomes reliably, year after year. In short, sustainability is linked in the public mind with something which is completely unsustainable " - Foundation for the Economics of Sustainability, see Endnote [120].

A part of understanding what real sustainability is involves understanding how the economic system itself is fundamentally flawed, especially the financial and banking processes that underpin its operations, and understanding how the current banking system provides vast financial benefit to a very small group of people at the expense of everyone else.

The Brundtland definition influences political sustainable development strategies

Thus, we see that many people are misled or confused about what real sustainability actually means and entails. The financial, corporate and political world has hijacked the term to mean sustaining growth, but continuous growth and a never-ending pollution and depletion of the world's resources that are finite is impossible/unsustainable. Peoples' confusion can now be traced back to the definition of "sustainable development" which was introduced by the United Nations Brundtland Report, *Our Common Future*, in 1987. see Endnote [121]. The Brundtland definition states:

> "Sustainable development is development that meets the needs of the present without compromising the ability of future generations to meet their own needs",

However, then the Report states:

> "Meeting essential needs depends in part on achieving full growth potential, and sustainable development clearly requires economic growth in places where such needs are not being met. Elsewhere it can be consistent with economic growth provided the content of the growth reflects the broad principles of sustainability and non-exploitation of others."

In other words, sustainable development is linked with growth, and many people therefore think that "sustainable development" and "sustainable growth" are the same thing. However, sustainable growth is an oxymoron, it is simultaneously 'polluting and resource depleting', and it is impossible on a world with finite resources. So 'sustainability' has been linked in the public consciousness with something which is completely unsustainable, i.e., GDP growth. The real problem is the Davos group corporate agenda, but UN Agenda 2030/climate change narrative places the blame squarely onto the individual, who is emotionally blackmailed to save the planet and unwittingly induced to get on board with the UN agenda, toward what actually amounts to complete faceless corporate control of everything.

Global political mechanisms for sustainable development all incorrectly endorse corporate globalisation and its economic growth narrative, for example, the above often quoted UN Brundtland Report and also the Rio Declaration produced at the UN Earth Summit in 1992. All national governmental strategies for sustainable development endorse economic growth. The Brundtland Report continues to influence political thinking on sustainable development. The Brundtland scenario has been estimated by Professor Olsen in 1995 to increase the environmental impact levels per person by 2.5 to 5 times.

The failure/flaws of decoupling, resource substitution or eco-efficiency strategies

In the late 20th century ways to decouple resource use from economic growth were hypothesised by environmental economists. A hypothesis called the environmental Kuznets curve (EKC) predicts increasing decoupling of resource use from GDP per capita, as technology improves and material substitution occurs. In some cases, this accurately describes reality. In other cases, the resource flow continues to increase with increasing GDP per capita. An EKC hypothesis has never been validated. If it were validated then it would imply that economic growth is the means to environmental improvement. The EKC has never been shown to apply to all pollutants or environmental impacts, and evidence exists that challenges the notion of the EKC in general, see Endnote [122].

In 2009 Professor Tim Jackson Chair of the U.K. Government's Sustainable Development Commission authored the policy document called *'Prosperity without Growth'*. The report describes the myth of decoupling of environmental impacts from GDP growth as follows:

> "(Decoupling) As an escape from the dilemma of growth it is fundamentally flawed. Ever greater consumption of resources is a driver of growth. As industrial ecologist Robert Ayres has pointed out: 'consumption (leading to investment and technological progress) drives growth, just as growth and technological progress drives consumption.' Protagonists of growth seldom compute the consequences of this relationship" - see Endnote [123]

Therefore, it is no surprise that the UN sustainable development strategy of decoupling GDP growth from environmental impacts, which is promoted or given lip service by every government worldwide, has failed utterly. Decoupling, resource substitution or eco-efficiency strategies will not solve the worldwide environmental problem. Sustainable development policies include efforts to decouple (separate) GDP growth/economic activity from environmental impacts, however, over the past three decades these efforts at decoupling have not been successful in any significant way, see Endnote [124]. In my view such efforts never will be successful because absolute decoupling is most likely impossible within a paradigm of globalisation and is not truly a priority for the main players of the GDP growth paradigm. Given the vast quantities of waste and toxins produced by current industrial society, so called decoupling is very unlikely to be achieved in any significant way in the coming decades in my opinion.

Sustainable development makes use of various decoupling policies and concepts such as eco-efficiency, eco-innovation, and sustainable consumption and production. However eco-efficiency may actually result in greater resource use. This counterintuitive result known as the Jevons or "rebound" effect. Consider that efficient or technologically advanced firms are able to lower prices, gain market share, and increase wages and salaries to employees. As this phenomenon propagates through the economy, more money chasing cheaper goods and services results in increased consumption/pollution (back to where it would have been, or close, had the technological innovation not happened). Green consumerism is still consumerism and its modest gains can be nullified by the Jevons paradox. Resource-efficiency can be also be outweighed and outpaced by effects of the paradigm of GDP growth in which it exists.

Authentic innovation and rediscovery of ancient technologies has definite merit, however, for many decades it has been hijacked, suppressed or bought out, by the corporate powers-that-be and the gatekeepers of the system that have their own agenda of control for world society. The globalists do not communities or towns or cities to be independent and self-sufficient, they want everyone to be dependent on the banker-owned globalised corporate system and controlled by the narratives of UN Agenda 2030 and the WEF technocratic system currently being promoted. The WEF reset is comprehensively exposed in my book *'Transcending the Covid-19 Deception'*.

Much of sustainable development worldwide has amounted to a dishonest 'greenwashing' of the existing environmental destructive economic system which by design instigates boom-bust cycles. Part of the political sustainable development strategy has been a delusional attempt to "decouple" environmental impacts from GDP growth. This decoupling strategy has failed, was never going work and I doubt it ever was intended to work. This is evidenced by a BIOS Research Institute study that reviewed **179 scientific studies on decoupling published between 1990 and 2019**, a period of nearly 30 years, and found, in short, that:

> "the evidence does not suggest that decoupling towards ecological sustainability is happening at a global (or even regional) scale." - (6)

BIOS Research Institute is an independent multidisciplinary scientific organisation that has previously advised the UN Global Sustainable Development Report on the risks of emerging biophysical limits to endless economic growth. The de-coupling concept has been utilised as a ploy to placate people concerned with the environmental impacts of rampant GDP growth, nevertheless, rampant globalisation and environmental degradation continued unabated for decades.

> "Based on insights revealed by 2005's Millennium Ecosystem Assessment, new approaches under consideration suggest that productivity can be decoupled from environmental degradation. Imminent critical thresholds require that this decoupling proceed at once." - United Nations

Environmental Programme UNEP Year Book 2009: New Science and Developments in Our Changing Environment, pg 9

The flawed mantra of politicians, bankers and mainstream neo-orthodox economists in almost every country is *"we must create sustainable growth"*. We can conclude that the political strategy of 'decoupling' GDP Growth from environmental impacts has not worked, and in my opinion was never intended to work. This is evident in that the Hartwick Rule, a theory of environmental economics upon which de-coupling is based, has not been proven, it has only been validated in some few resource cases.

After decades of the use of this de-coupling policy, no significant de-coupling of environmental impacts from GDP growth has occurred over the past 40 years aside. Some relative decoupling of economic growth from materials and energy consumption has been achieved by a number of EU countries, however 'sustainable development', which includes efficiency policies, has not achieved absolute decoupling of economic growth and resource use in the EU. In addition, hidden imported goods are linked to hidden resource flows/ ecological impacts that are not measured.

> "Although resource productivity is steadily increasing (relative decoupling), Europe's absolute resource use remains at a high level, with economic and environmental consequences. Policy measure should therefore focus on an absolute decoupling of resource use and economic growth. DMC as an indicator for resource use does not include hidden flows ("ecological rucksacks") that arise from the extraction or processing of resources. In particular, imported goods are linked to large hidden flows. Europe is currently improving its resource productivity by increasing resource imports. The environmental burden connected to resource extraction is increasingly shifted to other countries." – *'Eco-innovation – putting the EU on the path to a resource efficient and energy efficient economy'*, Wuppertal Institute for Climate, Environment and Energy 2009.

This deceptive narrative is also evident in additional fiasco of words in a study conducted by scientists at the Department of Ecology and Environmental Science, Umea University. The study finds that the ecological footprint across 135 countries did not decrease at high levels of GDP per capita. The improved eco-efficiency, which is seen in many wealthy countries, is associated with economic growth which increases the global ecological footprints of these countries. One example of this 'catch 22' is that

> **"Finland, a wealthy and eco-efficient country has been classified as both the most sustainable country (Devitt and DeFusco, 2002) and the country that caused the fifth largest per capita ecological footprint in the world** (Loh, 2002)" – *'Eco-innovation – putting the EU on the path to a resource efficient and energy efficient economy'*, Wuppertal Institute for Climate, Environment and Energy 2009.

Decoupling has failed, yet the deceitful mantra of sustainable development, which is not real sustainability, is continually pushed by the UN. Despite substantial long-term efforts of de-coupling in some western and European countries, GDP growth has not been 'de-coupled' in any significant way from causing environmental and resource degradation. The reality in the globalisation paradigm is that the more GDP growth occurs, the more resource depletion and environmental damage occurs. By prioritising short-term GDP growth above all else in order to make interest payments to international banks and bond markets, governments are damaging the resource base upon which we all rely, instead these resources should be managed sensibly and not be subject to an economy in which ongoing usury has been one of the prime objectives.

Some governments are now utilising environmental resource economics, but this will not solve real environmental problems either. Resource economists have proffered, Hartwick's rule, a theory of resource economics, as a solution to resource issues, however Hartwick's Rule has been shown to only be viable in some instances and is not a proven theory. Therefore, there is no economic solution for creating sustainability in the current world-wide globalised economic system. Hartwick's Rule defines the amount of investment in produced capital that is needed to exactly offset declining stocks of non-renewable resources. This investment is undertaken so that the standard of living does not fall as society moves into the indefinite future. A study titled *'Intergenerational Equity and Exhaustible Resources'* by Robert Solow, see Endnote [125], shows that, given a degree of substitutability between produced capital and natural resources one way to design a sustainable consumption program for an economy is to accumulate produced capital sufficiently rapidly so that the pinch from the shrinking exhaustible resource stock is precisely countered by the services from the enlarged produced capital stock. However, the following point was made by Perman et al. in the book *Natural Resource and Environmental Economics* see Endnote [126], in relation to substitutability and an environmental Kuznet's curve hypothesis:

> "An "environmental Kuznet's curve" (EKC) hypothesis proposed by Kuznet has not been validated…If it were validated then it would imply that economic growth is the means to environmental improvement."

In the absence of effective de-coupling and resource substitution, it is clear that alternative systems and models must be considered. Human society must be enabled to function in such a way that it works with rather than against natural laws and processes of nature. The knowledge to do this already exists within the texts of humankind's ancient past. For those that people that choose it, a golden age involving a re-discovery and implementation of real knowledge of a how to create successful healthy society in harmony with nature is already well underway and emerging world-wide.

International policies for 'sustainable development' incorrectly endorse GDP growth

Governments rely on debt money that is created from nothing by the privately-owned international banking cartel, and must pay interest to that cartel, this is known as usury. This system has always needed GDP growth to ensure the interest payments keep rolling in, however, because GDP growth is directly linked with environmental pollution and resource, it can be asserted that **the usury system is a root cause of the environmental problem**, and the modern-day worldwide adopted religion of consumerism and materialism. This root cause is not addressed by the flawed political solution of sustainable development; thus, all governmental environmental laws and policies worldwide operate within the confines of the paradigm of economic GDP growth. The environmental laws amount to some slowing down of the real polluting and depletion effects of the system to land, air and water, but do not stop its overall trajectory. I am not referring to carbon emissions or methane from cows as pollutants, these are not real pollutants. There are real pollutants in emissions from fossil fuels, but carbon is not one of them.

The science of measuring sustainability demonstrates clearly that GDP growth and environmental protection are not the same agenda and are in conflict, but international organisations, such as the UN, the WEF etc, and virtually all national governments try to sell us the lie that they are the same agenda. While I worked at the UN, I viewed an advance copy of the Report of the UN Secretary General's High-Level Panel on Global Sustainability, see Endnote [127], which states:

> "Today we see with increasing clarity that economic growth, environmental protection, and social equity are one and the same agenda: the sustainable development agenda. We cannot make lasting progress in one without progress on all."

The above statement is a politically produced lie and is not backed up by evidence. We have already established that no significant decoupling of GDP growth from resource use and environmental impact has been achieved worldwide over the past 40 years. The oxymoron has already been described, for example, the Wuppertal Institute for Climate, Environment and Energy has estimated in a report, see Endnote [128], that:

> "Since the 1980s, total global extraction of both abiotic (fossil fuels, minerals) and biotic (agriculture, forestry, fishing) resources has increased steadily. Between 1980 and 2005, resource extraction levels grew from 40 to 58 billion tonnes. A total of about 80 billion tonnes is predicted by 2020 - 200% of 1980 figure (Giljum et al. 2008). While the global share of extraction by the BRIICS countries (Brazil, Russia, India, Indonesia, China and South Africa) and the rest of the world (non- OECD) is increasing, the global share of the OECD countries is shrinking".

Technologies, strategies and processes for local energy and sustainable living already exist, but have been suppressed (or not supported) by governments if they are in conflict with the paradigm of continuous GDP growth, corporate and banking profit, and so-called globalisation.

It is also notable that the flawed political solution of sustainable development does not list or acknowledge the fractional reserve banking system as a root cause of the environmental problem despite the fact this flaw has been pointed out by many academics and environmentalists, including Professor Tim Jackson, Chair of the now defunct UK Sustainable Development Commission, and Professor Herman Daly in his book '*Steady State Economics*'.

Green economy/green growth strategy is destructive globalisation painted green

The UNEP describes:

> ".a fresh, Green Economy approach—one that rewards greater resource efficiency, vastly improved natural asset management and decent employment across the developed and developing world" - UNEP (2009)Year Book 2009: New Science and Developments in Our Changing Environment

In January 2012, the Global Green Growth Institute, Organisation for Economic Co-operation and Development, UNEP, and the World Bank signed a Memorandum of Understanding to formally launch the Green Growth Knowledge Platform (GGKP). The GGKP's mission is to enhance and expand efforts to identify and address major knowledge gaps in green growth theory and practice, and to help countries design and implement policies to move towards a so-called green economy.

UNEP's Green Economy approach retains the current economic and monetary model, but with greater emphasis on resource efficiency and natural asset management. The term 'Green Growth' is now used, but essentially this Green Economy approach endorsed GDP growth but emphasises resource efficiency and as I have already described above resource efficiency alone will not solve the worldwide environmental problem – in fact resource efficiency may even make the environmental problems worse due to the Jevons Paradox. The 'green economy/ green growth' approach ignores the main drivers and inter-related root causes of environmentally destructive GDP growth, i.e., the fractional reserve banking system which imposes an absolute need for governments to continually grow their economies as the number one priority, thus we see that the green economy is simply business as usual rebranded.

UNEP's approach will at best slow global environmental degradation rather than stopping it. As long as the worldwide economic model is based around a debt-based money system and fractional reserve banking, and as long as corporate profit is legally enshrined as a higher priority for corporations than anything else, the current economic system will continue to degrade our environment. Political terms such as 'sustainable development' and 'green economy' are simply marketing wordplay and will never significantly reverse or lessen the environmental degradation caused by the current worldwide system.

Clive Spash, an ecological economist, has criticised the use of economic growth to address environmental losses, and argued that the Green Economy, as advocated by the UN, is not a new approach at all and is actually a diversion from the real drivers of environmental crisis".

The UN incorrectly promote GDP growth thus causing environmental impacts

The UN promotes a policy, financial and regulatory environment endorsing and conducive to economic GDP growth, for example UNECE's Committee on Economic Cooperation and Integration, see Endnote [129], and the Report of the UN Secretary General's High Level Panel on Global Sustainability, see Endnote [130], states:

> "Today we see with increasing clarity that economic growth, environmental protection, and social equity are one and the same agenda: the *sustainable development* agenda. We cannot make lasting progress in one without progress on all."

The above UN statement is incorrect and highly misleading. It is incorrect because economic growth is causing and continues to cause environmental destruction, yet it has been packaged as part of 'global sustainability'. The UN Report provides no evidence base for the above statement because there is no evidence base to support it. The fact is environmental destruction has not been decoupled from economic growth in any globally significant way. As already stated, Wuppertal Institute has estimated that a total global resource extraction of around 80 billion tonnes in 2020 (200% of the 1980 value) will be necessary to maintain global economic growth and states:

> "Scenarios anticipate a total resource extraction of around 80 billion tonnes in 2020 (200 % of the 1980-value), necessary to sustain the worldwide economic growth.".

Some of the resources of nature are finite so there is obviously a conflict here. In addition, the prioritisation of growth, without any evidence to support that priority, is also demonstrated in a letter dated 30 January 2012 from the Co-Chairs of the United Nations High-level Panel on Global Sustainability addressed to the UN Secretary-General, see Endnote [131], which states:

> "Our mission as a Panel was to reflect on and formulate a new vision for sustainable growth and prosperity, along with mechanisms for achieving it.

Amidst the pro-growth rhetoric exists a contrasting UN' report that correctly points out the flaws of the growth-based economy. It is titled *'Building a Sustainable and Desirable Economy - in Society – in Nature'*, and its authors include Professor Tim Jackson and Professor Herman Daly. The report describes the need to transition away from a growth-based economy to a steady-state economy.

Blaming population growth rather addressing the root causes

> "Depopulation should be the highest priority of US foreign policy toward the third world" – Henry Kissinger

The globalist-owned and controlled corporate media and international institutions spin the narrative that the population level is to blame for the resource problems of the world. However, my analyses indicate that the worldwide population level is not the main cause of unsustainability in the current worldwide system, rather a real root cause is the debt-money system and fractional reserve banking system that we are all born into – it is this system that drives a never-ending treadmill of debt, consumerism, environmental destruction and unsustainability. The UN, an un-elected, un-accountable international organisation, has policies for population control and reduction in the name of sustainable development. Malthusian-type population reduction policies were initially proposed at the UN 1994 Cairo Population Conference on the genocidal assumption that population expands faster than food supplies. Sir Julian Huxley was a founder of the British Eugenic Society, director of the Abortion law Reform Association, and became the first Director-general of UNESCO, which pushes for population reduction.

The agenda also stems from the Club of Rome, an organisation established in 1968 with a Malthusian agenda for genocide. In 1972 they published *Limits to Growth* claiming that the Earth could not sustain the current population expansion in the age of depleting resources. Their 1992 report *The Global Revolution* leaves no doubt as to their real agenda: "In search for a new enemy to unite us, we came up the idea that pollution, the threat of global warming, water shortages, famine and the like would fit the bill. "They concluded "The real enemy is humanity itself.", see Endnote [132].

In truth, if people knew how to live and thrive in self-sufficient communities and regions, the world's resources could easily support the existing level of human population, and much more. However, we have all been born into a dependency on a trans-national system, and most of us appear to have lost have the knowledge to live in a self-sufficient community that our forefathers had.

> "A study by the University of California's Division of Agricultural Science shows that by practicing the best agricultural methods now in use the world's famers could raise enough food to provide a

meat-centred diet for a populations ten times greater than that at present… If people would be satisfied by an equally nourishing but mostly vegetarian diet, a population 30 times greater than that at present could be fed. A switch to a vegetarian diet would also bring many environmental improvements, less destruction of rain forests, less air pollution, less water pollution… "- *'Divine Nature: A spiritual perspective on the environmental crisis'* by Michael A. Cremo and Mukunda Goswami

7. Globalisation – a destructive paradigm

The tragedy of the commons and the privatization of everything

'The commons' is a term that describes the 'common land' that was under shared ownership by the common people worldwide for the welfare and sustenance of all for hundreds, if not thousands of years. Various authors have described how the ruling classes of early modern times instigated the destruction, and takeover, of the commons, in order to create a culture of dependence in which the masses depended on the schemes of the ruling classes. Over the past 300 years ruling classes of early modern times instigated the takeover of the commons. This was done via various political and legal mechanisms in order to create a culture of dependence of money and wages earned from labour rather than having relative self-sufficiency from use of the commons land for agriculture, grazing animals, wood for building, herbs for medicines, and other resources, etc.

> "The ruling classes of early modern times determined to create a culture of dependence with themselves replacing the popes as the dispensers of favour; those favors now being decided by money…To achieve this the former social customs of shared ownership, mutual aid, and the commons had to be destroyed… There were four significant social developments that were required for that long standing arrangement to be changed. One was industrialisation and markets for the goods produced, the second was a pool of labourers, the third was a paper money economy that could provide people with sustenance seemingly independent of the land, and the fourth was the development of the modern state… These changes in the social structure were accomplished, as they typically are in Kali-yuga by force… in England from the 16th through 19th centuries a series of 'enclosure laws' were enacted to eliminate the use of village lands and the commons…. The enclosure laws were specifically intended to eliminate their means sustenance making the peasants dependent on wages... " – Dhanesvara Das, Author

It was now the law of the (anonymous) market that condemned a man to work for starvation wages. Leo Tolstoy described the situation as follows: "Money is but a new form of slavery, distinguishable from the old (slavery) simply by the fact that it is impersonal - there is no human relation between master and slave." In this way a co-operative society of times past was gradually replaced by a competitive society in which each man was compelled to be for himself alone as he had to acquire paper money in order to survive, and to do this he had to work under the schemes of those who controlled the money supply.

> "The various powers had determined that the way of life was going to change to what is now called the 'modern' way of life. It more properly deserves to be called money slavery, since everyone,

without exception, is a slave to obtaining money simply to survive… We have the impression that we are governed by a certain political arrangement called democracy, or a constitutional republic,.. Nothing could further from the truth. We are in fact governed by money, or more specifically, by those who control money, as attested to by Rothschild. " - Dhanesvara das, Author

'Give me control of a nations' money (creation) system and I care not who makes its laws.' – Mayer Amschel Rothschild, Banker

In contrast to the times when people had shared use of the commons, in modern times virtually everything has been privatised and nothing is available to, or owned by, the common people. The land and water of the world, nature, seeds, the sky (the airwaves), even life itself via the advent of patenting and bio-piracy of genes, foods, plants, animals, biodiversity and resources of nature, and life-forms including pathogens, genetic markers, and so-called viruses! In almost all cases you will find it owned by corporations – whereas all these natural resources used to be called the commons and were shared and used by everyone.

"The law doth punish man or woman, Who steals the goose from off the common, But lets the greater felon loose, Who steals the common from the goose" - 18th Century Anti-Enclosure saying

"In the village communities of many areas of medieval Europe, land was held and use in ways that were not very destructive to the environment. Pastures, forests and water resources were held in common and their use was carefully regulated by councils of village officials... The agricultural system was directed toward local self-sufficiency, With the decline of the medieval God-centred world view and the rise of materialistic science and industry, this subsistence type of agriculture dwindled. Between the years 1500 and 1700, it was gradually replaced by production for the emerging market economy. The application of industrial methods of production to agricultural set-in motion a process that is even now destroying traditional village economies and the environment… began the rapid depletion of Europe's forest's... trees were cut to expand farmland… and to supply fuel and raw materials for factories" - 'Divine Nature: A spiritual perspective on the environmental crisis' by Michael A. Cremo and Mukunda Goswami.

"The medieval economy had been based on organic and renewable energy sources – wood, water and wind. The emerging capitalist economy was based not only on the non-organic (and polluting) energy source coal and non-renewable, but on… metals… the refining and processing of which further depleted the forests. " – Carolyn Merchant

"It was the tendency of industrialisation to focus power and money in the hands of a select few that Gandhi saw as most dangerous. It spelled the end of millennia-old village economy of India because it took away from the individual and the community the means of controlling their own livelihood. Nearly one hundred years after… we can see how the concentration of production and capital in the hands of a tiny minority of the world… has spelled the ruin of traditional lifestyles in every corner of the globe – lifestyles that were organically in harmony with nature and trod lightly on the earth. " – Ranchor Prime author of 'Vedic Ecology – Practical wisdom for surviving the 21st century'

"The Brazilian government estimates that 97% of the 4000 patents taken out on natural products in the country between 1995 and 2000 were by foreigners. **Biopiracy** is rampant, taking advantage of weak laws, hiding behind the mask of 'scientific cooperation' and 'ecotourism'... Mexican farmers were dismayed to find their indigenous landraces widely contaminated by genetically modified corn. They were even more outraged to hear that companies might want to charge them for using the contaminated strains as they now contain patented transgenes. Another imminent danger is the flood of rice gene patents that may affect farmers' rights to use and sell existing varieties or to develop new ones, now that the rice genome has been sequenced. China's Beijing Genome Institute has scored an impressive victory for the developing countries by joining the sequencing race late and coming out ahead. The Beijing Genome Institute has deposited the rice genome sequence in the public database, while Syngenta is hoarding its data on its own website. This has dramatically changed the power politics of agriculture, hitherto under the predominant control of the rich developed world. It remains to be seen, however, whether China can put a stop to the rampant gene-patenting that has occurred when the human genome sequence was announced in 2001." – (see Endnote [133])

"Scientists should work much more closely, if not directly, with local communities... priority must be given to revitalising and protecting traditional agricultural and healthcare systems from biopiracy and globalisation, and to developing sciences and technologies appropriate for the community... Apart from the obvious criteria that the technologies should not be harmful or toxic, there are other features to consider. They should respect human rights and ethical concerns of society. They should not compromise the conditions of life for future generations while benefiting the present." - Source unknown

Corporations prioritize profit above all else

"colonial powers brought destruction to indigenous peoples around the world. Violence is the base of such economic expediency and this modus operandi continues even to this day – the demonic plunder from behind the mask of corporations, freely roaming the world for every opportunity of profit at the expense of others." – Dhanesvara das, Author

"Corporations (are legal fictions that) continue to enjoy privileges not available to an individual person... Chief among these privileges are favourable tax structures, or no taxes at all; the anonymity provided to both the owners, and managers who act not in their own name, but in the name of the corporation... Corporations are an illusion of modern society because they have no existence in fact. They are a fiction agreed to by those who hold power; the rest of us merely go along with the established order as we do other fictions.... And there is now a movement to rescind the legal status of corporate personhood... There is no Monsanto, but only the people who act in the name of Monsanto... " – Dhanesvara das, Author

A company or corporation is a legal entity formed by a group of individuals to engage in and operate a business commercial or industrial—enterprise. These legal entities are designed to enable the creation of profit, see Endnote [134], and are central to the GDP growth paradigm. Almost all corporations in all industries are designed to prioritise profit over all other priorities. **They are legal fictions that their owners can hide behind, free from liability, whilst the corporation can be utilised to implement actions for which**

any individual would be jailed, such as major environmental pollution, etc. Corporations have no national identity. Bayer, a German company, was allowed to produce aspirin unabated in the US during WWII, and Ford and General Motors, supposedly US companies, ran factories in Germany throughout the war and then successfully sued the US government for damage to them!

The extremely wealthy few that hold the majority of the shares of the mega-corporations of the world have received vast incomes over the past decades. Meanwhile, environmental sustainability and the social wellbeing of society is not prioritised. Any concerns about the environment or the wellbeing of the people are usually a secondary corporate consideration to maximising profit. If a CEO does something positive for a community or the environment, he/she could even be ousted by shareholders if they deem the action is not a maximisation of profit.

This worldwide corporate structure continually contributes to worldwide resource degradation and pollution in order to use resources to maximise profits. Corporate social responsibility and corporate sustainability have become an increasingly common aspect of the corporate world, and some limited improvements in environmental performance have taken place. However, creating profit is always the overriding objective.

The vast majority of the world's population has become dependent on corporate trans-national food and energy production systems that are dependent on the resource of oil. There is a general lack of local systems for self-sufficiency in food and energy. A transition away from the trans-national environmentally destructive corporate profit-making machine and more toward self-sufficient co-operative local enterprises is needed.

Corporate globalisation – a design for mega-corporate rule of the world's resources

"… sold as a panacea for all problems, economic globalisation has not lived up to its advertising. It has not lifted the poor, it has instead brought record disparities in income and wealth between rich and poor nations. It has greatly inhibited democracy and social justice; it has destroyed local communities and pushed farmers off their lands. And it has accelerated the greatest environmental breakdown in history. The only real beneficiaries of globalisation are the world's largest corporations and their top officials, and the global bureaucracies they helped to create." - *'Alternatives to Economic Globalisation'* edited by John Cavanaugh and Gerry Mander (see Endnote [135])

"to date eco villages have been swimming resolutely against the dominant socio-economic paradigm of our age – globalisation…where globalisation is predicated on the notion that we can grow our way out of our social and ecological problems through ever greater specialisation, accumulation and trade, eco villages are living manifestation of a philosophy of voluntary simplicity and greater self reliance" - Robert Dawson, Author, see Endnote [136].

The modern era of globalisation is a design for corporate rule of the world's resources. Many corporations have utilised environmental and corporate sustainability initiatives over the past decades, yet these in most cases manifest as add-ons or end-of-pipe reductions that do not significantly alter the overall impact of the corporations' activities. Such initiatives do not change the fact that the corporate holy grail is to maximise shareholder profit. More successful corporate sustainability approaches involve the utilisation of whole-systems based sustainability frameworks, such as The Natural Step framework, see Endnote [137]. This framework has been utilised by some companies to redesign entire systems and supply chains toward a strict definition sustainability. However, the uptake and implementation of such useful sustainability approaches has not been not sufficient to negate the environmental impacts of globalisation, i.e., the process of decoupling environmental impacts from rampant ongoing GDP growth.

The problems associated with globalisation are described in the book *'Alternatives to Economic Globalisation'* edited by John Cavanaugh and Gerry Mander. The book describes how globalisation was in effect born at the Bretton Woods conference in 1944 attended by world's leading bankers, economists, politicians and corporate figures. Out of Bretton Woods the institutions of the World Bank and the International Monetary Fund (IMF) were formed. The General Agreement on Tariffs and Trade came later and then the formation of the World Trade Organisation (WTO) and other free trade agreements. According to the authors these instruments embodied a power shift away from national, state and local governments and communities toward unprecedented centralisation of power for global corporations, bankers, and global bureaucracies at the expense of national sovereignty, community control, diversity and the natural world.

The globalisation model is described as having key features including: promotion of hypergrowth and unrestricted exploitation of environmental resources and new markets; privatisation of public services and community commons; intense promotion of consumerism; corporate deregulation; and replacement of traditional powers of nation states and local communities by global corporate bureaucracy. The institutions above are described as an unholy trinity whose job is to align all of the world's national economies behind a central formula that involves the deregulation of corporate activity, privatization of whatever is public, preventing nations from protecting natural resources and opening the free flow of investment and trade. The authors recommend getting corporate influence out of politics as part of the addressing these problems. Corporate law enabled corporations to be treated as legal persons and is designed to prioritise profit above environmental or human rights issues. I note that a book by John Perkins, *Confessions of an Economic Hitman describes* some of the horrific social and environmental effects of corporate globalisation:

> "Ecuador had suffered under a long line of dictators and right-wing oligarchies manipulated by U.S. political and commercial interests... the corporatocracy had made major inroads there. The serious exploitation of oil in the Ecuadorian Amazon basin began in the late 1960s, and it resulted in a buying spree in which the small club of families who ran Ecuador played into the hands of the international banks. They saddled their country with huge amounts of debt, backed by the promise of oil revenues... International engineering and construction companies struck it rich — once again.... in 1968, this tiny country had evolved into the quintessential victim of the corporatocracy. My contemporaries and I, and our modern corporate equivalents, had managed to bring it to virtual bankruptcy. We loaned it billions of dollars so it could hire our engineering and construction firms to build projects that would help its richest families. As a result, in those three decades, the official poverty level grew from 50 to 70 percent, under- or unemployment increased from 15 to 70 percent, public debt increased from $240 million to $16 billion, and the share of national resources allocated to the poorest citizens declined from 20 percent to 6 percent. Today, Ecuador must devote nearly 50 percent of its national budget simply to paying off its debts." – John Perkins, Author

There are endless examples of fake sustainability and horror stories in the corporate mining, and oil sectors; and in the water sector by companies including Coca Cola and Nestlé in India, Brazil, Mexico. In the US, Nestlé has been in a battle with the Osceola Township, in Michigan, where residents complain the water extraction techniques are ruining the environment. Nestlé pays the State of Michigan US$ 200 to extract 130 million gallons of water per year in 2018, see Endnote [138]. Public water use by private corporations also results in trillions of used plastic bottles ending up as waste, in the sea, and on the land.

Aligned with the worldwide private banking cartel, a feature of globalisation is the debt enslavement of entire countries. This process was described in my book *Globalism Unmasked: The Truth about Banking and the Reset of Society*, and by authors, such as John Perkins. Massive loans are provided to a country under the promise of wealth from investment and when this does not materialise the country is forced to sell off assets, such as oil companies, water systems, land or resources, cheaply under conditionalities.

> "Because the loans have been arranged such that they can never be repaid, compounding interest only increases the debt. There is simply no way out. If the country defaults on the debt then they are cut off from all international funding." – John Perkins, Author

The IMF, for example, via the process of structural adjustment, controls the economic activities of countries that have received IMF loans, often resulting in economic, social and cultural devastation. This process has been applied by the IMF in over 150 countries resulting in what author Michael Chossudovsky calls the *globalisation of poverty.*

Globalisation also results in huge income disparities, for example, in 2005 a fulltime minimum wage worker in the US earned $10,500 per annum and the CEO of Exxon-Mobil was paid $13,700 an hour – more than 2,600 times what the minimum wage earner makes, see Endnote [139]. Yet, when a corporation fails it is never the common people that benefit, as the world witnessed with the case with the looting of Enron. Before it collapsed it was looted by the company's executives who received more than $744 million in payments and bonuses in its last year alone. At bankruptcy however, Enron workers lost $800 million from their pension funds.

In addition to the detrimental effects of the GDP growth system already listed, the effects of globalisation have hindered the creation of local sustainability. Local sustainability or local self-sufficiency are not part of the remit for the public institutions that foster the paradigm of GDP growth and globalisation. In this era of globalisation, national governments and public institutions have become subject to the policies of the international institutions of globalisation whose agenda is GDP growth. The process of politically defined sustainable development has always also endorsed GDP growth.

Local self-sufficiency initiatives have not generally been part of the industrial or scientific development remit of national governments, corporations or research and development institutes. Criteria for allocating funding for new projects in the era of globalisation has typically been based on the potential for job creation and profit creation. This paradigm has also resulted in the gradual loss of local and indigenous knowledge as people were forced to change their traditions for Western models. For example, the widespread use of industrial agricultural monoculture has resulted in reduced soil fertility, and a decline of traditional farming methods and associated knowledge involving seed production, crop varieties, soil fertility, and regeneration of the land.

Another aspect of globalisation is what some have called the economics of destruction. Armin Risi, author of the book *'Transcending the Global Power Game'* describes it as follows:

> "Consumption has to be continually increased by the creation of new artificial needs, by new ways of propaganda, and by opening up new markets. If that is no longer possible, consumption has to be expanded by yet another method, namely by increasing destruction. As history has shown, the most effective means to this end are economic crises, financial crashes and wars. In such cases, the winners – those who secretly incited the destruction – can start to build things up again. Obviously,

the power of the global players is based on a vicious circle: systematic destruction as a means to increase production." – Armin Risi, Author

" – the true nature of America's 'war on terrorism'.. is that it is actually a pretext for a 'New World Order' – wars of conquest for the purpose of serving the moneyed interests: Wall Street, the US military-industrial complex, i.e., oil, corporate and other interests who profit in death and destruction. " - Michel Chossudovsky, Author

To address the detrimental effects of globalisation, David Korten, author of *'When Corporations Rule the World',* recommends removal of a corporations' rights as an individual and reform of the Bretton Woods institutions i.e., the World Bank, the IMF and the World Trade Organisation. In addition, the publications of 'The Centre for Research on Globalisation', *see* Endnote [140], an independent research organization and media group of writers, scholars, journalists and activists that publishes articles on globalisation and its effects, are of note. Robert Dawson, author of the book *'Eco villages',* maintains that there are solid reasons for believing that the age of globalisation is coming to an end. He states:

"There are solid reasons for believing that the age of globalisation is coming to an end –perhaps even in the relatively short term – most obviously the long supply lines of products being transported hither and thither around the world – the ingredients of a typical Sunday lunch have been calculated to travel up to 49,000 miles – are highly vulnerable to increases in fuel prices associated with peak oil. Large scale plantation agriculture as it is currently practised is also very fossil fuel dependent…. Globalisation could be bankrupted by the rise in fuel prices;" a drop in food supply due to a reduction in chemical inputs; decreased availability of water and/or loss of soil fertility; melt down in the financial markets following a major debtor country default; terrorist attacks on vital supply lines such as oil lines" – Robert Dawson, Author, see Endnote 136.

The World Bank and the IMF – terrorist organisations devastating the developing world

Let us take a closer look at these two most powerful organisations in world trade and finance. For decades the World Bank and the IMF have been implementing Structural Adjustment Programs (SAPs) on developing countries. The SAPs require governments to cut public spending, privatise state enterprises, increase exports, and reduce barriers to trade and foreign investment; and are thus supposed to reduce debt and poverty within the developing country. However, we find that the exact opposite has occurred. According to a 2002 report prepared in collaboration with the World Bank, national governments and civil society, SAPs have been:

"expanding poverty, inequality and insecurity around the world. They have torn at the heart of economies and social fabric… Their effects, particularly on the poor are so profound and pervasive that no amount of targeted social investments can begin to address the social crises that they have engendered." - see Endnote [141].

Furthermore, US political domination of the World Bank and the IMF ensured these organisations would become instruments of US foreign policy. This was epitomised by World Bank president, Robert McNamara, who had been US Secretary of Defense before being transferred to the World Bank by US President Johnson in 1968. By promoting "export-oriented growth", McNamara accelerated the Third World's integration into the corporate globalisation, see Endnote [142]. In the 1980s, the World Bank and the IMF imposed SAPs onto many developing economies that needed to borrow money to service their debts. By 1986, the IMF dictated the economic conditions of life to over 1.4 billion people in 75 countries, in effect subjugating these economies with disastrous consequences. Between 19884 and 1990, Third World countries under SAPs transferred $178 billion to Western commercial banks, leaving these countries in a state of spiralling poverty and hunger.

"The United Nations Economic Commission for Latin America and the Caribbean stated "the levels of [poverty] are still considerably higher than those observed in 1980... Under SAPs, Africa's external debt has increased by more than 500% since 1980 to $333 billion today... African countries have paid their debt three times over yet they three times as indebted as ten years ago... the World Bank and the IMF... are merely instruments for the imposition of US imperial design upon Africa and the rest of the Third World " – Dr Sahadeva Dasa, Author, see Endnote 142.

Corporate control of the food supply

The world's food supply is now controlled by a mere handful of corporations. In the book *Food Fascism – Corporate Control Of Our Food Supply*, Dr Sahadeva Dasa describes that 95% of all grain reserves worldwide are controlled by six agri-business mega-corporations. Corporate control has resulted in more processed foods, industrial factory farms, loss of family farms and rural communities, and more pesticide and GMO usage.

"The Canadian Department of Agriculture figures states that (under GM) canola yields have decreased at least 10%.... The reality is that the nutritional content of all crops are down fifty percent of what they were before GMOs were introduced and now we have less yields and more chemicals used, exactly the opposite of what Monsanto promised." – Dr Sahadeva dasa

Major pesticide and GMO mega-corporations include BASF, Bayer Dupont, Dow Chemical, Monsanto and Syngenta. They own a vast number of seed, pesticide and biotech companies. Monsanto was responsible for the introduction of GM crops and toxic chemicals, such as aspartame, DDT, Agent Orange, petroleum-based fertilisers, rGBH, glyphosate, and more. In addition, the godless corporate practice of patenting nature itself is carried out by such companies, and has displaced thousands of years of traditional agriculture and farmers' rights. The World Trade Organisation's Agreement on Trade-

Related Aspects of Intellectual Property Rights (TRIPS) has facilitated the granting of patents to all genetic material, including seeds, plants and animals.

> "By May 2002, there were 1,457 biotechnology companies in the US with a total value of $224 billion…. consolidation is acute, 70% of patents on staple food crops are held by six multinational corporations who can set the market price for them and block competition for 20 years, thereby monopolizing the market… The developing world, where 75% of people's livelihoods depend on agriculture, is the source of 90% of all biological resources. Yet transnational companies based in the developed countries hold 97% of global patents…. patenting of life goes against the sharing of knowledge and the preservation of biodiversity and culture" – Dr Sahadeva das, Author

Consequently, farmers in developing countries are now not permitted to store seeds without paying corporations for the privilege, but who gave corporations this privilege? This issue is known as 'bio-piracy'. In India, millions of farmers borrowed money to purchase corporate-produced GM seeds that were around 1,000 times more expensive than traditional seeds, but when the crops failed these farmers were left with huge debts. The situation was compounded by the fact that the GM seeds contain terminator technology, so that famers had to buy new seeds each year. This crisis resulted in over 250,000 farmers committing suicide in India between 1995 and 2009, see Endnote [143].

Another major trend is the headlong corporate rush to buy huge tracts of land in the developing world for crop production, for example, the multi-national Daewoo Logistics secured 1.3 million hectares of land in Madagascar, to grow crops for biofuels. Madagascar is a country in which a third of the population and 50% of children under 5 are malnourished, see Endnote 143. This worldwide trend has resulted in vast deforestation to clear land for crop production; and also evokes images of crops being transported out of heavily protected factory farms as hungry locals starve. I am reminded of the genocide that occurred in Ireland in the 1800s when over a million people starved whilst endless shiploads of food produce and farm animals were being exported under the auspices of the British Crown corporation, and their occupation army forces, as detailed in the book *The Perfect Holocaust* by researcher, Chris Fogarty, see Endnote [144].

According to analyst Frederick Kaufmann, see Endnote [145], the world food inflation crisis is also a result of the manipulations of Wall Street mega-bank Golden Sachs. In 1991, Golden Sachs came up with a new type of investment product called the Goldman Sachs Commodity Index (GSCI). When, in 1999, the Commodities Futures Trading Commission deregulated futures markets, bankers could suddenly purchase a large stake in the grain futures market. A crucial aspect was that the GSCI did not include a mechanism to sell or "short" a commodity – it was a long-only strategy, requiring bankers to buy and keep buying regardless of the price, and to keep rolling their multi-billion-dollar backlog of buy orders into the next futures contract. According to Kaufmann:

> "since the deflationary impact of shorting a position simply wasn't part of the GSCI, professional grain traders could make a killing by anticipating the market fluctuations these 'rolls' would inevitable cause". As other banks entered the game, "the scene had been set for food inflation… that would send shockwaves throughout the world…. And so, from 2005 to 2008, the worldwide price of food rose 80% - and has kept rising… investment bankers have engineered an artificial upward pull on the price of grain futures… 250 million people joined the ranks of the hungry in 2008… all the while the index funds continue to prosper, the bankers pocket the profits, and the world's poor teeter on the brink of starvation." – Frederick Kaufmann, Author

8. The flaws of the GDP growth system

This chapter is available in the PDF download version of this book *Transcending the Climate Change Deception - Toward Real Sustainability*, which is available on my website www.mkeenan.ie. This chapter is also available in my 2020 book *Globalism Unmasked: The Truth about Banking and the Reset of Society,* which is available on www.amazon.com. It covers the following topics:

- GDP growth anti-ecological and detrimental to society / needed so interest can be paid to banks
- GDP growth causes increased environmental degradation and resource use
- GDP is more of an indicator of Gross Domestic 'Pollution', rather than the actual wellbeing of a national population
- This GDP growth paradigm and usury/debt money banking system has failed to create a sustainable society
- GDP growth is a flawed indicator for progress toward a sustainable society
- Flaws in GDP accounting as an indicator of the wellbeing of society
- Beyond a certain point, GDP growth does not increase human wellbeing, it impoverishes it
- The economic welfare of society, as estimated by the GPI, has decreased since 1978
- The myth that GDP growth and globalisation 'floats all boats'
- The illusion of money and the problem of hyperinflation
- Constraints to GDP growth and the potential end of GDP growth
- A prosperous sustainable society without GDP growth and fractional reserve banking

9. Contemporary economics is a flawed ideology / pseudo-science

This chapter is available in the PDF download version of this book *Transcending the Climate Change Deception - Toward Real Sustainability*, which is available on my website www.mkeenan.ie. This chapter is also available in my 2020 book *Globalism Unmasked: The Truth about Banking and the Reset of Society,* which is available on www.amazon.com. It covers the following topics:

- Contemporary economics is a flawed ideology or pseudo-science it is not a scientific discipline
- Putting a financial value on the environment is an insufficient environmental policy
- The UN property rights 'regime'

10. Systemic problems, oil dependency, constraints to growth, and collapse

The serious implications of oil availability – constraints to GDP growth

In addition to the systemic problems of the banking and economic system, it is important to note that the current globalised society and industrial economic system of the world is extremely dependent on the availability of affordable oil. **'Peak oil' does not mean there in no more oil left in the ground, peak oil occurs when the cost of oil extraction exceeds the price consumers will pay**, see Endnote [146].

Aside: Some commentators maintain that peak oil itself is a myth, and is not due to a physical limitation or economic constraint, but is actually due to the availability of affordable oil being intentionally limited by geo-political forces or by a globalist cartel. Whatever your view on this, the fundamental issue is the same, i.e., the vulnerability of society to a lack of affordable oil.

Aside: The current mainstream theory is that oil is formed via the degradation of trees over millions of years and is therefore limited. However, I note that this theory is unproven. This subject is not within the scope of this book.

Without an ongoing supply of affordable oil, the structures of the current trans-national economy will become increasingly dysfunctional. For example, current systems of transport and industrial agriculture are hugely dependent on oil. The issuing of vast amounts of credit, the process of quantitative easing, and creating debt-money from nothing cannot by itself maintain the flawed GDP growth paradigm. Without the energy input of oil that can be extracted economically the GDP growth system cannot be maintained, as worldwide industrialised society is hugely dependent on oil. Over the past decades there has been very little political focus by the governments of the world on creating local systems of self-sufficiency and thus the whole of so-called modern trans-national industrial society is extremely dependent on trans-national oil supplies. David Korowicz, author of a report titled *'Tipping Point Near-Term Systemic Implications of a Peak in Global Oil Production',* see Endnote [147], states:

> "The key to understanding the implications of peak oil is to see it not just directly through its effect on transport, petrochemicals, or food say, but its systemic effects. A globalising, integrated and co-dependent economy has evolved with particular dynamics and embedded structures that have made

our basic welfare dependent upon delocalised 'local' economies. It has locked us into hyper-complex economic and social processes that are increasing our vulnerability, but which we are unable to alter without risking a collapse in those same welfare supporting structures… There is much we can do. Not to prevent or defer a collapse, rather to prepare to some degree ourselves and communities for some of its impacts." – David Korowicz, Author

An article I wrote in 2011 began as follows: "As the banking system scrambles to save itself from collapse (at the unjust expense of ordinary citizens), we also face the challenges of 'peak oil'… which will impact citizens' buying power, and the stability of our societies. These events represent an opportunity for a re-evaluation of the values that our economic system is based on and an opportunity for transition toward a more sustainable, resilient society."

Fast forward to 2022, and the exact same words still apply. The banks and asset management corporations have yet again received a multi-trillion-dollar bailout in April 2020 in the U.S., and there has been very little preparation for the consequences of peak oil, an issue that was raised decades ago. The warnings by various systems analysts over the past decades about the serious implications of peak oil, and the consequent possibility of societal collapse, have been side-lined by governments, corporate media, and the existing 'orthodoxy' for decades. These warnings were also ignored by influential and deluded contemporary economists and governments who continued to shout the mantra of promoting GDP growth they were blindly fixated upon. The following quote by Dr Louis Arnoux should give the reader serious pause for thought:

> "Unless alternative primary energy sources are brought in rapidly enough the Oil age as we know it will have fizzled out by circa 2022." – Dr Louis Arnoux, former head of Alternative Energy Research, New Zealand Government

Furthermore, a Finnish government research report, see Endnote [148], warns that the economic viability of the entire global oil market could come undone within the next few years.

> "We are not running out of oil, but it's becoming uneconomical to exploit it… A government research report produced by Finland warns that the increasingly unsustainable economics of the oil industry could derail the global financial system within the next few years…the report arrives at the shock conclusion that the economic viability of the entire global oil market could come undone within the next few years, see Endnote [149]" – Dr Nafeez Mosaddeq Ahmed, Journalist

The reality is that the unsustainable aspects of the debt-money banking and GDP growth paradigm have been manifesting and the entire economic system is in a cul-de-sac of its own making. The large rates of GDP growth that have been created in the past decades cannot be maintained by creating more debt money or by utilising human labour alone.

The current globalised economy and GDP growth has been reliant on a cheap source of energy for decades, i.e., oil. There are indications that that peak oil has occurred and the days of using oil as a cheap energy source to drive the worldwide GDP growth system may be permanently over. Should this prove to be the case, there are potentially massive consequences for the extremely wealthy few of the current corporate, political and banking orthodoxy, as well as the rest of humanity that has become dependent on current systems of transnational supply lines to acquire goods and food.

We have been living in a fake unsustainable economy, as it is based on money created from nothing and backed by nothing, and is heavily reliant on the availability of the resource of affordable oil. Many politicians and governments blinkered by short-term analysis have for decades failed to appreciate or understand the fundamental reliance of the GDP growth system and the whole of the trans-national worldwide economy on the availability of 'cheap' oil. Furthermore, for decades, governments have pointedly neglected to support the development of more self-sufficient communities, towns and regions or mechanisms for society to function without affordable oil. Without affordable oil the house of cards upon which the worldwide economy and industrial society has been built could come quickly crashing down.

Analysis published by the Foundation for the Economics of Sustainability

The Foundation for the Economics of Sustainability has published articles, see Endnote [150], by Mr. Tim Clarke that analyse the issue of peak oil and implications for society. Referencing data and analysis of various experts and systems analysts, the articles indicate that 'peak oil' has been reached and that, therefore, GDP growth on a worldwide basis can no longer be maintained. He has kindly provided permission for the following extract:

> "Before the current Covid-triggered global economic slowdown began, the global economy was already perched on the edge of a major correction... (there is) a systemic and fundamental problem with the global economy which is getting more serious as time passes; showing that continuous on-going economic contraction is from now on baked into the cake of our global industrial economic system. It is more than ever vitally important for us to understand the root cause(s) of the economic malaise to help prepare ourselves, our families, communities and businesses, and plan appropriate strategies for the future...
>
> Most economists do not understand that the economy runs on energy – not money! Money is a claim on goods and services that are created by the use of energy. Without energy there can be no human economic activity... Of all the planet's energy sources, oil plays a fundamental role in the economy, partly because it powers 95% of all transport, 100% of shipping and air transport, and is key to production of most mineral resources and the majority of global food supply...

"In the early twentieth century, the Energy Returned on Investment (EROI) of fossil fuels was sometimes as high as 100:1. This means that a single unit of energy would be enough to extract a hundred times that amount. But since then, the EROI of fossil fuels has dramatically reduced. Between 1960 and 1980, the world average value EROI for fossil fuels declined by more than half, from about 35:1 to 15:1. It's still declining, with latest estimates putting the value at between 6:1 and 3:1." - see Endnote [151].

According to Mr. Clarke the current EROI is too low to sustain industrial economies, and he maintains the following:

"greening the economy will NOT enable further economic growth… The inescapable fact is that the exponential economic growth of the last 250 years or so, made possible by the "money-creation as debt-with-interest" Ponzi scheme, and powered by the seemingly endless bonanza of cheap high-net energy fossil fuels, is now over. We have entered a new challenging era of permanent net-energy contraction and economic decline… with the probability of major disruptions to global supply chains including food production, and the failure of banks and currencies….

To keep the ship afloat, central banks have promised to throw more and more "money (debt) at the problem, which will cause "fiat" currencies to hyperinflate and banks to collapse under the weight of non-performing loans. Thus, a complete reset of the financial system is inevitable. This reset is now being openly discussed by the WEF (See Endnote [152]), the BIS and other global financial institutions.

Do not be misled by the hyperbole. As pointed out, greening of the economy will not enable continued economic growth. These initiatives are designed to preserve and strengthen the position and status of the few. The reality is that as economies contract, people and countries will be increasingly impoverished and societal unrest will grow. Is it any surprise that all over the world governments are now instigating drastic surveillance and social control measures in the name of C-19..?.. Our policy makers here, busy firefighting what they believe is a conventional fire of recession and determined at all costs to create more growth, appear to have no understanding of the root causes of the gathering global economic collapse, and no idea how incredibly serious this will get…

For instance, struggling at all costs to maintain the exploitive money-creation by debt-with-interest financial system, which has financed economic growth until now, will fail and make things so much worse because this system is NOT compatible with degrowth. Unfortunately this is the likely route the world and Ireland will take as global privately owned central banks print trillions of new debt-money which they can conjure out of "thin" air, and this straw is seized gratefully by drowning governments, businesses and people… " – Tim Clarke (Quoted with kind permission).

11. Modern day attempts to scientifically define 'real' sustainability

The problem of reductionism

> "the purpose of the scientific method is to select a single truth from among many hypothetical truths …. But historically science has done exactly the opposite. through multiplication upon multiplication of fact, information, theories and hypotheses, it is science itself that is leading mankind from single absolute truths to multiple, indeterminate relative ones. The major producer of the social chaos, the indeterminacy of thought and values that rational knowledge is supposed to eliminate is none other than science itself. and what phaedrus saw in the isolation of his own laboratory work years ago is now seen everywhere in the technological world today. Scientifically produced anti-science – chaos" – Robert Pirsig, Author of *'Zen and the Art of Motorcycle Maintenance'* (pg 119)

Author, Robert Pirsig identified a trend in science toward reductionism over the past 200 years. The vast amount of information knowledge in the world is more than anyone person could hold, and thus it is divided into many specialist areas and into the province of professionally employed specialists. Most are expert in their own knowledge silo but ignorant of the other silos. This has led us to a narrow reductionist view of the earth. A holistic view, which views the whole from the outside is just as important as viewing something in multiple separate pieces. Today there exists a vast number of specialized research and development sectors and, yet, there is no strict scientific definition of sustainability being applied across the entire development sector. Thus, these silos are often behaving independently of one another without a common beneficial 'end goal' for humanity – the result is the scientific chaos and godless scientism we see in the world today. The only commonality over the past decades has been the central ideology of making a product or technology that can be sold for profit, regardless of environmental or human impacts. Furthermore, with a huge diversity of specialist research areas, specialists in one sector seldom understand the specialists in another sector, and lack a common language or framework for societal and environmental sustainability in their profit driven endeavours. They are unable meaningfully communicate with each other. And lack a common language to tie the silos together in a truly meaningful way that is beneficial for society as a whole.

In a reductionist world most people only recognise certain individual trees of the metaphorical forest of knowledge, but cannot see or even fathom the whole forest, i.e., the whole system of knowledge. We are inundated with thousands of chunks of information, in essence we are drowning in knowledge, whereas what we actually need is a 'whole systems view' of what is happening in the world and to understand what is the net effect of the entire system of parts.

Scientist Jay Forrester, see Endnote [153], maintains that humans have trouble understanding and managing current social, economic, and environmental systems because these systems are too complex for the human mind to grasp. However, I do not think it is correct to assume this – it certainly is not true of everyone. In my experience, there are many people worldwide that do understand what is occurring in the world today, and are expert in research and pattern recognition, but their voices are not aired on the corporate-owned media systems. Many truthtellers and whistle-blowers have been censored and smeared by the orthodoxy that owns the 'system'. Thus, contemporary industrial, economic, political and technological mechanisms have largely been left to their own tragic devices, un-fettered, un-restrained and un-aligned with the operating rules that are built into nature itself.

Thus, in 2022 there exists thousands of mostly separated research silos of knowledge, but without a whole-systems framework tying them all together. Without a whole systems sustainability view the direction of each separated silo of development is not compared to any fundamental guiding principle of sustainability. The result is multi-directional development chaos with no understanding of the long-term consequences of technologies in fields such as industrial production, bio-technology, genetic modification, nanotechnology, vaccines, pharmaceuticals, wireless communications etc.

The application of a correct definition of sustainability in the system as the 'end goal' would potentially connect all these diverse silos together, and drive all research, knowledge and development in the right direction, i.e., a direction that is beneficial for the long-term wellbeing of human kind, and for the quality, quantity and resilience of nature's resources. One of the main remits that is currently being applied worldwide is the UN IPPC remit to de-carbonise the entire world economy, and reduce methane emissions and that of other GHGs, but as we know, this is a deceptive agenda, and not a real sustainability agenda.

Many 'environmentally friendly' technology solutions exist throughout the industrial world, but all of these exist and operate within the ongoing paradigm of globalisation, GDP growth, reducing carbon emissions, creating greater efficiencies, etc., and these technological 'stopgaps' alone do not, and will never, reverse the overall trend of real environmental degradation. Rather than 'putting out individual fires', what is needed is an overall systems design solution in which the fires of unsustainability do not occur in the first place.

What is needed is to address the 'real sustainability' issue, and address real pollution to land, air and water systems; and to create self-sufficient communities, not just within technological sectors, but across the entire societal system. Peer reviewed whole-systems scientific frameworks for sustainability do actually already exist. A successful example of such a solution is The Natural Step (TNS) Framework for Strategic Sustainable Development (FSSD), pioneered by Professor Karl Henrik Robert. The framework uses a scientific definition of sustainability, which was endorsed by 170 scientists in the Science of Sustainability Report 2006, see Endnote [154], as a peer reviewed scientific definition of sustainability.

It has been implemented by hundreds of communities, companies and local governments since the 1980s. An unfortunate flaw (in my opinion) in the interpretation and implementation of the framework, is the inclusion of the narrative that 'carbon and methane emissions' cause climate change. Without the inclusion of this flaw the framework is a very useful tool for transitioning local, corporate and government systems toward more environmentally sustainable systems. The uptake of a solution like TNS would need to be in the many millions of projects, or implemented at the national or international level, to make a significant difference in the worldwide situation.

The precautionary principle has been ignored in science

"Science is value free. The inability of science to grasp quality as an object of enquiry makes it impossible for science to provide a scale of values." – Robert Pirsig, Author of *'Zen and the Art of Motorcycle Maintenance'* (pg 347)

To acquire funding, scientists and research and development teams are required to estimate the profit-making potential of the research or of the applications of the new technology. This has resulted in 'real sustainability' and the 'pre-cautionary principle' becoming an almost irrelevant aspect of the vast majority of scientific research. Various current technological industries generate many billions, or even trillions, of dollars in revenue, but have uncertain or unknown long-term impacts on human health and on the environment. These sectors include: GMOs, LMOs, nanotechnologies, thousands of manmade chemical compounds, vaccines, wireless-communications that emit high frequency microwaves / electro-magnetic fields, etc. The pre-cautionary principle should be prioritised as a fundamentally important to all technological use and innovation.

Modern-day research on the scientific basis for defining sustainability

I have been exposed to numerous contemporary definitions of sustainable development and sustainability in my environmental career. Most of these definitions lack a scientific basis and are based on loosely worded aspirations that can be interpreted in different ways and cannot be measured in the real world. In this sub-chapter I focus on a definition that I believe was a genuine attempt to scientifically define sustainability. What would the world economic system look like if, instead of being designed by profit-seeking globalists, it was designed using 'real science' to behave in balance with the environment we all rely on? To design such a system, we must examine the detrimental effects of the current flawed economic system and then define a system without those detrimental effects. Professor Karl-Hendrik Robert, Founder of The Natural Step organisation, an organisation which utilises a scientific peer-reviewed definition of sustainability, stated in a lecture I attended in Dublin, Ireland, in 2008:

> " the biggest single obstacle to sustainability is not climate change, but the lack of shared political understanding of what sustainability is."

RSBS was a five-month project in 2005 to investigate the scientific status in seven fields relating to environmental sustainability. Based on an extensive review of global literature, interviews and questionnaires with some 170 leading experts and scholars in Japan, the US, and Europe, the report was released in 2005. The objective of the project was to focus on clarifying the view of science and urge political and business decision-makers to base their decisions and actions on a solid scientific foundation. The report endorsed the Sustainability definition pioneered by The Natural Step organisation as the Scientific Definition of Sustainability; and Herman Daly's Three Conditions of Ecological Sustainability as the Economic Definition of Sustainability.

A scientific understanding about how ecological and social systems work is critical if we are to know what to aim for in creating a sustainable future. The Natural Step framework provides four concrete principles to guide a creative process that can envision sustainable outcomes as part of a planning process aimed to arrive at a specific destination – sustainable activity for humans on Earth. The principles quickly highlight that the current success model for our society has inherent design flaws that are placing the systems of nature and human social systems under ever more strain. The Natural Step's four principles, see Endnote [155], are derived from the following realities:

> "Our society is built around a reliance on digging up materials from the Earth's crust that then are allowed to accumulate in the biosphere as polluting waste. This includes the atmospheric accumulation of hydrofluorocarbons from refrigerants and aerosols; and the accumulation of heavy metals in water and soils from various industrial processes and IT equipment such as computers and mobile phones.

Our society produces and uses large numbers, over 100,000, of different synthetic chemicals which are also allowed to accumulate in the biosphere as polluting waste. Many of these chemical compounds are foreign to nature and do not easily break down. This includes pharmaceutical chemicals, like antibiotics, that accumulate in water, pesticides and insecticides that build up on water and soil systems and enter the human food-chain; and industrial chemicals used for plastics and mining.

The growth of our society has relied upon consistently increasing its encroachment upon and alteration of natural and ecological systems. We dam rivers for power, or drain water from them for irrigation reducing the flow to a mere trickle. We have removed vast amounts of forests, over-fished the oceans, destroyed soil systems with mono-culture and intensive agricultural methods, and we have dramatically reduced the prevalence of wetland systems that purify water and control flooding. In the process the amount of biodiversity has plummeted, with species extinction now estimated to be up to 1,000 times the natural background rate. Many biologists believe we are now heading towards a man-made mass extinction event.

The gap between rich and poor is now at epidemic proportions. A study by the World Institute for Development Economics Research at United Nations University reports that the richest 1% of adults alone owned 40% of global assets in the year 2000. And, the three richest people in the world possess more financial assets than the lowest 48 nations combined. Working conditions, pay rates and labour rights for many in the developing world, where much of the world's manufacturing industry is based, are poor. Even in the rich countries, democratic processes and personal freedoms have been systematically eroded, largely under the auspices of national security and the war on terror. Working hours have generally increased, with many people having less time to spend with family or on recreation."

According to peer-reviewed TNS definition of sustainability, modern industrial society alters the Earth and causes environmental degradation in three significant ways:

"1. Society mines and disperses materials faster than they are returned to the Earth's crust. Industrial societies have extracted pollutants that were previously stored for millions of years as fuel and mineral deposits.... Many of the mineral deposits are toxic for example mercury and cadmium, basic elements that cannot be broken down into less toxic components.

2. Society produces polluting substances faster than they can be broken down by natural processes and many manmade substances cannot be broken down at all. The chemical industry has created tens of thousands of new man-made chemical compounds that are released and leak out into natural systems. A number of these chemical substances being released are damaging to humans and to environmental systems. Industrial society is producing persistent artificial compounds and the global eco-system had not previously confronted these substances throughout billions of years. Humans are not equipped to deal with these new artificial substances and the significant health risks associated with them. Many of the substances are organic compounds of chlorine, fluorine and bromine and include polychlorinated biphenyls (PCBs), dichlorodiphenyltrichloroethane (DDT), dioxins, and chlorofluorocarbons. Manmade chemicals such as PCBs that do not break down, accumulate in the body and stay there. The term persistent organic pollutants (POPs) refers to substances that are not part of nature, that interfere with organic systems and are not degraded by physical, chemical or biological processes. Even in low concentration POPs can harm humans. The

slow movement of pollutants, the accumulation of toxins in the food chain, the emission of chemicals from products and waste, and interactions between artificial and natural compounds can result in uncontrolled environment degradation and significant public health risks. Exposure to chemical pollutants has been documented as playing a major role in determining children's health. (See Endnote [156]).

3. <u>Society depletes or degrades resources faster than they are regenerated</u> (for example, through deforestation and overfishing), or by other forms of physical degradation of ecosystems (for example, paving over fertile land or causing soil erosion). As a consequence of the physical destruction of the environment the restorative capacity of eco-systems is being reduced, while the outputs of industrial wastes are increasing. (See Endnote [157])."

Thus, the RSBS report lists the following TNS definition, see Endnote [158], as the peer-reviewed definition as the Scientific Definition of Sustainability:

"In a sustainable society, nature is not subject to and we must eliminate our contribution to:
▶ increasing concentrations of substances extracted from the Earth's crust (e.g. heavy metals)
▶ increasing concentrations of chemicals and compounds produced by society (dioxins, PCBs, POPs, etc..)
▶ degradation and physical destruction of nature, (overharvesting forests, destroying natural habitats, etc).
▶ and in that society people are not subject to conditions that systematically undermine their capacity to meet their needs."

The conclusion is we must transform our industries and align societal processes so that they function in harmony with scientific conditions for sustainability.

Balancing material flows with nature's capacity via sustainable design

Material flows in society must be such that the concentrations of pollutants, such as heavy metals and toxic chemical compounds, produced by society do not systematically increase. Therefore, innovation can have the following aims:

societal biological flows of matter must be incorporated into those of nature's systems;

societal technical nutrient flows of matter must be kept separate from nature's systems, or societal technical nutrient flows of matter must be gradually reduced in order to enable nature's systems to process them.

The volume of natural systems should therefore be increased, for example, by planting trees. The balance of material flows can be influenced upstream by choices regarding industrial designs and production volumes, by societal competence in safeguarding toxic substances and by international cooperation under legally binding international instruments, , see Endnote [159]. In nature there is no since thing as waste. Waste from one organisms or process is used by another, thereby realizing a closed-loop symbiotic relationship. The sustainable design challenge is for human systems to emulate nature's cradle to cradle (zero waste) design. Efforts have been made by various companies over the past decades to redesign our existing systems to emulate the zero-waste design that exists in nature's systems.

Cradle to Cradle design

One such approach is Cradle-to-Cradle design. McDonagh and Braungart the authors of the book 'Cradle to Cradle' (C2C), see Endnote [160], describe C2C as a biomimetic approach to the design of sustainable systems. C2C as well as sustainability frameworks, such as the TNS framework, see Endnote [161], are examples of useful sustainability approaches that have been implemented by hundreds of companies, communities, and local governments. According McDonagh and Braungart:

"In this approach materials are viewed as nutrients circulating in either biological (natural) or technical (manmade) metabolisms. To be sustainable the flows should be kept separate. Biological flows can therefore be returned safely to the bio-sphere and technical nutrients should remain within the technical flow so that nutrients can be re-used. C2C seeks to create systems that are essentially waste free. In this context sustainability is defined as a system in which the biological and technical flows function separately with zero waste. Sustainable Development in this context is the creation of products and services that utilise these design principles."

"Take biomimicry. The cooling system of the Eastgate Building in Harare, Zimbabwe was inspired by towers built by termites. It saves 90 per cent of the energy compared with a comparable building". - *United Nations Environmental Programme (2009) Year Book 2009: New Science and Developments in Our Changing Environment.*

C2C provides an innovation roadmap process for change that a community or industry can use to transform itself. The authors discount the concept of eco-efficiency and recommend eco-effectiveness. Materials are viewed as nutrients circulating in either biological (natural) or technical (manmade) metabolisms. To be sustainable the flows should be kept separate. Biological flows can therefore be returned safely to natural systems and technical nutrients should remain within the technical flow so that nutrients can be re-used. C2C seeks to create systems that are essentially waste free. In this context sustainability is defined as a system in which the biological and technical flows function separately with zero waste, and is the creation of products and services that utilise these design principles. The authors maintain that being less bad is no good i.e., that eco-efficiency or other policies that may simply slow down environmental destruction, are not viable solutions that will create a sustainable society. They maintain that the scientific community as a whole is paid for reductionist research of problems rather than implementing broad strategies of change.

"The Cradle-to-Grave Legacy. Manufacturing systems of the Industrial Revolution are based on a one-way, cradle-to-grave stream of materials - a model that takes, makes, and wastes… The advent of modern industrial processes has had the added consequence of making many processes and materials more toxic… profoundly affecting the air we breathe, the water we drink, the diseases we suffer from, and global politics.

Today, with our growing knowledge of the living earth, our designs can reflect a new spirit… Ideally, products of human industry designed from biodegradable, ecologically safe materials participate in the biological metabolism after use through decomposition.

The Technical Metabolism. Industry can also be modelled after natural processes to create technical metabolisms, systems that productively cycle industrial materials. These materials, valuable for their performance qualities and typically 'non-renewable,' are technical nutrients, designed to circulate safely and perpetually through cradle-to-cradle product life cycles of production, use, recovery, and re-manufacture… "

"Eco-efficiency i.e., doing more with less. It has been successful and profitable to some extent, but it just slows environmental damage at best… Relying on eco-efficiency will slowly finish us off. Being less bad is a failure we need to be 100% good." – McDonagh and Braungart, Authors of Cradle to Cradle

Note however, the overall trend of environmental degradation far outweighs the advances made by these pioneering modern-day corporate sustainable design and corporate sustainability framework initiatives. I note also that, in almost all modern-day sustainability initiatives, there is a complete lack of knowledge on how ancient human cultures lived in balance with nature.

Sustainable design and innovation are only a part of the sustainability solution. By itself it will not solve the overall problem or move humanity through a major paradigm shift into a 'real' sustainable and resilient society.

Sustainable design, eco-efficiency or eco-innovation has failed – it is not enough

Corporate processes of sustainable design, eco-efficiency or environmental technology innovation have not been not enough and will never be enough, on their own, to create a 'real' sustainable society worldwide as long as the polluting globalisation / GDP growth paradigm continues. Environmental innovation is currently far outweighed by the rampant environmentally destructive globalisation paradigm and its polluting industrial processes, and is incorrectly focused on the flawed agenda of combatting climate change. Any authentically environmental innovation will always be playing 'catch up' to new environmentally-damaging and human-health-damaging technologies that are continually funded within the GDP growth/globalisation paradigm. It is like trying constantly to 'grab the donkey by the tail'.

Born in the unsustainable matrix – ideological delusion (not fact) in education and politics

"Politics is a very interesting game for people who have no talent, and have nothing much to say, and wish to advance themselves... It's for very energetic mediocrities" – Gore Vidal

It's not just the economists that are in living in delusion. We find ourselves being led by politicians who do not understand the flaws of the system, lack the ability of whole-systems analysis, and are often more concerned with wielding power and gaining status than anything else. The development and self-realisation of each individual person should be the goal of an enlightened society; however, the current education system and economic system does the opposite - it moulds people to fit into the system like cogs in a wheel. In addition, the pseudo-science of contemporary economics accounts for a person as merely a unit of labour and production and consumption only. We have become cogs in a flawed system rather than free people working to create a world of better quality and real sustainability. Living outside the realms of current insane system is not an option for most people because most of humanity has not yet created the structures for anything except the so-called 'rat race', in which everyone must work hard, pay the mortgage, and become a slave to materialism and endless consumerism.

With some notable exceptions academia has been slow to understand these 'systemic' problems; and remains mired in reductionist solutions and reductionist research, failing to address the bigger picture or the 'elephants in the room', i.e., the systems of globalisation, GDP growth, privately-owned world banking, debt-money and usury. Too often comfortably shackled to corporate funding, the mantra of profit, and corporate-technology development, our universities and research institutions have failed to elucidate the problem of inherent unsustainability in the system itself. Academia and research have become as conditioned as the rest of society and is full of efficient worker-drones kneeling before the source of funding, and never seriously questioning or challenging that source. Free thinkers have become the radical enemy of the current academic and research orthodoxy. Mired in the mode of compliance with the money-masters, academia has become entirely bereft of unrestrained free-thinking geniuses who are now regarded as too difficult to work with, or politically incorrect. Thus, when the time comes, academia is destined to implode along with its master.

"The church of reason like all institutions of the system is based not on individual strength but upon individual weakness. What is really demanded in the church of reason is not ability but inability. Then you are considered teachable... a truly able person is always a threat" – Robert Pirsig, Author of *Zen and the Art of Motorcycle Maintenance* (pg 395)

Of course, our education system never teaches how money is actually created, or who controls and owns the worldwide private banking system. The human 'products' of the education system become indoctrinated and induced into a wide variety of economic sectors in service of the globalised economy, including accounting, advertising, marketing, business management, sales, engineering, law, media, etc., without ever being taught what creating a truly sustainable society actually involves. **Real sustainability or community self-sufficiency is never taught in the education system because these concepts are in conflict with the world system-wide orthodoxy that imposes complete dependence on debt-money produced by privately owned mega-banks, endless consumerism and the transnational supply chains of corporate 'globalisation', corporate profit and corporate resource control.**

The education system has largely vanquished the natural creativity of young people and instead they are taught to become automatons. To achieve high grades, they must replicate what they are being told, rather than question it. By the time they graduate from university young people have been tailored for the market economy office jobs of accountancy and big business, and for industries that rampantly consume nature's resources. Universities have become centres for imposing the bogus ideologies and material illusions of the economic system and are no longer centres for free thinking, or even free speech, as they used to be for many hundreds of years. Political correctness is paramount to get ahead in this system.

Rather than robotically serving the future worker drone interests of faceless legal entities called corporations and banks, an education system for real sustainability and community resilience could teach practical processes for local food and energy production, natural building methods, ancient knowledge on how to thrive in balance with nature, real health and healing, as well as emotional and spiritual development. Our true role as creative 'spiritual' beings needs to be nurtured and expanded not ignored.

In corporate-owned media sector, there is no remit for 'real' sustainability whatsoever. The functions of the corporate-owned media include to: promote endless consumerism; distract the masses with endless frivolous and increasingly perverse programmes; and indoctrination and mind control of the masses to comply with the ideologies and fake facts of the UN, governments, godless corporate scientism, corporate elites and the private banking cartel.

> "as a result of being caught up in our cultural trance, we in America no longer live in a democracy; we live in a 'mediacracy'. The media is so heavily influenced by its corporate sponsors that even the world's events are editorialised into opinion pieces… John Swinton, a writer at the New York

Times, was quoted as saying, 'the business of journalists is to destroy the truth.... We are the tools and vassals of rich men behind the scenes.'" - Alberto Villoldo, Author

Real sustainability should not be labelled with any 'political' ideology

Identity politics divides people and distracts from what real sustainability is and what it involves. Real sustainability is not communism or capitalism or socialism, all of which have been used in the past as systems of the 'haves' and 'have nots'; and is not so-called 'left' politics or so-called 'right' politics. Identifying with these labels is a divide-and-conquer trick which separates us and limits our thinking. It should not be labelled with any 'political' ideology. To become trapped in allegiance to so called socialism, communism or capitalism is to become trapped in duality or trapped in a dogma. One then may become averse to successful engagement and co-operation with other skilled members of the community around you.

Real sustainability involves a thriving real approach to life that works for you, your family, and community and must be based on respect for the natural resources that God provides and that we all rely on. It involves cutting our ties with dependency on a flawed and immoral system, and creating more local self-sufficiency that can be relied upon with confidence. If the globalised system collapses, these resilient local networks will survive, thrive and replicate. It is the freedom to live without the debt-money and usury systems of the international bankers; and without the unjust taxes of governments whose primary raison d'etre is to use these collected taxes to pay vast sums of interest to the international bankers that created the debt-money from nothing.

The success of any system whether it be based on capitalism, communism, socialism or even based on real sustainability principles, or none of the above, is always dependent on the 'consciousness' of the people involved and on the leaders in control. In a later chapter I describe the relevance of this aspect. A leader operating in a mode of goodness, fairness and truth is likely to produce a quite different societal outcome compared to a leader in a modes of authoritarianism, greed, power and control. Joseph Stalin who was a communist caused the death of millions of people in Russia and surrounding countries, and George Bush who was a capitalist caused the deaths of countless people due to his US-led invasions in the middle east. So, we can see that crimes against humanity can result in any system. Any power structure can potentially be used for good or for evil, thus the real solution to the problems of the world is to cleanse our consciousness. Each of us can, of course, start with our individual self, and this ultimately has a powerful effect on those around us.

12. A sustainable retreat – creating resilient local systems

Discarding false narratives and starting anew

Faced with UN Agenda 2030, the WEF reset, the fake covid-19 pandemic and fake climate change agenda, and ongoing corporate globalisation, how should we react? Firstly, we must recognise and state that these agendas are fake and deceptive and are designed to control and limit freedom and keep everyone subservient to technocracy of behind-the-scenes so-called globalist elites. Unless we label them for what they are then we are at risk of being carried along by these false narratives of the corporate media, and become at risk of indoctrination. These fake agendas are not good for you, your family, or your community. Thus, sooner or later, we must retreat from, and discard, these false narratives mentally, emotionally and physically.

We need education for how to create self-sufficient communities - not education for UN-defined sustainable development. The vast majority of third level courses on sustainable development are not based on 'real' sustainability and are a convoluted mixture of real problems and flawed solutions that are ultimately aligned with globalisation and the planned UN Agenda 2030 technocracy.

We must also recognise that real environmental pollution does exist and real resource depletion does exist and that if we are not to be dependent on the globalist system we must create our own local systems, based on 'real sustainability' and real resilience. Most people are reliant on the globalised corporate system so we must chart a gradual 'sustainable retreat' from it and create self-autonomy and local-autonomy. Many people have already started to do this worldwide. A new golden age is manifesting in which robust local and regional systems are being co-created to fulfil our fundamental human needs, physically, mentally, emotionally and spiritually.

The most valuable part of these systems is the self-development and self-realisation of the individual and his or her life skills, or mission in life, also known in the ancient Vedas as *dharma*. This self-development aspect in conjunction with a connection with spirit, is the opposite of the system of globalisation in which people are conditioned to be robotic cogs in the system machinery and hierarchy of the money masters. In the golden age, the current flawed system will not be able to compete with the higher quality of wonderful local systems and networks that emerge for food, energy, and services. Natural toxic-free processes for housing, health services, transport, and many others areas will emerge or be re-discovered based on ancient knowledge and a re-connection with nature.

A sustainable retreat is needed not so-called 'UN sustainable development'

People are overly dependent on the current trans-national economic system. I believe a sustainable retreat toward creating real sustainable self-sufficient local communities, and away from the fraudulent usury economy, is needed. However, a widespread pro-active retreat is unlikely to happen. To move away from the current paradigm is a difficult task for most people – the vast majority of people are dependent on the current system and many are trapped in debt. Like people as batteries in the movie '*The Matrix*' they know no other way of life. To change their way of life is for many a difficult task, should they even be interested in such a change or challenge.

Society is not jumping en masse into the concept of local self-sufficiency and resilience. Who has the time? Most of us have been like hamsters running on a wheel just trying to survive the 9 to 5, to 'get by', to pay the rent or mortgage, and spend some time with friends and family, after work at the end of the day. Yet as the flaws in the current paradigm become more apparent many people are questioning the current system. There is a better path than living life as a debt slave to the private banking system and having to work as a cog within a fraudulent economic system that serves the interest of elites ahead of yours. By embracing new possibilities, establishing self-autonomy and re-discovering our own creativity, we can empower ourselves and those around us to forge a better society.

Is it possible to re-align the current 'system' toward 'real' sustainability

Could humanity simply re-align the mainframe of our current political, economic, social and technological systems and its leadership, with real local sustainability, self-sufficiency and environmental objectives? I believe attempts to do this have been futile because the controllers and leaders of the existing system are mired in the mode of greed, and are not going redesign a system that serves their own narcissistic objectives of societal control. There is a growing awareness of the increasingly desperate lies of the so-called elites in control of the current system. This represents an opportunity for a widespread re-evaluation of the values and mechanisms that our current human society is based on.

To redesign the current system, it is obvious that as initial steps: we must keep 'short term' economic analyses of GDP growth from being the main policy driver; the process of fractional reserve banking should be replaced by full reserve banking; fraudulent usury on money the private bankers create from nothing must be stopped; and governments or local autonomies should consider taking the money creation process back from the private banks and back into public or local ownership. However, it is equally obvious that such a redesign is very unlikely to happen any time soon. Therefore, the present system will likely continue until it collapses, or is subject to some unforeseen readjustment, reset or game-changing external event. Recall that the fake covid-19 pandemic and the scary narrative that the 'world will end in 12 years' due to climate change are the orchestrated 'game changers', and that UN Agenda 2030 and the WEF reset contain technocratic measures of control that you have no say in. This includes plans for moving everyone into so-called smart cities, restricting peoples access to land, eliminating the use of cash and introducing a new digital currency that people have no control over. These are the type of 'solutions' the globalist corporate/communist elites are trying to sell you.

Governments could begin to base policy on the 'real' science of sustainability (not the bogus science of climate change) and help create systems for local resilience, but they are not doing so. Instead, they unwittingly or wittingly, imposing the UN lie of manmade climate change on the world's population. If politicians wish to truly serve the people, they should help create self-autonomous, self-sufficient local communities, and disavow the UN, the WEF and the banker-led worldwide corporate moneyocracy.

The unelected UN and WEF top-down policy framework are part of the problem. The real solutions can be implemented locally by intelligent and determined people in local and regional networks. A truly thriving society that nurtures the creativity, development and wellbeing of people, should be much more than just a technology platform for globalisation and so-called environmentally friendly-industries. It has to be guided by a vision of what a 'real' sustainable society should look like in the long run. Sustainable is actually an insufficient word for the amazing potential of the human spirit.

Sustainability or Collapse? – the risk of societal collapse

There is a significant risk that the current globalisation paradigm that prioritises endless GDP growth, regardless of resource depletion or pollution, will have an impact on the stability of our current globalised system of production and consumption. An extensive re-design of that system has long been needed, but has not been implemented. Decreased access to resources results in increases in the prices of energy, food, and raw materials and will impact citizens' buying power and the stability of our societies dependant on those resources. Communities, regions and nations that are prepared for the challenges ahead will be better placed to deal with the 'systemic shocks' and to build thriving sustainable futures. Societies that have not prepared will be forced to quickly adapt or fail. We have become dependent on vast international supply chains that are in turn dependent on fossil fuels. We all take the trans-national system for granted, but current access to fossil-fuels is reduced or removed, the systems of our current society would be crippled.

Generally speaking, the new renewable energy technologies have a low EROEI and are not sufficient to act as a replacement in the existing system, and will not save a collapsing society. Therefore, appropriate intermediate level technologies used at the local level that are easily maintained via local resources and local people are vitally important.

Over the past decades, various groups have been preparing for what they view as the inevitable detioration or collapse of the current globalized production and transportation system for goods and services. Such groups have tried to raise awareness or change the existing system, but are quickly faced with short-term thinking of politicians or the intransigence of the existing orthodoxy. These groups have been preparing for what they view as the inevitable consequences of system collapse, and have been pro-actively creating local systems for food, energy, services and currency etc. Dmitry Orlov, an author on the subject of collapsing societies, maintains that we must prepare for a non-industrial future. He describes in his writings and articles, see Endnote [162], how to adapt to life in a 'collapse' scenario and addresses topics including de-financialisation, de-globalistion, re-localisation and social collapse best practices. I recall listening to a lecture by Mr. Orlov in 2007 – I paraphrase one of his memorable remarks: *"If you see me on television someday take your shotgun and run for the hills!"*, the purport I take to be, in part, that you've left it too late to create a resilient local network.

Moving away from dependency on fossil fuels, in particular oil and gas

A sustainable retreat must be cognizant of the dependency of society on current fossil fuel powered energy systems. The globalized consumer society is highly dependent on fossil fuel for the production and transport of food and goods, as well as for heating and electricity. Local energy production technologies that are alternatives to fossil fuels have, according to some sources, been suppressed by corporate elites over the past decades; and thus, society is addicted to oil, that will kill if suddenly withdrawn. We cannot switch off our fossil fuel powered civilisation without crashing the trans-national system of transport, food and goods production, energy production etc. If food stops being delivered to ports, supermarkets would be soon be empty of imported food. This can also occur oil and gas availability is reduced due to shortages, inflation, production problems, or intentionally orchestrated geo-political issues. It is clear that if fossil fuels availability is reduced, we will need to focus on the development of local systems for self-sufficiency.

Resilience planning and creating sustainable communities/regions

According the UK government's 2005 National Sustainable Development Strategy (NSDS):

> "Sustainable communities should be... active, inclusive and safe... well run... environmentally sensitive... well designed and built... well connected... thriving... well served... fair for everyone" - (pg 121)

What the above words actually mean is anyone's guess because they are vague and open to different interpretations. "Well run" by whom? Does self-autonomy exist or do totalitarian type councils exist to impose UN agenda 21 on you? "Well designed and built" with what? Natural materials or with materials that contain toxins and chemical compounds that can impact human health? "Well connected" by what? "Fair for everyone" Who decides what is fair and what is not? Furthermore, in an era of volatile energy and food prices, the UK NSDS does not mention anywhere that communities should be moving toward self-sufficiency, self-reliance and resilience, and does not mention the benefits of co-operative local enterprises. The document does, of course, pay homage to the mantra of GDP growth, i.e., globalisation.

> "The possibility of sustainability achieved through participative co-operative enterprises is not even mentioned in the UK strategy" - UK Commission for Rural Communities document, Planning for Sustainable Communities report (2008, pg 8)

Society can be enabled to function within the limits of the environment and its resources and in such a way that it works with rather than against natural laws. A strong concept of 'real' sustainability is needed coupled with ancient knowledge, in which society nurtures nature's pure untainted resources, rather than seeks polluting technological or synthetic substitutes that may fail to deliver the same range of functions and services. To begin creating more sustainable regions and local communities' the following actions could have been implemented decades ago.

Today's economy (unsustainable)	A sustainable thriving society
Charges interest on debt money	Abolishes usury / implements interest-free banking to curtail GDP growth OR at a higher level of consciousness a gradual transition to a moneyless economy
Competitive hierarchy	More co-operative enterprises / the creation of self-sufficient local communities

GDP growth economics	An economy designed using the real science of sustainability and utilising ancient knowledge
Degenerative (keeps using up resources)	Regenerative (regenerates resources and conserves vital stocks)
Products lacking quality and longevity	Qualitative and designed for longevity
Pollutes the environment with toxic chemicals	Refreshes and renews the environment upon which we rely
Unsustainable design of systems, products, buildings	Non-toxic sustainable design of systems, products and buildings, utilising natural materials / use of Cradle-to-Cradle design and The Natural Step framework, a rediscovery of traditional and ancient knowledge of how communities can thrive in balance with nature
Oil dependent	Oil independent, the adoption of 'intermediate-level' technology and a re-discovery of ancient knowledge and suppressed technologies for local self-sufficiency
Oil dependent industrialised food production	Permaculture, organic farming, bio-char fertiliser etc
Corporate ownership of 'the commons' (natural world)	Reclaiming 'the commons' for stewardship or sustainable non-polluting use by the people, a rediscovery of traditional and ancient knowledge of how communities can thrive in balance with nature
Destroys and consumes animals and species	In higher consciousness we respect the right of all animals to live unharmed by human activity

Due to resource constraints, whether real or geo-politically imposed, in particular, in relation to energy supplies, there are systemic risks to the current trans-national systems for acquiring energy, food, goods and services. It is important therefore that local and national resilience planning is promoted by communities, and local and national governments. The question of meeting fundamental human needs for food, clothing, and shelter can usually be dealt with on a small amount of land and with local resources available within a 10-mile radius.

To meet these needs in the years ahead, co-operative local ventures will become increasingly vital, especially if the cost of oil and material resources continue to rise. Co-operative enterprises for community self-sufficiency are already operational in various village-based initiatives throughout the world, for example, Cloughjordan in Ireland, Govardhan village in India, Krishna Valley in Hungary, see Endnote [163]. Yet, the possibility of sustainability achieved through participative co-operative enterprises is usually not promoted in governmental strategies.

> "ecovillages and local government alike need to offer the welcoming hand of friendship, the one to the other." - Johnathon Dawson, Author, see Endnote [164].

Very little adherence to local sustainability principles has left many countries, including Ireland, overdependent on foreign oil, foreign investment, foreign goods and borrowing. We have built little 'self-reliance'. More support and planning need to be directed to creating more 'self-reliant' communities. Such a redesign should be cognisant of the flaws of the debt-money system and should consider local currencies, and the prudent issuance of debt-free money by national governments. Otherwise, societies will remain vulnerable to the austerities of the debt-money banking system and inevitable (or intentionally orchestrated) boom-bust cycles, or worse the WEF 'reset' and UN Agenda 2030.

We must prioritize resilience in food, energy, water, social fabric, natural systems, local and intermediate technology, local currencies, and strength of spirit. The Transition Towns network, see Endnote [165], as well as eco-village networks throughout the world are additional examples of initiatives to create more resilient self-sufficient communities, but unfortunately some of these networks appear to have been hijacked or hypnotised by the cult of manmade climate change. See also the GEN database, see Endnote [166], and the Sustainable Communities Network, see Endnote [167]. Another interesting example is the Sarvodaya movement:

> "now active in over 4000 towns and villages, opening programmes for health, education, agriculture and local industry... it has not tried to apply any readymade solutions or development schemes from above, instead it has gone to the people to draw forth the strength and intelligence that are innate in them and are encouraged by their age old traditions... no programme will be effective if it tries to separate the economic aspects of life from both the cultural and spiritual aspects, as do both the capitalist and socialist models of development. With their sole emphasis on the production of goods they neglect the full range of human wellbeing.... Needs that include satisfying work, harmonious relationships, a safe and beautiful environment, and a life of the mind and spirit, as well as food, clothing and shelter... Sarvodaya has committed itself to a dynamic nonviolent revolution, which is not a transfer of political, economic or social power from one party or class to another, but the transfer of all such power to the people.... each person must awaken to his or her true needs and true strengths if society is to prosper without conflict and injustice..." – Dr. A.T. Ariyaratne and Joanna Macy

Sustainable communities often utilise food production approaches, such as permaculture, see Endnote [168]. The benefits of such systems compared to industrialised food production potentially include: a 2-to-10-fold energy saving on switching to low-input organic agriculture; a 2-to-3-fold increase in crop yield using compost in comparison to chemical fertilisers; organic farming that performs as well or slightly better than conventional industrial farming; and generating twice as much money for the local economy compared to buying food in supermarket chains.

An alternative culture for health and natural medicines, natural (non-toxic) building methods, and other beneficial natural methods and technologies has long existed in more self-sufficient villages and faith-based communities in parallel with the mainstream corporate system, but has been increasingly suppressed. Some years ago, I personally interviewed a scientist that had invented technology for community-scale energy and fertiliser production fuelled via pyrolysis of easily grown plants and organic waste. This technology was being successfully implemented, but was suppressed in various ways. Governments and energy corporations do not want us to be independent and self-sufficient, they want us dependant on the grid.

The wisdom of E.F. Schumacher

E.F Schumacher was a forefather of the real sustainability movement of the 1970s, a movement that was subsequently hijacked by nefarious political processes. The following quotations by E.F. Schumacher (1911-1977) are relevant to the task of creating a successful society. I am very grateful to the Verena Schumacher for kindly providing permission to publish these quotations.

> "Fuel and food he saw as two basic necessities for survival and sustainability. All communities should strive to be self-sufficient in these as far as possible – otherwise they become economically and politically vulnerable" – Diana Schumacher

> "he exhorted all to rely on people power and their own mental and physical inventiveness rather than basing their futures on capital and energy intensive technologies" – Diana Schumacher (referring to E.F. Schumacher)

> "Societies should aim to produce goods with eternal, rather than ephemeral value to avoid a culture of poverty. This is a direct challenge… to our throw away society, with its built in obsolescence."

> "there is no such thing as the viability of states or of nations, there is only the problem of the viability of people: people; actual persons like you and me, they are viable when they can stand on their own feet and earn their keep." – Author, by E.F. Schumacher from 'This I Believe',

> "Production from local resources for local needs is the most rational way of economic life"

> "The economics of giantism and automation are a left over of 19th century thinking and they are totally incapable of solving any of the real problems of today..(we need) a system based on attention to people, and not primarily attention to goods – the goods will look after themselves.. production

by the masses rather than mass production.. but people can be themselves only in small comprehensible groups. Therefore, we must learn to think in terms of an articulated structure that can cope with a multiplicity of small scale units. If economic thinking cannot grasp this it is useless"

"Economic growth, in itself is neither a good thing nor a bad thing. It all depends on what is growing and what is being displaced or destroyed."

"taken by itself the American car industry is of course highly efficient; but how could this efficiency ever offset the monstrous inefficiency of needing nearly 4 million cars for (every) 7 million people...
"

"I launched the Intermediate Technology Development Group to research and reintroduce some of those middle level technologies which are human friendly, environment friendly and which render considerable help to farmers around the world without the depletion of resources and loss of employment that high level technology involves"

"The free and independent 'middle class' capable of challenging the monopolistic power of the rich disappears in step with the 'disappearing middle' of technology" (for example, technology suitable to empower local communities has not been made available)

"The development policies of the last twenty years have been virtually exclusively based on the assumption that development can be most speedily achieved by transferring the high technology of the rich countries to the Third World. Where this transfer has been effected, the result has been a concentration of development upon big cities; a massive migration of rural populations into these cities which consequently have become infested with enormous slums; mass unemployment; stagnation of life in rural areas; and sharply increasing energy requirements. The view is now gaining ground that what the world needs more urgently than anything else is an 'appropriate technology… one of the primary criteria of appropriateness is 'small-scale'"

"Silviculture and forest farming are the only way to safeguard our future and the health of the planet"

"This modern system of food production is so dependent on fossil fuels, primarily natural gas and oil, that if we thought we could feed the whole of humankind… with this system of green revolution agriculture, we would find that all the known resources would be absorbed by agriculture alone in less than 30 years."

"the rest of the country being left practically empty; deserted provincial towns, and the land cultivated with vast tractors, combine harvesters, and immense amounts of chemicals. If this is somebody's conception of the future of the USA, it is hardly a future worth having"

"During the past 25 years… the fuel requirements of agriculture in the advanced countries, including the fuel requirements of agricultural inputs as well as those of food processing have increased by a far higher factor than the increase in agricultural output."

"In 1949, an average of about 11,000 tons of fertiliser nitrogen were used per… unit of crop production, while in 1968 about 57,000 tons of nitrogen were used for the same crop yield. (efficiency decreased 5 fold)" "agriculture should be relatively independent of fossil fuels, which means independence of large scale mechanisation and intensive chemicalisation. At least agriculture should be so organised that it can in case of crisis, absorb large amounts of labour… many successful farmers around the world… are today obtaining excellent yields without using any products of the chemical and pharmaceutical industries."

"Huge modern bureaucracies never achieve anything. They just amble along; the problems don't become smaller they become bigger and bigger. If we think we can solve problems by monster size. We are mistaken"

"Mushrooming cities, surrounded by ever growing misery belts (slums), infested by a largely unemployed proletariat without nourishment for body or soul can be found all over the world…the rural areas tend to sink into ever deeper decay. Every gifted person tends to migrate into the city, to escape from rural misery, and this irresistible brain drain makes the problems of the rural hinterland ever more intractable. At the end of this kind of development lies social chaos, the degradation of man and his environment."

"A country's development policy may be geared primarily to the development of goods or it may be geared primarily to the development of people."

"The poor cannot be helped by our giving them methods and equipment which presuppose a highly developed industrialism. They need an 'intermediate technology; they need the stepping stones of self help. "

"Insane work cannot produce a sane society"

"The question of what the work does to the worker is hardly ever asked, not to mention of whether the real task might not be to adapt the work to the needs of the worker rather than demanding of the worker to adapt himself to the needs of the work – which means of course primarily to the needs of the machine"

"A sane society cannot emerge.. if millions of men and women are condemned most of their lives, to do work which destroys their initiative and rots their brains; or, indeed, if all – or most of – useful productive, creative work is handed over to machines controlled by giant corporations, while people – real living people – are told to find their fulfilment in leisure activities."

"can we take it lightly that so many of them (teenagers) now refer to their participation in adult life as 'joining the rat race'? There could hardly be a greater sign of human failure than this."

The bio-char solution to soil management and desertification

The soil beneath our feet is a living and breathing substance, the top few inches of which is the basis of all life on dry land. In the Amazon basin, large expanses of dark fertile soil called *'terra preta'* have become extremely valuable to farmers and ecologists alike. The soil, which contains charcoal and compost, is believed to have been created by pre-Colombian civilisations. It is believed, by some, that in 1542, the Spanish Conquistador, Francisco de Orellana, whilst exploring along the Rio Negro, one of the Amazon Basin's great rivers, found a network of farms, villages and even huge walled cities that utilised the terra preta.

Terra preta has an ability to maintain nutrient levels over hundreds of years. Studies have shown that even chemical fertilisers cannot maintain crop yields into a third consecutive growing season, yet terra preta remains fertile year after year. Terra preta is rich in charcoal, incompletely burnt wood. It is believed that the charcoal holds the nutrients in the soil and sustains its fertility. This is the great secret of the early Amazonians: the process for nurturing the soil towards sustainable productivity and increased fertility. Carbon was added to these soils using low intensity smouldering fires. A thousand years after its creation it is so well known in Brazil, that it is sold as potting soil. Modern day experiments have shown that adding a combination of charcoal and fertiliser into the rainforest soil significantly boosts yields compared with fertiliser alone.

Inspired by the properties of Terra Preta, biochar (also called charcoal or biomass-derived black carbon, sometimes called agri-char) was identified as a means to radically improve sustainable soil management. Today, the International Biochar Initiative provides a platform for the international exchange of information and activities in support of biochar research, development, demonstration and commercialization. The Japanese government has approved charcoal as an official land management practice. Many studies worldwide, have shown increased crop yields of 20-50% and total biomass yields increasing as much 280%. Such studies led Kansai Electric to fund a reforestation research plantation in Australia with Dr Syd Shea for producing charcoal and returning it to grow more trees and crops in the arid west of that country. Relevant information resources on bio-char and pyrolysis are listed in Endnote [169].

Re-discovering the power and dynamics of horses

I have not owned a car for the past 10 years, I have cycled almost everywhere I go for the past 7 years, and have not flown in a plane for the past 5 years, this is mostly to do with personal preference to live a simple lifestyle. Driving around in a metal box that weighs almost half a tonne has always seemed alien to me. I also see no reason why men and women, communities or society as a whole cannot re-discover their ancient strong relationship with horses for travel and other purposes, rather than relying on hundreds of millions of expensive moving metal boxes produced by industrial mining, which does cause horrific 'real' pollution to water and land systems and consequent human health impacts.

Horses have unique characteristics, abilities, affinities, and ancient connections with human culture and remain an exceptional aspect of the gestalt of human enterprise to this very day. Humankind is now starting to re-discover the full potential of our relationship with horses and how we can more successfully collaborate with horses. The utility of horses has obvious significance in terms of developing strong local communities, amidst the nonsense of electric cars, the production of which cause vast pollution from industrial mining, and amidst reduced oil availability. According to Dave Doherty, at Horsetech market report:

> "Unlike dogs we haven't just co-evolved with horses we have been selected by them because the abilities of a horse are so intimately related to the rider. In many ways we haven't just bred horses to be more like us. They have, in a sense, selected us. Our ancestors' ability to understand and emotionally connect with horses gave them enormous advantages in terms of hunting, farming, fighting and protecting the community. It is no exaggeration to say that the tribe that had a better understanding of horses would, all else being equal, have vanquished or even wiped out the tribe against whom it was competing for scarce resources. Our genetic lineage was decided, at many different points in history, by the cooperation between humans and emotionally intelligent horses. We are here, in part, because our ancestors knew how to train horses. " – Dave Doherty

Natural house construction

In *The Gaia Natural House Book* by David Pearson (2000), health, ecology and spirit are described as the basis of a whole-house design approach to designing a home that is in harmony with the natural systems around it. Pearson states:

> "He says we "are exposed in our homes to the hidden effects of gases and vapours from synthetic materials made from petrochemicals, to heavy metals and pesticides in water and food... Bad health resulting from exposure to this complex mix of pollutants is increasing - allergies and undiagnosed illness are affecting more and more people. Sick building syndrome is a term we have all heard. Our health is under threat from the constant and insidious pollution pervading the home caused by the massive increase in chemicals and synthetic materials... since the largely synthetic free world of 1925 – by 1980 4 million new manmade chemicals had been recorded of which 60,000 are in common use...

> your home is likely to contain rafters treated with toxic fluids, insulated with potentially unhealthy materials, roofs that may contain asbestos, cavity walls containing foam that may contain formaldehyde, walls that are painted with petrochemical paints or vinyl wallpaper that off gas more dangerous vapours especially when new. Wooden floors and stairs may have been chemically treated. Synthetic carpets which contain formaldehyde, furnishings that contain flammable toxic treated polyurethane foam and upholstered with synthetic fabrics, glues in furnishings and plastics in kitchens – all these off-gas particles that we breathe in are not natural to our bodies. Phenols in cleaning products cause unpleasant symptoms such as rashes and breathing difficulties and should be avoided. Plastics and PVCs are harmful can cause birth defects cancer bronchitis and skin diseases... we are also polluting the environment every time we use aerosols, wash the dishes or

clothes with polluting detergents… Use… materials and products that are non-toxic, non-polluting sustainable and renewable" – David Pearson, Author

The proliferation of problematic or toxic chemical compounds that damage human health or the environment is a worldwide problem and is rife even in the so-called sustainability sector. For example, the Sustainable Energy Authority of the Government of Ireland (SEAI) claims to be an organisation promoting sustainability. However, in my opinion, the SEAI house insulation programmes utilise chemical materials that can cause allergies, and other health problems, via off-gassing. The wall-pumped insulation material that is used contains chemical-based glues, and I have medically-verifiable personal experience of allergies being caused by this material. The process involves filling the walls of your house with material enveloped by chemical-based glue.

A transition to a gift economy? - the moneyless manifesto

As an alternative to the current debt-money system some self-sufficient communities utilise local currencies. Another concept that is relevant is the 'gift economy', which has been advocated by Mark Boyle, author of *'The Moneyless Manifesto'* and creator of the Freeconomy group. Boyle describes an illusion of separation in which we have become disconnected from what we consume. The following quotes (provided with kind permission) describe the concept:

> "Consider the water you drink from the stream (or these days, the tap) – do you believe that it is part of you? It makes up between 30-90% of your body, once it is inside you, so you probably ought to. But what about that split second before you cupped it in your hands and drank it, when it was still labelled a stream – is it still separate from you then?"

> "When the illusion of this (separation) myth also fades… me charging you for the gifts I bring to the world… is no less daft than me charging a tree for the nitrogen in my urine when I pee under it, and it then invoicing me for the oxygen it produces and supplies to my lungs. Nature, like me, abhors bureaucracy and administration, so it simply gives unconditionally,.. "

> "A pure moneyless economy, in my definition, is the meeting point of the gift economy and the 100% local economy, and I believe that the physical and spiritual benefits of combining both are huge. Until the day that such an economy is either desirable or possible for you, just apply the aspects of I that work for you... keeping one eye on the converging crises that we all have to face together." – Mark Boyle, Author of 'The Moneyless Manifesto'

Vedic communities and ancient knowledge for thriving in balance with nature

A successful model of a more sustainable self-sufficient community is exemplified by the Vedic farm communities of the worldwide Hare Krishna movement. For example, the well-known Krishna Valley community in Hungary, and Govardhan village in India. These communities have a strong spiritual focus exemplified by the phrase *simple living high thinking.* The *Vedanta Sutru* says that human life is meant is for understanding the spirit, which alone can bring real fulfilment. The communities utilise as far as possible, natural processes for the provision of food, clean water, and energy; as well as intermediate technologies, manpower, and animal power, that is not dependent on oil or gas or the globalised system. They keep cows and bulls and use organic techniques to grow their own food. The bulls are utilised for tasks usually done by machinery, including ploughing, transporting, grinding grain and generating power for simple mechanisms. The communities utilise methods for the production of grain-based fuels, methane gas, composting, waste management, crop rotation and natural pest and weed controls.

Rediscovering the splendour of ancient forest villages

The question was posed in an earlier chapter "even if current human society had full access to nature's forests and the natural world, would we treat nature the way it deserves with purity, respect and love?" The answer is that most of us, having been, born into, and conditioned by the current materialistic society of exploitation, have lost our ancient connection with the forest and the natural world. This is evident in that 80% of the Earth's original forests have been exploited and no longer exist. We require a higher level of consciousness to re-establish our ancient pure connection with the forest.

The world's oldest traditions and practices and spiritual values offer a way toward resolving the real environmental flaws of today's industrial world. For many thousands of years our forefathers and ancestors lived in balance with the world around them and as caretakers not abusers.

Ancient practical wisdom is evident in nature itself. Every physical object in nature has a natural God-given function, or reason to be here, and symbolises some aspect of reality. We could even say that every substance and object in nature has its own 'mission in life'. In Vedic texts this specific property or function, is called *dharma*. Pure water, for example, has the properties of flowing, giving life and healing. A forest, for example, symbolises totality combining all life in a single, interdependent whole. The vast ancient forests also provided mankind with everything needed to live, including trees bearing fruits, edible plants and roots, herbs for healing, wood for construction of homes, fodder for cows and animals, shelter from bad weather for people and animals, protection from invaders. The trees ensured the fertility of the soil and the purity of the air and the water; and rainwater was harvested in large ponds surrounded by trees.

"The whole life of trees is to serve. With their leaves, flowers, fruits, branches, roots, shade, fragrance, sap bark, wood and finally even their ashes and coal, they exist for the sake of others. "
– Srimad Bhagavatam (ancient Vedic text), 10.22.33-35

We can see that real sustainability was and still is a property of God's creation. By destroying indigenous forests, and by introducing thousands of manmade chemicals, plastics, nanotechnologies, GMOs, and industrial by-products that alter or pollute land, air and water systems, modern society has been destroying the original 'quality' that sustained us and ensured our wellbeing. In contrast, ancient villages cared for the forests as the forests provided for their needs. These 'cared for forests' were like forest gardens surrounding the village, and contained mango groves, edible flowers, etc, and the most useful trees were arranged close by. By growing up in this way and learning from the qualities of nature, people knew how to live sustainably as a natural function.

Balance with nature was achieved via three types of forest patches: untouched forest sanctuaries; dense woodland that could be used for collecting dry wood, leaves, herbs, flowers etc, and a small amount of needed timber; and cared for groves of planted fruit trees.

The close-knit relationships in the community and a common bond to create an ideal community ensured that the welfare of all was catered for. The forest and streams with pure healing water also provided an environment that was peaceful and healing for the mind, body and soul. Sages and holy persons were naturally attracted to living simply in forest ashrams, as described in the ancient Vedic texts. For example, the *Ramayana*, describes the royal prince Rama and his wife Sita living happily in the forest before going to war against an evil king. Spiritual truths were an inherent part of ancient life and rebelling against those truths was known as the path to disaster. This is exemplified in the Vedic text, the Bhagavad Gita, when Krishna, God personified, promises enough of everything, so long as we take only what we need.

200 years ago, the world was still covered by vast areas of natural forest and even some 'cared for' forests. In India, however, the forests were nationalised and exploited in service of the British ship building industry, and public access to forests was restricted. Villagers were denied access to the forests that had always been 'the cared for commons' for the welfare of all. This exemplifies the death of this original human-forest connection worldwide. According to Banwari, editor of *Jansata*, a daily newspaper in Delhi, India,

"if the state gives up its control of the forest and returns its to the villages, India will blossom again. " – see Endnote [170]

Ancient Vedic culture – a thriving God-conscious society in balance with nature

Throughout the ancient Vedic world, in forest villages, larger communities and larger royal households, sanitation as based on local recycling of human and animal manure;

cottages and royal palaces were built from local materials; and cleanliness was prioritised. The lanes and streets would be clean and free from dust and places of worship especially were especially cared for. Villages featured a common for grazing of cows; a co-operative dairy; schools for teaching practical skills, and would produce their own milk, grains, vegetables, and fruits. The use of bullocks was a natural, reliable and non-polluting method for transporting goods locally. In Vedic cities, kingly and warrior classes protected the society from evil and took advice from the Brahmanas, the wise elders well versed in the practical and spiritual knowledge as detailed in 'original' ancient scriptures. As the original caretakers of the land. would advise the kings how to protect and manage the land. This system was known as *varnasrama*.

The Vedic texts prescribed the most ideal, sustainable and simple form of economic development, in harmony with nature, and state "*Produce only what you need*". Production of food and utilisation of nature was never meant to be a profit-making enterprise. As soon as the aspect of the market is introduced, exploitation begins – exploitation of the land, animals and mankind.

Ayurvedic medicine is an ancient medical science that is prominent to this day and is once again gaining in popularity. (Aside: In the current profit-driven corporate bio-pharmaceutical era era, there have been cases in which cures (including natural cures) for diseases have been suppressed and their developers have had their names smeared, or have even been jailed or killed. Big Pharma does not want the truth about cancer to be known, that would stop their hundreds of billions of profits. Ayurvedic specialist Andreas Moritz described the truth about cancer and a toxic body's natural healing process in his book "Timeless Secrets of Health & Rejuvenation".)

Note that the Vedic society is documented to be our planet's most ancient civilisation and that the philosophy behind Vedic social organisation is detailed in the vast Vedic texts, the oldest known texts. This is not Hinduism; in fact, the word Hinduism does not even appear once in the Vedic texts. The Vedic texts provide an insight into a culture and a civilisation far beyond sectarian religious beliefs and deal with concepts with exactitude and science. Vedic culture is documented to have existed worldwide in various forms, for example, ancient Vedic symbols are clearly visible on ancient standing stones in Ireland and other parts of the world. Old shrines of Vedic worship remain at the Agni Temple at Baku, Azerbaijan, and have been uncovered all over Asia. Vedic culture balanced material and spiritual dimensions of life as advocated in the original form of the Vedic system of *varna* and *asrama*. This should not be confused with the modern interpretation as currently exists in parts of India, which is a distorted flawed version of the original system. I believe that it is inevitable that human society will re-establish its ancient, pure and necessary connection with forests, the natural world, and with ancient knowledge. This process is already beginning to take place.

Bible (Genesis 1:26)

I note here the influence of modern-day Christianity on consciousness, specifically an interpretation (or translation) of the Bible stating that God has given man 'dominion' over nature. The word dominion in the Bible (Genesis 1:26) has often been misinterpreted by some Christians to mean that God gave man dominion of nature and the animals that man the right to exploit nature and the animals at his disposal, literally. However, dominion does not mean exploiter or abuser. In traditional biblical use, the original Hebrew for the word "dominion" is *yirdu*, and it means a type of stewardship in which were commanded to care for nature and the animals – not to eat them. For example, a king was said to have dominion over his subjects, but that does not mean that he should eat them. In fact, in Genesis 1:29, God recommends to us a vegetarian diet, prohibiting the use of animals for food. God says "I have given you every herb-yielding seed which is upon the face of the earth, and every tree in which is the fruit of a every tree-yielding seed – to you it shall be for food". God does not beat around the bush – from the very start he emphasizes the vegetarian diet. Many of the early Christian fathers were vegetarian.

Furthermore, early Greek manuscripts of the Bible refer to 'Jesus the Nazerene'. This is important because it tells us more than he was from Nazereth, it tells us that he was 'a Nazerene'. 'The Nazerenes' were a sect that followed the Essene principles, including vegetarianism. Furthermore, evidence indicates that the teachings of Saint Peter, Jesus's direct follower, condemn all kinds of meat-eating and abuse of animals, see Endnote [171].

This incorrect interpretation has been an encouragement to exploit nature to the fullest degree rather than implementing the original biblical meaning, i.e., man's 'stewardship' of nature. It is not the original doctrines of Christianity that are at fault, but the manner in which the Roman and Protestant churches chose to understand them.

> "Christianity… not only established a dualism of man and nature but also insisted that it is God's will that man exploit nature for his proper ends… Christianity (as taught by the Christian institutions) made it possible to exploit nature in a mood of indifference… " – Dhanesvara das, Author

In contrast to this mis-translation or mis-interpretation, the Vedic *Isopanisad* tells us that we have a right to only as much as we can make productive use of. God created the world for the benefit of all the living beings who are here by His arrangement. Any claim to ownership is therefore temporary because God is the real owner of everything.

'Everything animate or inanimate that is within the universe is controlled and owned by the Lord. One should therefore accept only those things necessary for himself, which are set aside as his quota, and one should not accept other things, knowing well to whom they belong." - Text 1 of the Isopanisad

A Vedic perspective on the importance of cows in self-sufficient communities

In ancient times cows were revered and they provided the miracle food of high-quality milk with all the nutrients the human body needs, and which was beneficial to the brain and higher thinking. Ancient brahmans and sages could live on milk alone. Such was the importance of cows in ancient cultures that they were considered as members of the family and given names.

For thousands of years mankind drank raw milk – any impurities can be eliminated by simply boiling it prior to drinking it and this is the best way to drink milk. I spent some months living at a Vedic rural farm community in 2015 and I was amazed at the delicious nutritious high-quality milk that the Jersey cows provided. The milk did not go through the modern enzyme destroying process of pasteurisation and was used raw for producing ghee for cooking, and was simply boiled before drinking. These cows were nurtured and cared for in natural ways very different to commercial dairies. The animals themselves were clearly of a much higher quality breed biologically in comparison to commercial dairy cows. In Vedic cultures and ancient cultures worldwide cows were not regarded as mere commercial commodities to be sold and exploited, they were an essential part of a functioning community.

Note also that raw milk is much more beneficial to the human body and easier to digest than pasteurised milk. We have drunk raw milk for at least 5,000 years, but today it is illegal in various countries to sell or produce raw milk, for example, in Canada under the Food and Drug Regulations since 1991. I note also that in the US, in 2011, Judge Patrick J. Fiedler made an astonishing unjust ruling… "no, plaintiffs do not have a fundamental right to produce and consume the foods of your choice… no right to contract with a farmer… no right to own a cow…" Three weeks later he resigned from his position as a Judge and joined a law firm that represents Monsanto, a major producer of rBGH growth hormones for commercial dairy cows, see Endnote [172]. In response to such injustice some towns in the US have been approving food sovereignty initiatives that allow food producers to sell food without with federal or state interference.

In addition, in times past, cow dung and cow urine were utilised in multiple ways. Few people realise that cow dung is extremely anti-septic – to this day, believe it or not, it is the custom in India to mix cow dung with water to clean the floor and walls, to apply it to the skin for cleansing and moisturising, or to use it in dry form mixed with straw as a fuel for cooking. To this day, in Ayurvedic medicine ghee, which is made from milk, is used to improve memory and reduce mental tension; and cow urine is used as an effective treatment in kidney disorders and in prevention and control of bacterial infections.

The need for traditional farming decoupled from a government-controlled system

With the onset of monetisation, commercialisation, government taxes, globalisation, government regulations, etc., the traditional dairy farm culture that existed for thousands of years has been largely displaced worldwide, one could even say forcibly displaced by these impositions. Farmers today, especially in the Western world, have been born into times of commercialisation, government taxes, government regulations, the use of vaccines and growth hormones for cows, etc., none of which were ever needed in traditional farming cultures, and much of which did not exist two or three generations ago.

Farmers are the stewards of the land and the providers of food for the people of the world, we should therefore provide farmers with the respect they are due. Just like everyone else, farmers are just trying to survive and make a living whilst paying taxes in this government-imposed system.

This commercialised system, includes an unjust tax system, in which taxes collected by governments mostly go to pay vast fraudulent national debts (for example in Ireland €6 to €10 billion is paid each year to foreign financial institutions to pay the interest on the national debt). Society, including the farming sector, is therefore compelled by governments to maximise production volumes rather than maximise quality, so that more tax monies can be collected to service the national debt.

I am aware there are some famers that wish to embrace more traditional and organic farming practices and the production of higher quality produce, but within this current system, being subjected to government taxes and regulations, it appears they have insufficient scope to do anything other than continue industrial farming practices.

I foresee that dairy farming, and all farming, must be become free from government taxation and over-regulation to have the scope to truly develop and thrive in new ways. Farmers that wish to embrace traditional farming practices, forest farming, etc., and produce higher quality produce would then have the financial leeway to do so. This will create a culture in which local communities can purchase high quality produce from local farmers and local farming co-operatives. In this way farmers will skip the middle-man of large foreign-owned corporate supermarket chains and food mega-corporations (that dominate the food industry sector worldwide) and will receive more money, or local currency, for their produce. Using local currency mans that the money stays within the local community rather than being funnelled away into government tax payments or to foreign-owned supermarket chains. This principle can be utilised in all countries for local resilience.

Traditional farming is more labour intensive and therefore, young people may begin to find employment working in these farms, utilising intermediate technologies and learning to become farmers, perhaps in exchange for accommodation and board with high quality organic food. As other farms join this process, farms will assist each other and become collaborative centres of excellence. The long-term end-goal could be to create self-sufficient co-operative local community networks for food, energy and necessary goods, whilst utilising local currency. In this way a strong resilient community is created in which farmers and people are no longer dependent on increasingly expensive foreign food imports, the availability of imported oil, oil-based chemical fertilisers, etc. Additionally, friendships, integrity, and a stronger local spirit is cultivated.

Today, modern day commercial dairy farming produces milk that differs from that produced just two generations ago in that it has become laced with growth hormones, manmade chemicals, pesticides used on farms, ingredients from vaccines, GMOs, etc. In addition, the modern process of pasteurisation destroys valuable enzymes making the milk harder to digest for some people.

In contrast to the practices of traditional dairy farming, modern commercial dairy cows are artificially stimulated to provide up to 12 times more milk than is normal - they are artificially impregnated and forced into a cycle of permanent lactation. This practice of overmilking is linked with mastitis in cows, and the problem of the milk being contaminated with bacteria. Consequently, these commercial cows also have much shorter lifespans than is normal. In contrast, in my experience, the milk from cows that are not being artificially stimulated to produce much more milk than is natural for them, is tastier and of higher quality, and the cows live longer healthier lives. Consequently, I foresee that more farmers will be producing milk in the original traditional way, and some people will keep their own cow to produce milk for their own domestic milk, just as many of our ancestors did.

In an ideal world, the animals on commercial farms would be treated much better than is currently the case. Unlike ancient and traditional framing practices in which the cows were an integral and nurtured part of self-sufficient communities, due to commercial pressures modern dairy farms have had no other option, but to operate as commercial businesses that utilise cows for profit, little different from chickens in a chicken factory. This is in large part due to the paradigm of government-induced globalisation.

I also note that rearing animals for meat industry slaughter is very land-intensive, and the long-term trend may be that it makes more sense financially to focus on dairy production rather than meat-production, but of course there are political and market forces that I cannot predict. In addition, more and more people are moving away from a meat-eating diet for various reasons. For example, research has shown that eating meat reduces the human life span and is also a cause of excessive acidification in the body, which can lead to cancer. When we are drinking high quality raw milk like our forefathers and ancestors did, all the proteins, enzymes and nutrients that our body and brain needs are provided, so why would we need meat?

As more people transition away from a meat-eating diet, the pressure on the land of rearing live-stock for slaughter is greatly reduced, freeing it for other uses. This free land can then be used to increase the number of cows in the dairy herd, grow fast-growing trees and plants for timber, fuel, and even for clothing (as in the case of hemp).

Consciousness and dharma in a spiritual civilisation of wellbeing for all

Despite its advanced technologies, today's society is akin to a prison. Many people have become enticed by, distracted by and habitually connected to advanced technological concoctions, such as smartphones, TVs, electric cars etc. This elaborate dependency has imprisoned the human spirit – like a bird in a cage, the human experience is bereft of its original links with nature and the spirit is starved of its natural eternal functions. As we know, such technological products, also violate environmental integrity via their production, distribution and disposal.

All our 'systems' should benefit and serve the human spirit. Wellbeing, health, happiness, truth, joy and spiritual development would ideally be embedded in how a society functions, rather than being something esoteric to aspire to after the long grind of working a day job as a robotic cog of the globalised corporate system. The current system treats each person as simply a unit of production and a payer of debt interest to the private bankers, but is that all we are here to do? Our objective should be to follow our *dharma*, or mission in life, and to uncover and express our true self both materially and spiritually. Otherwise, what is the point of being here? Note that *dharma* should not be mis-interpreted as some religion or faith, it is the essence of something, its most intrinsic quality or nature.

To create a society of higher quality therefore we must follow our *dharma*, and raise our consciousness by re-discovering knowledge of the spirit, re-establishing our spiritual identity and re-establishing our connection with God, the creator who has given us all the qualities we need to live and thrive. The original Vedic system of *varnasrama dharma* is an excellent example of how this approach was successfully structured and implemented in ancient societies. The *varnasrama* society provided life-long aptitude-based learning in which individuals were educated in the varna in which they were most suited to. This was not based on birth right; it was based on ability. Individuals were educated as either *Brahmanas* (knowledgeable advisors in spiritual and material matters), *Ksatriyas* (leaders, warriors and administrators of the kingdom), *Vaisyas* (providing goods and services) or *Sudras* (agricultural workers who also assisted the other classes), but all were regarded as spiritually equal and worked in harmony together for the welfare of all, cognisant that God is the highest authority and is connected with each person.

Furthermore, in the Vedic spiritual approach to designing society it was recognised that all people and animals in the world are worthy of respect as living entities and have the right to exist without being killed for needless human consumption. God provided humanity with sufficient nutrients in fruits, vegetables, grains and milk to live healthy long lives. Real sustainability is a function of God's creation and is a fundamental aspect of original God-given knowledge as described in the 'original' ancient scriptures of the world.

A metaphorical 'mountain of success' – a 'successful society of higher quality'

The philosophy of real sustainability and real quality should underpin everything that we strive for. We have the capacity to create systems that value and respect people and communities, and we can choose not to participate in systems that ultimately benefit the 0.01 % of the population that own the world's major corporate and banking systems. It is up to us – increased 'quality' is always within our capability. Societies and co-operative human networks can emerge that value fundamental human needs, quality of life, and local systems that nurture the environment and significantly increase human health and wellbeing. Education, co-operation, optimism and leaders with vision are needed for the transition.

If we view the ideal of a success as the top of the highest mountain, we can say humanity has begun its journey toward the mountain top – toward an ideal society of higher quality for all humans and for the natural world. Determined skilled people and visionaries are walking through the high valleys mapping successful approaches to the summit. All are approaching the higher taste of 'quality' from their varying locations and perspectives.

Each of us can perceive the mountain top from our own point of view or particular circumstance – in doing so we can strive to resolve violations of real sustainability that occur in our various sectors of society, i.e., reduce and eliminate real pollution to land, air and water systems and needless overuse of resources. There will be difficulties along the way, but those souls that resolve the issues on their particular path will have stories of meaning that will resound for generations to come.

Humanity has the potential to successfully reach a metaphorical mountain top of success in the Earth-human relationship. It is a journey worth taking. If this is achieved in the coming decades or generations it will be a most impressive milestone signifying our higher abilities and wisdom. The challenges described also represent an opportune moment for embracing higher levels of consciousness. There will come a time when we all thrive in harmony with the Earth again, just as our ancient ancestors did, rather than polluting it. Real sustainability in society is inextricably linked to the human condition.

The worthwhile challenge is to achieve a sustainable earth-human relationship. However, the underlying causes of the damaging impacts to environmental and human wellbeing have not been addressed via current sustainable development mechanisms and are embedded in a matrix of control and illusion. This matrix includes the economic paradigm of GDP growth, the banking system that creates money from nothing and charges everyone interest for it, as well as the political, govern-mental (mental = mind/govern your mind), and corporate mass media networks and online media systems that dominate and influence most people's lives and mindsets. It is important to recognize that the reason all governments prioritize GDP growth is in order to pay interest to the privately owned international banking system, which creates debt money from nothing via fractional reserve banking.

In a global power game dominated by banking and corporate profits, political control systems and greed, current systems are dominated by the GDP growth and fake manmade climate change narratives. There is no evidence that over the past decades the orthodoxy behind these systems has been re-aligned to embrace the real sustainability and resilience at the local level. UN Agenda 2030 and the UN sustainable development goals are deceptive and illusory aspects of the current flawed system, that actually perpetuate the corporate agenda. Effective change must emerge at the local level.

In later chapters, I examine the modes of human behavior and the role of higher consciousness and spiritual values in potentially transcending an overly materialistic way of life. What are the motivations and character traits of the group of people that have created and perpetuated this flawed system which pollutes and destroys the very place where humanity live? Is there a realistic chance that humanity en-masse will transcend the obstacles of the current flawed paradigm to embrace a future of higher quality in harmony with nature? Ultimately there is no other choice for communities and societies that wish to survive and thrive long term.

These flawed systems that we have been born into are a product of human consciousness. Is there one group of people in particular that has perpetuated this system or are we all to blame? If you have read the earlier chapter on banking and the corporate super-entity, the answer should be obvious to you. Yet, to succeed, we must create something new rather than waste too much time or energy attacking the old flawed paradigm and those responsible. Nurturing the human spirit and a connection with God, the all-attractive creator, enables us to move toward higher consciousness, awareness, intelligence and truth. We can transition away from bogus ideology, godless scientism, or the illusions of 'the matrix', and take a higher quality path for human life. This involves distinguishing reality from the illusion.

13. The trap of the materialistic illusion

Materialism is not the answer to the problems of humankind

"As soon as we begin our plans for material happiness, mark it – this is where our conditions of distress begin." – Srimad Bhagavatam (7.7.42), Translation by Srila Prabhupada

"A conditioned soul tries to enjoy material happiness again and again. Thus he chews the chewed…sometimes… he becomes relieved from material entanglement by associating with a great soul.. a conditioned soul is always engaged in some type of sense gratification, but when he understands by good association that it is only a repetition of the same thing, and he is awakened to his real Krishna consciousness, he is sometimes relieved from such repetitive so-called happiness. " – *'Bhagavad Gita As It Is' 18:36 commentary.*

"Material life is all about desire. Subtly or explicitly, we lust. Items, situations, relationships, attitudes – we hanker to possess, control, and enjoy them. Thereafter we'll agree to material life's daily grind, accepting the competitive toil as necessary – 'the real world'…. (but) the desire to enjoy the material world and its affairs cannot award the inner satisfaction and fulfilment the real self needs." – Devamrita Swami, Author

The illusion that materialism, consumerism and financial wealth will make us happy has been promoted by corporate media culture for decades. Pervasive advertising for an endless variety of mostly un-needed consumer products is the norm. Creating slaves to the religion of consumerism is the aim. It is all mass-hypnosis for the promotion of a never-ending consumer culture that is aligned with, and designed for, the globalisation / GDP growth and usury-economy. Without the paradigm of endless and excessive consumerism, the vastly lucrative and fraudulent banking system of debt-money usury will not work – i.e., the bankers will not receive interest on loans they create from nothing. To keep the usury-economy going, the world has been turned into one large shopping mall. Rather than creating self-sufficient communities, in this merry-go-round society, for decades many people have been working in jobs they don't really like, in order to buy cradle-to-grave items they 'think' they need. In addition, countries with different and rich cultural heritages have become increasingly similar, with the same corporate logos and franchises tagged onto street facades.

"Real human progress kicks in when the mirage, the mass consensual trance, loses its attraction. When the constant stream of our material attempts exhaust us, when we are weary of the illusory matrix of consumer culture." – Author, Devamrita Swami

Through, sometimes bitter, life experience many people have realised that those who make money more important than their 'true' path in life have lower levels of life satisfaction. The ancient Vedic texts confirm that civilisations built solely on the consciousness of sense gratification cannot survive. It is a myth that money brings happiness, and it is a myth that 'more' technology brings wellbeing. In the book *Hiding in Unnatural Happiness,* Devamrita Swami makes a number of interesting observations relevant to a deeper understanding of the predicament we are in.

> "Unthinkingly focused upon strenuous labour – whether industrial or corporate – meagrely rewarded by moments of mind-numbing entertainment and exploitative sensuality, such inwardly poor participants in our material culture cannot persevere without artificial succor that intoxication delivers."

> "Our materialistic mantra – 'Work, buy, consume, die' – has manacled us, imprisoned the whole world. What a tragedy. If we turn to leaders who cannot offer any higher goal than the hedonistic treadmill, we can be sure that there will be no solution to human problems – neither today nor tomorrow… The materialistic dream that things will be better when as many humans as possible can dive into an ocean of material choices, goods and lifestyles has failed. Careful social investigation reveals that beyond a certain modest level of option availability and option-acquisition people are not going to become any happier – indeed they even become more distressed."

> "The struggle, the daily grind to squeeze true satisfaction from the rock of material nature has cheated us… a report by social scientists (shows) that a coolie carrying loads through the streets of Calcutta experiences the same level of life-satisfaction as the average American."

Shackled by the debt-money system, many of us have been compelled to continuously work to pay our debts. For example, if you have a mortgage, note that the bank that gave you the mortgage never actually had the money in the first place and you are paying interest on money created out of nothing via fractional reserve banking. In this way people in debt can be compared to slaves or human batteries that are powering a system that is feeding off their energy, as is portrayed in the science-fiction movie the *Matrix*. In the rat race of the current debt-money system people with mortgages or debts are compelled to work like hamsters on a wheel to continually pay interest to the banks who never had the money in the first place, otherwise he or she will not be able to pay their mortgage. If the hamster wheels stop turning the worldwide banking scam will not function.

In this insane system, consumerist gratifications and entertainment distractions are the norm - the corporate remedy to keep us as happy slaves and from questioning this strange reality. Some people can see the cage of the system they are in, and for others ignorance is bliss. Alcohol, drugs and other vices, are temporary and illusory escape routes from the drudgery of the 9 to 5. Expensive items in shops are displayed like prizes for those that have been the hardest working 'slaves'. The 'go-getters' are promoted to become 'captains of industry'. As if in the animal kingdom or in a game of musical chairs, a go-getter has to be fast and aggressive to grab a chair before his opponent. Is this what human life is really meant to be? Are we not meant for something more meaningful than this?

> "So many people can't express what's on their minds, nobody knows them and nobody ever will, until their backs are broken, their dreams are stolen and they can get what they want and their gonna get angry" – Matt Johnson, Musician

In this system to do what the heart really desires is a pipe dream for most. It takes a focused person to shun the current system and live 'outside' of it. Free souls, people with higher values, those who are more self-contented, creative, or spiritual, or, indeed, those with warrior-like determination and vision of how they wish to live, and how society can better function, are a potential threat to the globalist materialist system. Such free souls might be interested in more enlightened things other than endless consumption. The materialist system depends on people never finding real inner peace, they must continually be prodded to consume, and the world is thus constantly being inundated with new needs, problems, and products.

Eventually we reach the realisation that our attempts to find happiness in consumerism and material wealth have failed; and that we need a higher knowledge. After years of slogging through life with no knowledge of the true self, the inner spirit, or why we appeared in this world, more and more people are opting out of the 'system'. The realisation that you won't be able to get the information you need from the mainstream corporate media is leading people toward a higher path.

> "Most people in the world are wholly dependent upon 'The System' and cannot function without it. This system forces them to live in a debt cycle which never ends. The system perpetrates an addiction to materialism for the purpose of producing interest which is created from debt. Since debt does not really exist, then neither does interest. Hence, the national debt is a hoax perpetrated by the Powers That Be. The biggest con game the world has ever known was perpetrated by those who control education, law, media, churches, banks, medicine. They played upon our innate belief that we must earn our right to life, that we are unworthy, not to trust our intuition, that we must depend upon the authorities, that any punishment we sustain is justified and deserved, that we have no self-generated power, that what is outside our minds is real. They have confiscated our health, wealth, love, and peace of mind under this ruse. This scam is known as The Matrix.

> How did we ever get conned into believing that we are required to 'earn' our living? The perpetuation of this myth is destroying our true spiritual nature. If my Creator and I co-created my physical existence, then this makes me sovereign, right? Why would I do anything other than just be free to live, to experience? Someone thinks we must pay for the privilege ... who? How did this ever come about?... How did we come to be coerced to believe that we are required to 'earn our keep'? The movie, The Matrix states we are just batteries – the energy to fuel the pleasure of the

PTB, those who never did, never will, never even thought to work a day in their lives" – Author, Mary Elizabeth Croft (with kind permission)

The true purpose of work is to provide society with the correct goods and services that it needs for physical and spiritual wellbeing; to enable each person to perfect their God-given gifts like good stewards; and to align their work for the service of God. We must remember, that 'it shall profit a man nothing to gain the whole world if, in the process, he loses his soul'.

> 'Whatever gift each of you may have received, use it in service to one another, like good stewards dispensing the grace of God in its varied forms' - Peter, 4:10

> "the essence of civilisation not in a multiplication of wants but in the purification of human character… considering goods as more important than people and consumption as more important than creative activity is standing the truth on its head. It means shifting the emphasis from the worker to the product of the work, that is, from the human to the sub-human, a surrender to the forces of evil… An entirely new system of thought is needed, a system based on attention to people, and not primarily attention to goods…" – E.F Schumacher

The illusion of 'the economy'

There is no actual item or substance that is 'an economy'. Can you touch it? Show me one? There are goods and services and people, but the 'economy' is a word only – more than that it is a word that is used to control you. The 'global economy' is just marketing speak for mega-corporate control. The real reason we are encouraged to keep growing the economy (an increased level of work and production of goods) is so that interest on debts will continually be paid by governments to the worldwide private banking cartel. A cartel, which, by the way, intentionally orchestrates boom-bust-bailout cycles for its own benefit. We were born into this matrix type system and have been affected by its influences. We were trained from an early age to be a part of the 'economy' to feed the system of the money-masters, who, for decades have drip fed material and financial incentives to the captains of industry and commerce, like carrots leading a donkey. In order to pay debts or to save for retirement most people have seen no alternative but to work within the system. The development of your natural talents or the uncovering of your real self and true nature is not prioritised, or even mentioned, in this system. The faceless 'economy' just wants you to serve it as a worker and as a taxpayer. The harsh reality is that, through the dominant lens of contemporary economics, governments view you simply as a unit of production and consumption – nothing more.

> "subsistence farmers in India… planted what naturally grew well and did not over farm the land. then western economics introduced the belief that these farmers had to produce more than they could consumed in order to create wealth so that they could attain "quality of life". Consequently,

> Indians left their family land to live in squalor in cities such as new delhi, and subsistence farming gave way to huge farms and agribusiness. Today, between 250 and 300 million Indians who once farmed on family plots survive on less than one dollar a day; and they don't have clean drinking water, healthcare, education, or the prospect of a future for their children. Yet cling to the old dream that if they could just create more wealth or join the march of progress, their problems would magically disappear." - Alberto Villoldo

In addition, much of modern-day technology creates more problems than it solves. We should not put our ultimate faith in technological solutions to solve human issues. As technology has become more pervasive, our true spiritual nature seems to have remained suppressed. The result is that we are not in control of technology, rather, technology seems to be controlling us.

> "Although we expertly fabricate countless remedies to counter the miseries of life, these so called solutions in the material world eventually reveal themselves as more problematic than the predicaments they're designed to resolve. Therefore the only real cure is to engage in bhakti.." – Srimad Bhagavatam (7.9.17), translation by Srila Prabhupada

The fabricated matrix is a system of domination and exploitation

All governments are actually registered as corporations and are designed to tax you and thus control you. Note that 'govern-mental' means 'govern your mind'. A large swath of taxes collected goes directly to pay vast amounts of interest to the international privately-owned banking system. As long as this trick of taxing the population (on money that was originally created from nothing by banks) continues, society can never be sustainable in the real sense of the word, and the population will remain tied by an invisible rope to the economic 'hamster wheel' to generate enough money to survive and also pay tax.

Another aspect of importance is that governments have become morally degraded and often the political leaders are those that seek excessive power and control. The current situation was not always the case. In ancient times, good kings adhering to the word of God in 'original' scriptures, ensured the fair functioning of society, in which each person was accorded the right and facility to develop their full natural strengths and abilities. The original form (not the modern distorted form) of the ancient Vedic system of *varnasrama-dharma* is an example – in that culture, qualities of truth, duty, goodness and spiritual realisation were paramount.

> "Inherent in the system of Varna is the concept of duty of each segment of society to the others, with the highest orders, the vaisyas (people involved in organisation and productive activity), ksatriyas (natural leaders, kings and rulers) and brahmanas (wise spiritual persons providing direction to society) and having increasingly greater responsibility to the other orders. It was the duty of the higher orders to protect the lower ones, and especially to protect the weak and innocent such as brahmanas, women, children the elderly and the cows. Indeed, every living creature was

considered a citizen in Vedic culture and entitled to the protection of the king… Every member of Vedic culture traditionally followed their duty, because that was the culture. They were not motivated by desire for gain, or threat or punishment or loss. Because the culture was established in goodness people acted out of a sense of duty.." – Author, Dhanesvara das

In contrast, the modern-day fabricated matrix of economy, government, banking and corporate power is a dominator culture. It is a system of domination and exploitation by so-called ruling elites. The entire 'mainstream reality' is made up by the so-called elites who control the media and corporate system. In the book *'Escaping the Matrix – How we the people can change the world'* author Richard Moore writes:

> "The consensus reality that we see portrayed on television and in school history books is a fabricated illusion…. Civilization is not a reflection of human nature, but is rather a system of domination and exploitation by ruling elites. We are like animals in cages: our behavior under these stressful conditions is not representative of our nature, just as the pacing of a caged cheetah does not represent the natural behavior of that beautiful animal…. Environmental collapse and capitalism are merely the terminal symptoms of a chronic cancer… We need a culture based on mutual understanding and cooperation rather than on war and conquest… we sheep must finally cast aside our illusions, recognize our condition, and reclaim our identity as free human beings.
>
> Our societies and political systems are characterized by competition and struggle among cultural factions and political parties. When we try to change this system by forming adversarial political movements we are playing into this game – a game rigged so that elites always win. If we really want to change the system, we need to learn how to come together as humans, moving beyond the ideological structures that have been created to divide us from one another… the residents of a local community… are in the best position to manage their resources and economies wisely…There is no need for centralized governments, corporations, or institutions, which inevitably become vehicles for the usurpation of power by would-be ruling cliques.
>
> In our transition…one of the first steps will be for each community to repossess its commons – assuming ownership of all land, resources, buildings, and infrastructures that are currently controlled by absentee landlords, banks, corporations, and government agencies. Under the control of local communities and workers, conversion plans can be worked out, gradually repurposing existing facilities toward sensible and sustainable uses." – Richard Moore, Author (quoted with kind permission)

An interesting article, see Endnote [173], was published in 2015 titled *"The Six Grand Illusions That Keep Us Enslaved to "The Matrix"* by Sigmund Fraud.

> "We live in a world of illusion…. As we are indoctrinated into this authoritarian-corporate-consumer culture that now dominates the human race, we are trained those certain aspects of our society are untouchable truths (ideologies not based on fact), and that particular ways of being and behaving are preferred. Psychopaths disempower people in this way. They blind us with never ceasing barrages of suggestions and absolutes that are aimed at shattering self-confidence and confidence in the future. … Advertising is just the tip of the iceberg. When we look further, we see that the overall organization of life is centered around the pursuit of illusions and automatic

obedience to institutions and ideas which are not at all what they seem. We are in a very real sense enslaved. Many call this somewhat intangible feeling of oppression 'the matrix,' a system of total control that invades the mind, programming individuals to pattern themselves in accordance with a mainstream conformist version of reality, no matter how wicked it gets."- Sigmund Fraud, Anonymous Author.

Author Armin Risi described the human predicament of the manipulators and the manipulated as follows:

"All over the world, millions upon millions of people, while working in some office, factory or business, perform activities they ordinarily would not do, were it up to them. A constant pressure makes them spend their lives in busy-ness, stress and anxiety, as they all have to make money…. most of these occupations either directly or indirectly harm people's health or the environment. Yet still these artificial needs continue to be advocated and justified, in spite of all warnings and dangers. Why? A first answer is: because there are forces wanting it to be so. Otherwise, the course would be different. Exploitation, corruption, pollution, injustice and wars do not simply happen by chance. Without money and organisation, none of these achievements would be possible. It is a question of power. There are those who influence and those who allow themselves to be influenced. Both sides contribute their share, though featuring in different roles. This unequal power game is called manipulation… using other people to serve one's own interest. Manipulation is especially effective when the targeted people are not aware they are being manipulated. Voluntary cogs in the machine are easier to handle than forced ones. Therefore, manipulation is a stronger means of power than enforcement. **For manipulation to have its intended effect, it must secure a hold on people's consciousness**."

"The world situation cannot be properly assessed by passing the buck of responsibility… being manipulated means that one is part of the manipulation, having accepted the role of an ignorant or intimidated victim (by giving in to the illusion of being powerless and helpless).. the point of examining the global power game cannot be a hypo-critical criticism of some manipulators… the solution cannot be the judgement and blaming of others… we have to transcend the global power game… becoming aware of the higher perspectives in life."

"Looking at the excesses of today's world economy, war industry and secret politics, we get the impression that, indeed, there must be 'inhuman' beings at work. Would a normal human being wish to destroy his own environment, exploit the earth and slaughter his neighbour? How is it possible that destructiveness has become so pre-dominant?... both forces - divine and demoniac – are simultaneously present on earth." – Armin Risi, Author (quoted with kind permission).

"global entities are relying on you not knowing that you are sovereign and that you were given an inheritance. Instead of acting as princes and princesses, kings and queens of the land, we blindly accept our role as slaves to a completely artificial and contrived social construction, created and controlled by a hidden governing body that has been swindling off our energies and monies the moment we are born." – Lenu Pu, Author

Do you perceive this fabricated matrix? Are you enslaved to the matrix? The matrix seeks blind obedience in an attempt to dis-empower us. Do you wish to escape from the matrix to embrace a higher reality? The first step is to remember that all of this is merely an elaborate sales pitch. They can't sell you what you don't care to buy.

Recognising the dysfunctional state of CONfusion

Embroiled in this dominator matrix, most of mankind has been in a dysfunctional state of CONfusion that has been intentionally promoted for a very long time. CON meaning 'against', fuse meaning 'together'. Yet, there are many souls with a higher level of consciousness and with a warrior-like nature to live and work with full freedom and integrity unrestrained by the 'system'.

The words of enlightened people, as well the wisdom contained in original ancient scriptures, enable us to see that the real path to escaping the matrix is tap into our own spiritual identity and connection with God, for therein lies the source of our real power. Therefore, the task for each person is to identify and bypass the obstacles to establishing your true self-identity, both materially and spiritually, and thus lead a spiritually fulfilling life.

14. Beyond material consciousness

Are humans capable of 'real' sustainability?

> "The problem posed by environmental detioration is not primarily a technical problem; if it were, it would not have arisen in its acutest form in the technologically most advanced societies. It does not stem from scientific or technical incompetence, or from lack of information, or from shortage of trained manpower, or lack of money for research. It stems from the life style of the modern world, which in turn arises from its most basic beliefs – its metaphysics, if you like" – E. F. Schumacher

The subject of human behaviour is very relevant in the context of creating a 'truly' sustainable thriving civilisation. Whether it is to escape the fabricated matrix of illusions, create a society of higher values, or heal the real environmental problem, we must first heal ourselves and step into our spiritual identity. Each problem is, at its root, a problem of consciousness. People will only choose to pollute the environment if their consciousness is polluted. The real remedy for the problems of the world is the raising of the consciousness of humankind to that of goodness, purity and transcendence.

We have all been subjected to the illusions and false promises of consumerism, illicit sex life, greed and profit at the expense of others and of the environment. What are the deeper inner reasons that humankind has embarked on this path? Is there a realistic chance that humankind en-masse will transcend excessive materialism and move toward a thriving paradigm that enhances the individual, the community and fully respects the natural world? With all our material scientific knowledge why are we not doing that already?

> "Easy-going optimism that science will solve all problems or that we can somehow achieve a social-political system so perfect that no one has to be good, is the most current form of cowardice" – E.F. Schumacher, Author

To fix what is happening around us we need to fix what is happening within us - it is only by examining ourselves and our weaknesses will we be able to embrace the mode of goodness, transcEND incorrect action, overcome and evolve into such a paradigm. Humanity could be compared to a group of people trying to cross a fast flowing river - on the other side of the river is a successful resilient spiritual community. To get there we must cross the currents of excessive consumerism, unhealthy egoism, fear, greed, passion and ignorance that could sweep us further downstream away from our destination on the other side. Good souls with a strong moral spirit are needed to make the crossing.

Human nature, arrogance and greed has played a role in the emergence of 'real' environmental problems, including resource scarcity and pollution to land, air and water. Therefore, in order for humans to handle material nature and create a 'real' sustainable society, we need a higher knowledge and consciousness must play its part. Even in the unlikely scenario that the paradigm of debt money, usury, fractional reserve banking, polluting GDP growth, and corporate control was reformed; unless the darker elements of the human psyche are cleansed then humanity will simply 'rinse and repeat' and manifest corruption in some other form. The greedy ones, psychopaths, sociopaths and narcissists will still scramble for power, resources, and control, unless these habits are eliminated, until or a higher level of consciousness is the dominant aspect of humanity.

"And what is good, Phaedrus, And what is not good - Need we ask anyone to tell us these things?"

"The social values are right only if the individual values are right. The place to improve the world is first in one's heart and head and hands, and then work outward from there… If a revolution destroys a systematic government, but the systematic patterns of thought that produced that government are left intact, then those patterns will repeat themselves in the succeeding government. (There's so much talk about the system. And so little understanding.)"

"And now he began to see for the first time the unbelievable magnitude of what man when he gained power to understand and rule the world… had lost. He had built empires of scientific capability to manipulate the phenomena of nature into enormous manifestations of his owns dreams of power and wealth – but for this he had exchanged an empire of understanding of equal magnitude: an understanding of what it is to be part of the world, and not an enemy of it." – *'Zen and the Art of Motorcycle Maintenance: An Inquiry Into Values'* by Robert Pirsig

In relation to the question of whether humans are capable of sustainability, William Rees of the School of Community and Regional Planning, University of British Columbia published a hypothesis, see Endnote [174], stating:

"that modern H. sapiens is unsustainable by nature. Unsustainability is an inevitable emergent property of the systemic interaction between contemporary technoindustrial society and the ecosphere. I trace this conundrum to humanity's once-adaptive, subconscious, genetic predisposition to expand (shared with all other species), a tendency reinforced by the socially constructed economic narrative of continuous material growth. Unfortunately, these qualities have become maladaptive. The current coevolutionary pathway of the human enterprise and the ecosphere therefore puts civilization at risk..." – William Rees, University of British Columbia

Some academics maintain that humans are 'K-strategists' i.e., that the survival of the individual and overall success of humans depends on competitive superiority at high population densities under conditions of resource scarcity, and suggest that the failure of the sustainability project to date has much to do with the modern world's failure to face up to basic facts of human nature. William Rees' working hypothesis is that because of human traits, modern humans are biased against sustainability. It appears to me that Rees correctly identifies the systemic problem of unsustainability in society, however, I disagree with the implication that 'all' humans are unsustainable by nature or that 'all' humans are biased against real sustainability. We have all been born into an economic system that is unsustainable and environmentally destructive by its innate design, and the reality is there is only a relatively small percentage of humanity controlling that system. Most of us have been lacking the knowledge and/or realistic opportunity to live and function as part of resilient self-sufficient community in greater harmony with nature, but that does not mean that some people are not capable of doing so.

Humans do not have to be K-strategists, although they have been compelled to be - it is the economic and banking system itself, owned and controlled by a small group of so-called elites, that has foisted the paradigm of globalisation, and excessive and aggressive competition upon human society.

Most of us are conditioned early in life via school and media systems to become part of the current system. Many of us were saddled with debt early in life and jumped onto the treadmill of working for decades to pay off student loans, the mortgage etc. Without the pressure of the 'ratrace' induced by the debt-money system, we would have more scope to make better choices, and to explore options for living and working within co-operative more self-sufficient-communities.

The ancient Vedic scriptures describe the nature of each individual person as a mixture of the modes of goodness (correct action), passion (greed/lust) and ignorance (incorrect action/wars/murder, stealing etc). We can observe these different modes of nature operating in different people. Some people are more fixed in the mode of goodness, than others, etc. Thus, it is incorrect to tar all of humanity with the same brush. All of us are capable of improving ourselves, and many people are cognisant of and capable of co-creating a better future.

> ".. the worst of faults is wanting more…always… When action is pure and selfless, everything settles into its own perfect place" – extract from the Tao Te Ching 7th verse by Lao Tzu

> "The Latin names of the four cardinal virtues… denote higher orders of human excellence… temperantia, that is, the virtue of self control, discipline and moderation, which preserves and defends order in the individual and in the environment – we can see that this is the virtue most needed and at the same time the virtue most conspicuous by its absence in the modern world. Our obsession with so called material progress… recognises no bounds and is thus the clearest possible demonstration of intemperentia… the real cause of our troubles is intemperentia; how could we hope to bring pollution or the consumption of resources under control; if we cannot control ourselves and are not prepared to study the question of self-control." – E.F. Schumacher

The creation of sustainable self-sufficient communities' rests to some degree on suppressing our selfishness for material wealth, and moving toward co-operation with other determined souls. Therefore, we must re-evaluate the role of competition in society. Note that the virtue of non-competition does not mean that we allow other people to take unjust actions against us – far from it. We must also fight with knowledge and fight with correct action when required.

Breaking through the matrix of material illusions – transcending un-sustainability

Humanity would need to move toward a higher level of consciousness and awareness to shatter the matrix of material illusions, created by the current economic system and its architects. To do this we must address the obstacles, practical aspects and solutions referred to in the earlier chapters, yet the essential ingredient is the spiritual process of inner transformation. Without that real change will not occur.

Real sustainability in society is, and will be, a natural by-product of our journey toward higher quality and higher consciousness. It is part of becoming more conscious of how we are linked fundamentally with the health of our planet. Real sustainability involves being a person in the mode of goodness and understanding that it is a spiritual process that creates transformation in the world.

At this level of perception, we know that all we really need at the material level is (ideally pure) water, food, air, and level of safety and security for ourself, our family and community. Prioritisation of material wealth for self-gratification will not interest us when we are this level of perception, and we will no longer see ourselves as disconnected from the earth or other people. Individuals and communities at this level of consciousness will find that abundance naturally manifests and that true abundance is not just material, it also consists of abundant knowledge, happiness, bliss, and self-realisation. Real sustainability is a key aspect of unconditioned or purified human existence. When this manifests, people will treat other people and nature with reverence, in the knowledge that all life is a part of God's creation, and that each of us is a spirit soul, connected with God.

(Note that I am not advocating adherence to certain religious institutional dogmas that are evident in modern times, whereby various original teachings and scriptures have been distorted or altered, over time, for the benefit of those in positions of institutional power.)

Higher consciousness and interconnectedness – the Avatar movie metaphor

In 2009, the movie *Avatar* as well as being a blockbuster action movie raised some of the fundamental ecological, psychological and social issues relevant to living 'in symbiosis' with nature, rather than destroying nature. The movie portrays a fictional alien world where the humanoids, called the Navi, live in harmony and symbiosis with the natural environment cognisant of the interconnectedness and symbiosis that exists between all living things. Should that be so outlandish to us? On earth our ancestors also lived for countless generations in symbiosis with the natural world. It has been in relatively recent times that use of so-called modern technology has seriously messed up that natural balance. Everything we need to survive is provided by nature, and we are part of that interconnectedness, and we need to re-discover and embrace this connection. For example, on Earth, trees and plants are powered by sunlight, and utilise water from ground and carbon dioxide from the air, converting these materials into food for their use and for ours. In eating the plants of nature, we extract the energy that powers us, and in the process, we exhale carbon dioxide, which the plants then utilise to a make more carbohydrates. This is an incredible co-operative arrangement/design.

In Avatar, the Navi live in a state of vitality, peace, happiness and spiritual connection with the interconnected life on the planet, but, an invading human corporate army has arrived intent on ravaging the planet's resources for the purpose of greedy profit-making. The viewer is thus posed with a subtle question 'is the human corporate form of civilisation superior to the Navi civilisation, or vice versa?' The main human character is originally aligned with the corporation; however, he eventually evolves his consciousness to become part of the native Navi. He moves to a higher level of awareness or consciousness, and the Navi teach the courageous character to live in harmony with the planet, to take only what is needed, and to respect all living things. The Navi in this respect reflect the ancient teachings of humankind, for example, in ancient Vedic culture. Ancient human cultures were much more aware of how-to live-in balance with nature, but this knowledge has been largely lost.

Ancient Vedic cultures of the world were of a *sattvic* nature, pre-disposed to the mode of goodness. In contrast, under the imperative of debt-money and GDP growth economics, modern society has little possibility to function in the co-operative ethic that existed for many thousands of years in human history, instead we are mired in the economics of competition, greed and self-gratification. (Aside: Ancient human civilisations also had types of technology that have been lost amidst the sands of time. This subject is not within the scope of this book.)

The theme of the movie reflects what is happening here on Earth. The subtle message is that if humans learn to co-exist in symbiosis with nature, human quality of life will be increased, as the benefit and bounty of nature is manifested correctly in a pure form, not abused for profit.

Beyond the material consciousness - seeking a higher quality

"We must beak free of the illusions of the world of money, rediscover spiritual meaning in our lives." – David Korten, Author

"Completely rejecting all religious activities which are materially motivated, the Bhagavata Purana propounds the highest truth… The highest truth is reality distinguished from illusion for the welfare of all. Such truth uproots the threefold miseries." – Srimad Bhagavatam 1.1.2, translation by Srila Prabhupada

"One who is undisturbed by the flow of desires, as the ocean is unmoved by the incessant flow of rivers, finds peace." – Bhagavad Gita, 2.70, translation by Srila Prabhupada

The movie 'The Big Blue' (1988) is an interesting movie – it is not your typical Hollywood type production. The main character is a deep-sea diver and the water is the one place where he feels more like his true self - where he feels content. The main character has more than a 'love for diving' - he simply must dive, and it appears as if he is unconsciously seeking a deep fulfilment that he cannot find in the modern material world around him or in the relationship with his new girlfriend that he does not feel fully a part of and is not fully contented by. He appears to seek something beyond himself or something within in himself he has not yet fully grasped.

In the ocean he feels peace and happiness, more than that he feels blissful contentment there and seeks the unknown depths of the sea, the unknown beyond the world he does not really feel part of. Perhaps he seeks reconnection with his dead father or his friend Enzo or what lies beyond this material plane, perhaps he seeks 'a higher quality'. Is it money that provides those moments of pure bliss and life satisfaction? Rather, I suggest, those moments are often associated with expressing true yourself in an area that you love and have a natural affinity with whether it be: building, creating, designing or teaching; extending your body in sports or martial arts; playing beautiful music; climbing a mountain; being in nature; reading, writing and acquiring higher knowledge; being amongst real friends; living a happy simple joyful life; maintaining your health and cleanliness; finding peace through prayer, meditation, spiritual practices and love of God. The bliss of doing whatever honours your inner peace – and the path of your spirit is worth more than money can buy.

In seeking peace, contentment and bliss in our own lives perhaps we are simply seeking and choosing our natural state of being – a natural state that has been subverted by so-called modern technological life. In doing so perhaps some men and women subconsciously seek the highest quality of all – connection with the divine source of all life and all consciousness - God. My experience and research indicate that the concept of higher quality and the search for higher quality, sooner or later culminates in a search for

God. The writings of Robert Pirsig in his famous book *'Zen and the Art of motor Cycle Maintenance'* reflect man's search for a higher quality or *'what is the generator of everything we know'* - the generator of reality. These quotes from Pirsig's writings indicate to me that there is a higher quality in existence that our current profit-driven society has tragically failed to grasp.

> "The questions... the same questions... he's got to know everything. And if he doesn't get the answer he just drives and drives until he gets one and that leads to another question... endlessly pursuing questions, never seeing, never understanding that the questions will never end. Something is missing and he knows it and will kill himself trying to find it."

> "it is quality not dialectic which is the generator of everything we know"

> "Quality lay not only outside any academic discipline, it lay outside the grasp of the methods of the entire church of reason – it would take quite a university to accept a doctoral thesis in which the candidate refused to define his central term."

> "The result is rather typical of modern technology, an overall dullness of appearance so depressing that it must be overlaid with a veneer of "style" to make it acceptable... It's the style that gets you; technological ugliness syruped over with romantic phoniness in an effort to produce beauty and profit by people who, though stylish, don't know where to start because no one has ever told them there's such a thing as Quality in this world and it's real, not style. Quality isn't something you lay on top of subjects and objects like tinsel on a Christmas tree. Real Quality must be the source of the subjects and objects, the cone from which the tree must start." - Robert Pirsig, Author.

Pirsig's writings raise fundamental questions about where real quality comes from. I believe that higher quality comes from God. Let us consider, for example, the design quality of the human body, or of animals. So-called modern scientists cannot even do what a cow does, i.e., change grass into nutritious milk. The design quality of God's creations is perfect. In nature, in the human organism, in plants, in the universe, we observe supreme design quality, but our words are not sufficient to define that magnificent quality. Yet, it is something we can all identify with in some fundamental way because we are ourselves are a product of the quality of God's creation.

Walking a spiritual path

So how can we define ultimate quality? We are a part of God's creation, and a spark of God exists in each of us, but we are not the architects of God's creation. We are, therefore, unable to define ultimate quality – God being the highest quality of all cannot be fully defined by the limited speculations of mankind. This is not a cause for remorse because, in the original versions of the ancient scriptures of the world, God has provided the path of higher knowledge and spiritual realisation before us. Seek and you will find!

In contrast to evil personalities, divine souls cultivate an atmosphere of inner peace, contentment, self-control, purity, farsightedness, simplicity, purified consciousness, openness, and love. When we genuinely commit to a spiritual path we can begin to better recognise and appreciate the higher quality in nature all around us, in God's design and 'within ourselves'. Why is it that people experience much greater wellbeing, peace and spiritual harmony when they are in nature, as compared to being, for example, in an office block? The answer is that in nature we are in contact with the higher quality of God's creation as compared to man's creation. We should therefore acknowledge the importance of the higher quality of natural systems as essential to a truly sustainable society. Quantitative measures of wellbeing, such as economic GDP growth, have been described as the 'reign of quantity over quality'. Thankfully there are definite signs that this quantitative era is coming to an end.

Thus, for those seeking a higher quality, the real challenge is to walk a higher path in life; to uncover and express our true spiritual self; to raise our consciousness; to truly embrace a spiritual path in life with full self-respect, respect for others and for nature; and thus re-establish our original energetic spiritual nature and connection with God. How do we actually do this? The answer lies in the original spiritual teachings of the world. Ancient scriptures have provided spiritual wisdom for thousands of years, and all ancient cultures tell of divine teachings. My research indicates that all the original basis for these teachings was the ancient Vedic texts. The Vedic texts pre-date the texts of early Christianity, and those of eastern religious philosophies, such as Buddhism and Daoism. (I note there are various similarities (and differences) between the original versions of these texts - this is a large subject not within the scope of this book)

(Aside: With respect to those genuine souls that are members of modern-day institutional religions, I state plainly that my research indicates that various aspects of modern day institutional religious scripture appear to have been subtly distorted, altered or incorrectly derived from much earlier 'original' bona-fide scripture, sometimes for the purposes of institutional power, greed and control.)

The Dao of sustainability / the Tao of quality

I was raised in a Christian family and to this day I have an affinity with the original scriptures of early Christianity. Years later as a young man, I had some affinity with Daoist concepts, especially when I spent time hiking in the Wicklow mountains in Ireland. Daoism recognises the energy of this reality we live within, and reflects a sense of the importance of acting in harmony with nature, and with the natural rhythms and natural energy of this reality. The source of the energy is called the Dao. A typical online definition describes the Dao/Tao as follows:

> "Tao can be roughly stated to be the flow of the universe, or the force behind the natural order, equating it with the influence that keeps the universe balanced and ordered. Tao can be roughly translated into English as path, or the way. It is basically indefinable. It has to be experienced. It "refers to a power which envelops, surrounds and flows through all things, living and non-living."

Daoism thus points toward the obvious question. What is the Dao? Where does the energy of this reality come from? I note, however, that Daoism can be described as a philosophy of impersonalism because it does not recognise the personal aspect of God. Therefore, I assert that I am not a Daoist. Nevertheless, despite the incomplete aspects of Daoism, the words of the Daoist, Lao Tzu, author of the Tao Te Ching, provided me with some food for thought when I was a young man.

> "if you conform to the way, its power flows through you… your actions become those of nature, your ways those of heaven." – from the 23rd verse Tao Te Ching

> "do you think that you can take over the universe and improve it - I do not believe it can be done – everything under heaven is a sacred vessel and cannot be controlled – trying to control leads to ruin - trying to grasp we lose - allow your life to unfold naturally, know that it too is a vessel of perfection' 'to the sage all of life is a movement toward perfection" - from the 29 th verse Tao Te Ching

> "when man interferes with the tao, the sky becomes filthy, the earth becomes depleted, the equilibrium crumbles, creatures become extinct. " - from 39th verse Tao Te Ching

> "and whatever is against the tao soon ceases to be " – from 55th verse Tao Te Ching

Lao Tzu seems to suggest that behind the workings of nature there exists a reality of ultimate quality, that is evident in the design laws of nature itself laws of nature itself. Perhaps we could interpret the 23rd verse to mean if harmonise with the natural, zero-waste mechanisms of nature in our human processes, we will align ourselves with a higher quality, the Dao. The verse implies that human beings should cultivate the ways of nature, and reminds me of the concept of 'deep ecology'. However, despite providing various thought-provoking insights, I found Daoism unsatisfying. As I sought more knowledge, I noted that Daoism appears to negate the existence of the creator and does not show us a path to approach God or connect with God. Along with Buddhism, it is an impersonal approach that seems to imply that we can never begin to know God, never become closer to God, and never have a relationship with God.

The refusal of consciousness and denial of God in so-called modern science

All our problems are to do with consciousness. Consciousness can be loosely defined as the awareness of thoughts and sensations that we directly perceive and know that we perceive. Yet, so-called modern science deals only with mechanistic and material aspects of the world, and cannot explain the existence of consciousness and, thus, consistently ignores, this 'elephant in the room', or denies its existence. (Mechanistic science involves a theoretical system based on measurement and calculation). This 'elephant in the room' is actually the missing link to connect mechanistic science with spiritual science.

The scientific denial of the existence of consciousness is often coupled with a denial of the existence of the soul, denial of intelligent design in nature, and a dogmatic rejection of the possibility of creator of higher intelligence, or God. This godless scientism can be traced back to a hijacking of science in the 1800s by the atheistic society of freemasonry to deny the existence of God. Prior to this pivotal agenda most scientists believed in the existence of the creator. Charles Darwin, who proposed the theory of evolution in the 1800s had strong links with the Royal Society science institution, whose members were almost all atheistic freemasons. Driven by the network mechanisms of influential freemasonry, the completely unproven theory of evolution has been force fed to the world population for the past 150 years, and is the ideological basis by which 'modern science' denies the existence of God.

> "Freemasons thinking that Darwin theory of evolution could serve its aims played a great role in its dissemination among the populations… a group of volunteer propogandists promoted it, the most famous being Thomas Huxley who was called Darwin's bulldog. Huxley brought the world's attention to theory of evolution and was most responsible for its rapid acceptance. Huxley was a member of the Royal Society, one of England's most prestigious scientific institutions and like nearly all the other members of this institution was a senior Freemason. The society thus provided Darwin's theory with significant support.

> A fact that proves that Darwinism is one of the biggest deceptions of atheistic freemasonry is a resolution carried in a mason meeting. The 33rd degree supreme council of freemasonry at Paris carries a resolution reveals in its minutes its promotion of the theory of evolution as science while they themselves scoffed at the theory. The minutes read as follows "it is with this object in view, the scientific theory of evolution, that we are constantly by means of our press arousing a blind confidence in these theories, the intellectuals will puff themselves up with their knowledge and without any logical verification of them will put into effect all the information available from science which our agents have pieced together for the purposes of educating their minds in the direction we want. Do not suppose that these statements are empty think carefully of the successes we arranged for Darwinism.

> New age Magazine in its March 1922 issue stated that "the kingdom of atheistic freemasonry will be established by evolution and the development of man himself"… Masonists openly admit that

they will use the scientists and media which are under their control to present this deception as scientific which even they find funny. One of the main aims is to replace God with their godless myth of blind chance evolution. Darwin never claimed to have any verifiable evidence proving his evolution theory. Here we are 150 years later with sheeple convinced they are monkey men." – Eric Dubay, Author

"Masonry is based on Judiasm (Jewish Talmudism). Eliminate the teachings of Judaism (Jewish Talmudism) from the masonic ritual and what is left?" – Jewish Tribune of New York newspaper, October 28th 1927

Modern-day scientific institutions are reliant on government funding or corporate funding, and are thus beholden to the source of funding. As evidenced in an earlier chapter, the world debt-money system, banking, and corporate super-entity is predominantly privately owned by the international private bankers; and governments, being also beholden to the debt-money system, are mere vassals of this banking power structure. The dominant players are the Jewish banking families that have been operating private banking for generations, see page 78, and the historical intertwining of Freemasonry and Judaism is a well-documented fact.

"It has been ever universally admitted by the order, that to part Masonry and Judaism is impossible; in fact, to use a well known axiom amongst us, "Judaism is Masonry, and Masonry is Judaism." – Jewish Chronicle, December 20, 1867

Thus, the reality is that scientific institutions worldwide deny the existence of God, and scientists that have challenged the fake theory of evolution, or even hinted at the possibility of 'intelligent design', have been ostracised. This is evidenced in the documentary film *Expelled – No Intelligence Allowed,* in which multiple senior scientists and university Professors describe that their funding was cut or they lost their jobs when they mentioned the scientific possibility of intelligent design in nature and human biology, or the basis for the existence of God. Even Christian universities rigorously teach the ideology of evolution.

With God taken out of the picture, modern-day science also denies the existence of consciousness, and the individual soul.. Modern-science has adopted the view that individual consciousness or the 'self' is simply an interplay of processes within the brain that completely obey mechanistic science. This assumption is simply a lazy cop-out with no evidence whatsoever. Modern science ignores its failure to explain the phenomena of consciousness, inspiration, compassion, or the conscience, in which we instinctively know the difference between right and wrong, or good and bad. Consciousness is the unexplained missing link between material science and the higher qualities of spiritual science.

"We can admittedly find nothing in physics or chemistry that has even a remote bearing on consciousness. Yet all of us know that there is such a thing as consciousness, simply because we have it ourselves. Hence consciousness must be part of nature, or, more generally, of reality, which means that, quite apart from the laws of physics and chemistry... we must consider laws of quite a different kind." – Niels Bohr, 1922 Nobel Laureate, Physics

"The evidence is coming in from all sides: that physics and chemistry cannot account for more than a kind of substratum of phenomena and must be seen as being in the service of higher forces when it comes to matters like life, intelligence and consciousness" – E. F. Schumacher, Author

"The scientific community practices the art of 'refusal of consciousness' with perfection... survival will depend on our ability to overcome the 'refusal of consciousness' which defends totally outdated philosophies of economic progress and scientific truth" – E.F. Schumacher, Author

"We have discovered ourselves to be in a very, very deep spiritual crisis. An era which has been dominated by cartesian thinking and which has lasted for 250 or 300 years, has seen unbelievable developments in science and technology. This era is now drawing to a close. Having worked out the consequences of this type of thinking we find ourselves spiritually bankrupt." – E.F. Schumacher

Modern science heavily influences the strata of modern-day society, therefore, it is vital that people have access to scientific information that is reliable and true. In 2022, the lies of covid-19, climate change, evolution, and other topics, are becoming more apparent to the population of the world. Many millions of people can see that the 'institution' of modern science has failed us, and has been utilised to leave us bereft of spiritual truth in an ideological cul-de-sac not based on reality. By studying the material world, yet denying the creator of the material world, modern science is akin to the branch of a tree without its trunk and roots. So where should we turn to for real knowledge on the science of consciousness, and the science of spirituality?

Enlightenment can be a destructive process because it is a breaking down of false beliefs that have been promoted as truth. We need to search past the limited mechanics of material perception to acquire real knowledge on the science of consciousness. The reality is that a genuine science of the non-physical self, a science of the soul, is not only possible, it already exists, and has been known since time immemorial. In cultures worldwide, people have traditionally believed that the innermost self is an entity distinct from the physical body. The original source of that belief is the science of self-realisation as detailed in the Vedic literatures, the oldest known scriptures in the world. The next chapter provides lessons from the Vedic text, the Bhagavad Gita.

The satanic consciousness directing the climate change and covid hysteria

Luciferianism is the underlying globalist cult religion, and is the only ideological institution adopted by the UN, see Endnote [175], via the UN's relationship with Lucis Trust. Lucis Trust was originally called Lucifer Publishing Company, see Endnote [176], and still has a private library within the UN building today, see Endnote [177].

> "The demoniac person thinks: "So much wealth do I have today, and I will gain more according to my schemes… He is my enemy, and I have killed him, and my other enemies will also be killed. I am the lord of everything… the demoniac who are lost to themselves… engage in unbeneficial horrible works meant to destroy the world… the demon's lust is never satiated… they become attracted to two things: sex enjoyment and accumulation of material wealth." - Bhagavad Gita As It Is, translation by Srila Prabhupada.

> "At the present, especially on this planet earth… the representatives of… demons - have taken charge… This age is very dangerous because society is being managed by demons" - Srimad Bhagavatam 7.3.13 purport by Srila Prabhupada

This sub-chapter is derived in part with permission from the writings of a friend who is a Vedic monk. He has described the covid-19 vaccine as "the chemical messiah of demoniac scientism that will save everyone from death - problem is its a false messiah". Could this be true? Is the covid-19 vaccine the product of demoniac or satanic forces? For those people who have little or no spiritual knowledge or realization, and who are generally absorbed in the materialistic society, the message that a 'satanic influence' or 'satanic consciousness' is controlling the top echelons of the world's political, corporate and economic power structures is of such magnitude that it is quickly dismissed or certainly not easily understood or accepted. In March 2020, as the entire world grinded to a halt in the face of the covid-19 scare, most people had no idea of the deep significance of the events taking place. It was the first time that all nations were collectively brought to a complete standstill, and that all people, were simultaneously faced with the same threat of impending death. The fact that all the people of the world were simultaneously forced to 'stop', signalled that a major change in the world was coming. As this book has described the Covid-19 fake pandemic was a cover for a freedom killing economic reset. This was an ingenious demoniac attempt to takeover and control the entirety of world society.

The short-term changes of this reset are likely to be bad for many people, but the long-term changes will eventually bring an end to the present satanic system. This smokescreen has enabled the godless forces to further control the world's people and resources. If we accept this seemingly extreme perspective, then it follows that the devotees of God should not naively trust the official government narrative, or blindly accept the so-called remedial measures to the 'pandemic', i.e., the vaccines.

In relation to those godless forces who are intent on using climate change or covid-19, or any other manufactured crisis, to further their own ends, let all be assured that God has His own plans in action, and that any hidden evil will be eventually exposed to the world, with the resulting karma coming back on the head of the evil-doers.

The steadfastness, emergence and awakening of God-conscious people worldwide will eventually defeat satanic forces. In the Vedic scripture, the Bhagavad Gita, Krishna assured Arjuna that his victory over the demonic forces was a forgone conclusion, similarly, there are many assurances from God and his associates that the present godless system will be entirely annihilated. Whatever the short-term outcome, the end result will be the inevitable defeat of satanic government.

> "The conversation was wonderful because such an important conversation between two great souls never took place before and would not take place again. It is wonderful because the Supreme Personality of Godhead is speaking about Himself and His energies to the living entity, Arjuna, a great devotee of the Lord. If we follow in the footsteps of Arjuna to understand Krsna, then our life will be happy and successful…. Now it is concluded that wherever there is Krsna and Arjuna, there is victory." - Bhagavad Gita As It Is, Chapter 18, Text 74

In our own life-time we have lived under a political hierarchy, which though pertaining to be made of individual and autonomous nation states, is actually a one world government controlled by the world banking cartel and its mega-corporations. This hierarchy has stealthily introduced a poisonous atheistic ideology, an artificial monetary system that has caused economic enslavement to billions of people through-out the world, and a perpetual war machine which has caused death and injury to hundreds of millions of people through-out the world; it is a system which has introduced mass abortion, mass animal killing, illicit sex, gambling, and intoxication; it is a system that has introduced genetically modified foods, chemtrails, herbicides and pesticides, fluoridated water, toxic pharmaceuticals and vaccines, widespread ecological destruction, etc.; the list goes on and on.

Though individual politicians have been replaced by others, the same system of government has continued. Now in the midst of a 'covid-19' pandemic', we are expected to believe that this one world government is suddenly concerned for the lives and health of people threatened by the so-called virus. Does a vulture wish the cow to be alive or dead? And does a vulture government wish for the physical, economic and spiritual health of its citizens?

Many politicians are themselves unwitting pawns of the godless international hierarchy, which includes major institutions, such as the world's political and corporate organisations, finance and banking, military, education, health, and the media who, at the launch of the pandemic, employed nothing less than trauma-based mind control to convince the world's population that they are all likely to die from Covid-19 unless they do exactly what the world government orders and take an experimental gene-modification vaccine. Through various networks, such servants of the satanic forces are placed in positions of leadership, power, and influence, and then enact laws that allow society to become degraded, weak, easily controllable, and unable to perceive the nature of their material and spiritual captivity.

Is there a reason some people can see through the fake agendas, but most cannot?

The attempted UN Agenda 2030 and WEF / Davos group agenda will fail, over time, in my opinion and is already failing as millions of people are seeing through the manmade climate change lie and other manufactured hysterias. The real divide in society is not the media fostered left-versus-right punch-and-judy show', it is authoritarianism versus human freedom. The power seekers versus the freedom lovers. There are those that just want to be left alone and there are those that just won't leave them alone.

Yet there is another divide. Those people that could see the truth couldn't convince most other people of that truth no matter how hard they tried, and those believing the government narrative couldn't convince the 'conspiracy theorists' of their truth no matter hard they tried. It seemed like an invisible mental barrier manifested itself. But why can some people see through the fake climate change agenda and covid-19 fake pandemic, but others cannot? I noticed that an anonymous person posted the following thought-provoking statement online:

> "There has to be a reason why we the relative few who can see so clearly what the majority cannot are here at this particular time in the planet's history. Because if there isn't, if God had said you are going to incarnate on earth when pure evil is taking over, you are going to be given the ability to see right through these lies and deception with a relatively few numbers of others, you are going to acquire this knowledge and discernment, but there won't be a single thing you can do with these gifts, you will feel helpless in the mass insanity you see around you…
>
> we may be here to give alerts, signposts for future generations… it might be a spiritual test, it's how we face and deal with this evil that counts, not the end manifest physical result of standing up to, and if necessary, of going down fighting rather than submitting to slavery… it might be just another part of our soul journey and our spirits are being honed and refined in the fire of this current corona ordeal. Even if does turn out that we appear to have lost the physical battle in the far bigger and far more important spiritual journey level we will have proved our worth. Whatever there has to be a reason why we are here. Whatever the reason I will continue to hold the line to the very best of my

physical, spiritual, mental, and emotional ability. This is the last chance for those who refused to wake up after 911 and those who refused to wake up from the jackanory media."

Covid-19 was a fulcrum event, it created a mental split. There are those that fully accepted the government narrative, restrictions and wore the masks proudly, which by the way are a masonic symbol of slavery; and there are those more aware people that could see for themselves what was really happening.

The climate change agenda has a similar splitting effect in society. Our mental reality creates our physical reality. That is why it is so important to see the truth. If we live in mental fear that will be our physical reality. In contrast, spiritual knowledge enables us to bypass these limitations, in this higher knowledge we know that the spiritual spark, creates the physical reality, and each of us is a spiritual spark. We do not need to live in fear, we can create our own reality and successful future for our families and wider communities. This change of consciousness moves us away from fear.

Those that have been given the gift of higher discernment can more easily see through the lies of the criminal elites. When you see through the deceptions and manipulations, your mental reality is cleansed, you are set free from delusion, and the doors and possibilities for a better future can be opened.

Thus, the fake agendas could be perceived as a challenge for us all, we can choose to either be a slave to the system or, alternatively, to create and co-create an improved society, a world of integrity, truth, justice and wellbeing, along with the many millions of people who also realise what is happening. From an 'original' Christian perspective, and also from a Vedic perspective this means creating a God-conscious society. We can name the evil-doers all we want, but if we do not make sure our righteousness and actions exceed that of the evil-doers we are no better than they are. This may all be a spiritual test where everyone has a role to play - without the evil forces there would be no battle where the righteous ones can prove themselves.

The 'new normal' and the 'old normal' are not normal

It seems like most of the world has been desperate to return to the 'normal' world we had in 2019 prior to the fake pandemic, but the reality is that life pre-Covid-19 was far from normal, what exactly are people trying to get back to? Vastly excessive consumerism; hours stuck in traffic; the 9 to 5 hamster wheel to pay off the mortgage (mortgage is the French word for death grip btw); kids glued to harmful microwave-producing smart phones; mindless TV programmes designed to keep you 'programmed' and dumbed down; the whole world in unpayable debt to private bankers; an education system that indoctrinates everyone to become cogs in the system machinery of the criminal elites; mega-corporations polluting the earth; toxins in the food and water supply; Hollywood movie drivel; internet censorship; impotent art, music and culture projects that depend on corporate gatekeepers or state funding and, therefore, lack the balls to say what needs to be said; the list goes on and on. What is normal about any of that? All of it promotes fear, worry and distraction. The so-called alternative media is also littered with rabbit-holes leading you in the wrong direction. All this disconnects us from being our true selves.

We need a better paradigm, but obviously not the technocratic 'new normal' paradigm the elites have planned for us to keep us under tabs. It is time to leave it all behind – to hell with the new normal and to hell with the old normal. Is a slow comfortable death in the suburbs of the 'system' really what you are here on Earth for? With every payment we take from, and compliance we make to, a state that imposes freedom killing communism, our dignity is diminished. If we depend on the state, our soul is stinted by the conditions and rules they impose on us. Will you be a monitored, masked and muddled gimp in the new control system? Where each compliance sucks your energy into their system. The old system is based entirely on debt-money created from nothing, and the new system is based on technocratic control created from nothing except their narcissism and our consent. Only when people see there is nothing left to win in the 'system' because it is not based on real value, will they cast off their shackles and say "You can't tell me what to do anymore - now I'm FREE"

It is time for each of us to be our true SELF. Give it all up – all your expectations of fleeting fame and fortune in a system of corruption and perversion. It's TIME to BE what you NEED to BE, to cast off everything that holds you down.

Many will only see their predicament when they face the final trap of the technocrats, and then either fall into utter despair or transform into fearlessness. Why wait till then? The time is now. Local systems for food, energy, water and services are an essential part of escaping the coming technocratic system that is being cleverly wrapped around us. Start creating local self-sufficient systems. Overcome your fears! A transition is coming, a collapse of the old system is nigh. Start local currencies, home-schooling systems for practical skills, local skills shares, food production co-operatives, or work independently, and make contacts. Re-occupy 'the commons' land and property that the state and corporations have appropriated via a fraudulent money system and statute trickery.

Remember no politician, police or person has authority over you - unlock yourself from their mental prison. Only you can tell you what to do. God is the only true authority and is your ever-lasting well-wisher and guide. We must restore the true foundations of society - truth, integrity, love, fearlessness and respect for God.

God is the Supreme Controller. There is no cause to fear. Devotees of God will never perish. Those who have turned against God are controlled by the demonic system. God perhaps allows the demonic forces to perpetrate the fake pandemic because it forces people to choose between good and evil. We are just witness to some karma playing out. The world has to wake up to the evil system that they have been serving for so long. It's all a test to choose one side or the other.

The infiltration and manipulation of religious institutions

> "Asuras (demons) have a lot to do with religion. They fight it, and even more so they infiltrate it because that is a double victory for them; they have disunited all these people, and furthermore they can use them for their own ends. Therefore infiltration is much more effective than physical elimination. An infiltrated religion is no longer a threat, it is a tool!.. in one way or another, this matrix of (infiltrated) 'religion' was enforced all over the world." – Armin Risi, Author

In earlier chapter the links between talmudic Judaism, freemasonry, the banking sector and corporate media were examined. What about the other religions? Is there a new world order network in all religions? What about the heinous history of paedophilia within the Catholic church? What's going on at the Vatican? These subjects are so large they warrant a separate book. I note that the Roman Catholic Pope Francis appears to be a champion of the new world order and this is to the upset of many Catholics. He is co-operating with the UN, WEF, and the Chinese communist party, and running PR for the globalists on climate change. He advocated that even healthy young people get vaccinated, stood in the way of religious exemption for forced vaccinations, and sent a representative to Davos to bless and approve the WEF great reset. Pope Francis, even addressed UN member governments with a plea to support the UN goals. "The adoption of the 2030 Agenda for Sustainable Development ... is an important sign of hope," he declared, before demanding a UN "climate" regime as well. The Vatican is also in a publicised partnership initiative with the Rothschilds banking dynasty. I note the comments of Bishop Williamson:

> "The Vatican is full of freemasons".... "all of the religions that are going to be in the.. religious department of the new world order... religion is going to be entirely subordinate to politics... as puppets of the masters of the new world order what the politicians will do is make the catholic religion entirely subordinate to the state" - Bishop Williamson

According to author Dean Henderson, "the freemasons are the Christian component, the Muslim brotherhood are the Muslim component, the cabalists are the Jewish component, of the secret satanic network".

The programming of consciousness and how to transcend it

Author and Vedic Monk, Armin Risi, has described the programming of consciousness and how to transcend it. He states "The mind is like a mirror or an unexposed film which we constantly expose to certain sensory perceptions… These are the impressions that are reflected back into our consciousness, or to be more precise into our mind…. The mental body consists of a subtle substance (that) reacts to all conscious stimuli, registering (filming) each single one of them, either consciously or unconsciously… these impressions influence the direction of our consciousness… those in the position of materialistic power try their best to shape people's consciousness so as to secure and, ultimately, enforce subordination… It is difficult to force people to do something against their will. However, they will do the same thing without objection if they act under the impression that they are doing it voluntarily, or that it is necessary – for example, accepting new laws and enforced restrictions in the name of security, anti-terrorism, anti-cult information, or fight against new diseases. The easiest way to bring about total control is to create an atmosphere (atmos-fear!) of fear and intimidation. And this again starts in the mind." Clearly, therefore, we should be cognisant and selective of what impressions we allow to enter our consciousness. Living in a pure and conscious manner is important to avoid harming or weakening one's subtle material body.

15. Transcending the world power game – wisdom from ancient scriptures

This chapter is available in the PDF download version of this book *Transcending the climate change deception – toward real sustainability,* which is available on my website www.mkeenan.ie The chapter provides a perspective based on original Christian and earlier Vedic scriptures. It covers the following topics:

- Importance of a God-conscious society - respecting God as the only true authority
- Origen: A founding father of early Christianity
- Introducing the Vedic texts
- Human behaviours explained by the Bhagavad Gita
- Transcending lust and greed toward the economics of goodness
- Divine and demoniac consciousness
- The story of King Pariksit – the protector of truth
- His Divine Grace A.C. Bhaktivedanta Srila Prabhupada
- The importance of 'dharma', freewill and individuality
- Embracing your spiritual development - you are a spirit soul in a body
- The karmic reality of the current situation facing the people of the world
- The path of pure devotional service to God
- The 'Golden Age' - creating 'dharma nations'

Best wishes on your journey.

Mark

Printed copies of this book are available from www.mkeenan.ie **or** www.amazon.com

Endnotes

[1] Source: 'The Web of Debt' by E.H. Brown, pg 130. Second edition.

[2] For more information see https://clintel.org/

[3] The European Climate Declaration – There is no Climate Emergency is available at: https://www.thegwpf.com/european-climate-declaration-there-is-no-climate-emergency/

[4] Source: https://clintel.org/clintel-open-letter-to-bill-gates/

[5] Sources: https://www.youtube.com/watch?v=4JJ3yeiNjf4&feature=emb_title

https://www.youtube.com/watch?v=3FP7q86hzbc

[6] Source: www.clintel.org

[7] Dr. Willie Soon has demolishes the extreme weather panic and other hysterical arguments in the following lecture available at: https://www.youtube.com/watch?v=4JJ3yeiNjf4

[8] Professor Franco Battaglia has published a paper stating that the EU's energy policy of the last 20 years has been dead wrong. The full paper is available at: http://www.sepp.org/key_issues/soaring_energy_bills.pdf

[9] Source: Irish Climate Science Forum lecture titled *Testing Climate Claims 2021 Update* available at www.icsf.ie

[10] 100 years of climate data was deleted from a Canadian government policy report. Source: https://www.youtube.com/watch?v=3FP7q86hzbc

[11] The Irish Climate Science Forum website URL is www.icsf.ie

[12] Dr Nils-Axel Mörner was interviewed by Alan Jones on Sky News Live, Australia.

[13] Source: Irish Climate Science Forum lecture titled *What does IPCC AR6 say on scenarios and extreme weather?* available at www.icsf.ie

[14] Source: https://data.parliament.uk/DepositedPapers/Files/DEP2019-0718/Green_Finance_Strategy.pdf

[15] Source: http://www.wrongkindofgreen.org/2019/09/10/an-object-lesson-in-spectacle-excerpt-from-the-manufacturing-of-greta-thunberg-for-consent-volume-ii/

[16] Source: Video presentation by Whistleblower George Hunt with evidence of the UNCED documents, titled 'How the Illuminati gained control of the Earth' available on Bitchute.

[17] According to Hunt these are the same new world order banking families that funded, planned and orchestrated World War One and World War Two to further destructive geo-political agendas; create war profits; plunge governments into vast debt, create complete private banking control, set up the Jewish state of Israel on the lands of Palestine, and then create one world government control via unelected institutions, such as the UN, the World Bank, and the IMF.

At the Yata conference after WWII, Churchill, Stalin and Roosevelt (all high level freemasons) agreed on the formation of a communist style new world order, the UN. This is described in the documentary *Europa Last Battle* which is available on bitchute.com

[18] Sources: http://en.wikipedia.org/wiki/Climate_change

http://en.wikipedia.org/wiki/Global_warming

[19] Sources: http://en.wikipedia.org/wiki/Davis_Guggenheim

http://en.wikipedia.org/wiki/Jeff_Skoll

[20] Sources: http://www.americanprogress.org/experts/RommJoseph.html http://en.wikipedia.org/wiki/Joseph_J._Romm

[21] Sources: http://stephenschneider.stanford.edu
http://en.wikipedia.org/wiki/Stephen_Schneider

[22] Sources: http://www.meteo.psu.edu/~mann/Mann
http://en.wikipedia.org/wiki/Michael_E._Mann

[23] Sources: http://www.giss.nasa.gov/staff/gschmidt
http://en.wikipedia.org/wiki/Gavin_Schmidt

[24] Sources: http://www.eoearth.org/article/Santer,_Benjamin_D.
http://en.wikipedia.org/wiki/Benjamin_D._Santer

[25] Sources: http://en.wikipedia.org/wiki/Carbon_tax
http://en.wikipedia.org/wiki/Carbon_emission_trading

[26] Sources: http://www.state.gov/r/pa/ei/biog/122554.htm
http://www.whorunsgov.com/Profiles/Todd_D._Stern

[27] Sources: http://www.chicagoclimatex.com/content.jsf?id=122
http://www.time.com/time/specials/2007/article/0,28804,1663317_1663322_1669930,00.html

[28] Sources: http://en.wikipedia.org/wiki/Nicholas_Stern,_Baron_Stern_of_Brentford
http://en.wikipedia.org/wiki/Stern_Review

[29] Sources: http://www.unhistory.org/CD/Sachs.html
http://en.wikipedia.org/wiki/Ignacy_Sachs

[30] Source: https://thezog.wordpress.com/who-is-behind-the-climate-change-hoax/

[31] Source: http://www.climatecrisis.net/an_inconvenient_truth/about_the_film.php

[32] Jewish Population of the United States by State:
http://www.jewishvirtuallibrary.org/jsource/US-Israel/usjewpop.html

[33] Source: Article by William Engdahl at: https://journal-neo.org/2019/09/25/climate-and-the-money-trail/

[34] Source: https://www.wrongkindofgreen.org/2019/01/17/the-manufacturing-of-greta-thunberg-for-consent-the-political-economy-of-the-non-profit-industrial-complex/

[35] Sources: http://www.foxnews.com/politics/2009/03/25/obama-years-ago-helped-fund-carbon-program-pushing-congress/

http://northerngleaner.blogspot.com/2010/05/obamas-involvement-in-chicago-climate.html

[36] Source: http://www.chicagoclimatex.com/content.jsf?id=64
http://www.theccx.com/content.jsf?id=821

[37] Source:
http://en.wikipedia.org/wiki/Chicago_Climate_Exchange

[38] Source: http://www.examiner.com/x-14143-Orange-County-Conservative-Examiner~y2010m4d27-Scandal-Obama-Gore-Goldman-Joyce-Foundation-CCX-partners-to-fleece-USA

[39] The following article describes Tedros the head of the WHO as a member of a violent terrorist group: https://www.westernjournal.com/no-wonder-covered-china-director-prominent-member-communist-party

[40] The book "Sustainable Energy without Hot Air" by Professor David MacKay, Regius Professor of Engineering at Cambridge University and former Chief Scientific Advisor to the UK's Department of Energy and Climate Change, is available for free at: https://withouthotair.com/

[41] Source: Lecture by Dr Benny Peiser – *After COP 26 The looing energy crisis - Is there a realistic alternative to net zero?* Available on the Irish Climate Science Forum website www.icsf.ie

[42] Source: https://www.feasta.org/2020/02/07/end-of-the-oilocene-the-gathering-storm/

[43] Source: https://www.theguardian.com/environment/2012/aug/07/china-rare-earth-village-pollution

[44] The relevant article written by Elon Musk is available at: https://www.tesla.com/blog/secret-tesla-motors-master-plan-just-between-you-and-me

[45] The lecture *How to green the world's deserts and reverse climate change* by Allan Savory is available at:
https://www.ted.com/talks/allan_savory_how_to_fight_desertification_and_reverse_climate_change
https://www.youtube.com/watch?v=vpTHi7O66pI

See also the *Savory – Holistic Management* website available at: https://savory.global/

[46] An interesting documentary in relation to these topics is *NWO Communism by the Back Door*

210

[47] Source: *UK Sustainable Development Strategy*, HM Government 2005, pg 7.

[48] Source: *Natural Resource and Environmental Economics,* Perman 2003, pg 339.

[49] Sources: https://www.globalresearch.ca/coronavirus-causes-effects-real-danger-agenda-id2020/5706153

https://www.globalresearch.ca/agenda-id2020-continued-diabolical-agenda-within-agenda/5721717

[50] The Roise Koire writings are available at: https://www.democratsagainstunagenda21.com/#

[51] The American Policy Center website is www.americanpolicy.org

[52] Internet searches reveal the family connection between the WEF Klaus Schwab and the Rothschild banking dynasty.

[search result image showing "mother of klaus schwab" with photo captioned "Marianne Schwab" and text: "Marianne **Schwab**, née Rothschild: "I always feel a little homesick for Bad Homburg" Marianne was born in Frankfurt in 1919. She grew up in the town of Bad Homburg, where her father, Louis Rothschild, managed a bank."]

[53] There are thousands of scientific studies and research papers showing the harmful biological effects of electromagnetic and microwave radiation from mobile phones, WiFi, 5G, Smart meters, etc on our health and the environment. The following websites give detailed information and links to many of these studies:

In May 2011, the World Health Organisation and the International Agency for Research on Cancer (IARC) classified mobile phone and wireless radiation as a Class 2B Carcinogenic, the same category as DDT, chloroform and methylmercury. Press release available at: https://www.iarc.fr/wp-content/uploads/2018/07/pr208_E.pdf

See www.es-ireland.com

Canadians for Safe Technology: http://c4st.org/

US Naval Research Institute (1970) 2,300 studies by the US Navy showing biological impacts of EMF: https://apps.dtic.mil/dtic/tr/fulltext/u2/750271.pdf

A compilation of Scientific Studies on the effects of wireless microwave radiation and electromagnetic fields on the body – EMF Data. Available at: https://www.emfdata.org/en/studies

In May 2016 A National Toxicology Program Study funded by US Government confirms RF radiation from mobile phones breaks DNA and is a cancer risk/ Cell Phone Radiation Study available at: https://bioinitiative.org/cell-phone-radiation-study-confirms-cancer-risk/ and Microwave News available at: https://microwavenews.com/news-center/ntp-comet-assay

EMF Research is an independent research resource into electromagnetic fields (EMF) for public education purposes, focused primarily on Radiofrequency EMF (RF-EMF) and Extremely-Low Frequency (ELF-EMF) fields. Available at: https://www.emfresearch.com/

Wireless Radiation & EMF Studies published from August 2016 to September 2018 (335 pages). Compiled by Joel M. Moskowitz, Ph.D. School of Public Health, University of California, Berkeley. https://drive.google.com/file/d/1V3n0962PtWWB-gzcfF85TglEC4iZAOeq/view

March 2018 – Expert Panel to US National Toxicology Program on cell phone radiation concludes "clear evidence" of cancer. https://ehtrust.org/clear-evidence-of-cancer-concludes-the-expert-panel-to-the-us-national-toxicology-program-on-cell-phone-radiation-study-findings/

June 2018. Recent Research on Wifi Health Effects available at: https://www.saferemr.com/2015/09/recent-research-on-wifi-effects.html?spref=fb

Environmental Health Trust – Science. A comprehensive list of studies and research available at: https://ehtrust.org/science/

Emf-Portal.org. An extensive literature database with an inventory of 28,391 publications and 6,359 summaries of individual scientific studies on the effects of electromagnetic fields.

EMFacts Consultancy – Papers & Publications Research papers and up to date information available at: https://www.emfacts.com/papers/

Bioinitiative Report 2012
References 1,800 reports showing biological effects of electromagnetic fields available at: https://bioinitiative.org/

Pall, ML. 2013. – Electromagnetic fields act via activation of voltage-gated calcium channels to produce beneficial or adverse effects. Available at: https://www.ncbi.nlm.nih.gov/pmc/articles/PMC3780531/

Pall, ML. 2016 – Microwave frequency electromagnetic fields (EMFs) produce widespread neuropsychiatric effects including depression. Available at: https://www.sciencedirect.com/science/article/pii/S0891061815000599?via%3Dihub

Pall, ML. 2018 – Wi-Fi is an important threat to human health. Available at: https://www.sciencedirect.com/science/article/pii/S0013935118300355?via%3Dihub

Glaser naval medical research institute studies on microwave radiofrequency 1972 onwards available at:https://scholar.google.com/scholar?q=Glaser+naval+medical+microwave+radiofrequency+1972&btnG&hl=en&as_sdt=0%2C38

EMF Analysis – Science. A comprehensive list of scientific studies, research and links available at: https://www.emfanalysis.com/research/

"Cell Phones: Invisible Hazards in the Wireless Age: An Insider's Alarming Discoveries about Cancer and Genetic Damage" by Dr. George Carlo available at: https://www.amazon.com/Cell-Phones-Invisible-Wireless-Discoveries/dp/078670960X

The research of Professor Olle Johansson, a neuroscientist at the world-renowned Karolinska Institute. Available at: https://www.cellphonetaskforce.org/the-work-of-olle-johansson/

The research and lectures of scientist Barrie Trower, for example 'The Dangers of Microwave Technology' and and '5G Gigantic health hazard' available on YouTube.

[54] The report by Mark Steele is available at: https://www.weebly.com/uploads/1/3/7/4/137404875/mark_steele_expert_report_-_5g_radiation_emissions_in_context_of_nanometal-contaminated_vaccines_inc_c-19___antennas.pdf

[55] Evidence & Instances Of Geo-Engineering article: https://sandiadams.uk/evidence-instances-of-geo-engineering/

Proof of Weather Modification | NASA, HAARP & Chemtrail Technology: https://www.youtube.com/watch?v=wJBBlntDtEU

Weather Modification 'Operation Cumulus' Lynmouth 1952 Floods – UK RAF Military Cloud Seeding: https://www.youtube.comwatch?v=Oe3GJL9gWSo

[56] For example, see: https://brandnewtube.com/watch/trump-039-s-links-to-the-zionist-banking-cabal-a-puppet-just-like-obama-was-and-all-since-jfk_qMhQoq8nZ4Ro5ZU.html

http://www.alt-market.com/index.php/articles/4003-trump-vs-warren-and-the-fake-battle-against-the-elites

https://brandnewtube.com/watch/trump-039-s-links-to-the-zionist-banking-cabal-pt2-see-4-45-secs-the-banks-bailed-him-out-1980s_F7QSTNCQDwwgF5A.html

[57] The book "Sustainable Energy without Hot Air" by Professor David MacKay, Regius Professor of Engineering at Cambridge University and former Chief Scientific Advisor to the UK's Department of Energy and Climate Change, is available for free at: https://withouthotair.com/

[58] Source: https://www.feasta.org/2020/02/07/end-of-the-oilocene-the-gathering-storm/

[59] Source: https://medium.com/insurge-intelligence/green-economic-growth-is-an-article-of-faith-devoid-of-scientific-evidence-5e63c4c0bb5e

[60] Source: https://data.parliament.uk/DepositedPapers/Files/DEP2019-0718/Green_Finance_Strategy.pdf

[61] Source: https://theconversation.com/these-three-firms-own-corporate-america-77072#:~:text=Corporate%20American%20monopoly&text=The%20Big%20Three%20%E2%80%93%20seen%20together,Bank%20of%20America%2C%20and%20Citigroup

[62] Source: https://stockzoa.com/ticker/blk/

[63] Sources:
https://stockzoa.com/ticker/jpm/
https://stockzoa.com/ticker/ms/
https://www.fool.com/investing/general/2013/02/26/who-owns-morgan-stanley.aspx

https://www.fool.com/investing/general/2013/02/19/who-owns-jpmorgan-chase.aspx

[64] Source: https://www.investigate-europe.eu/en/2018/blackrock-the-company-that-owns-the-world/

[65] The study is available at: https://journals.plos.org/plosone/article?id=10.1371/journal.pone.0025995#s3

[66] Source: https://en.wikipedia.org/wiki/Morgan_family

[67] Source: https://www.thenewamerican.com/economy/economics/item/15473-world-bank-insider-blows-whistle-on-corruption-federal-reserve

[68] Sources: https://www.globalresearch.ca/the-federal-reserve-cartel-the-eight-families/25080

[69] Source: 10K Filings of Fortune 500 Corporations to SEC. 3-91

[70] Source: https://en.wikipedia.org/wiki/Morgan_family

[71] Source: http://theeconomiccollapseblog.com/archives/who-controls-the-money-an-unelected-unaccountable-central-bank-of-the-world-secretly-does

[72] Sources: https://www.globalresearch.ca/world-bank-whistleblower-reveals-how-the-global-elite-rule-the-world/5353130

http://theeconomiccollapseblog.com/

[73] Sources: https://www.therichest.com/rich-countries/the-only-5-countries-in-the-world-living-debt-free/

https://datatopics.worldbank.org/debt/ids/

[74] Source: The book 'Globalism Unmasked: The Truth about Banking and the Reset of Society', 2020, by Mark Keenan.

[75] Sources: https://www.rte.ie/news/2012/0122/311314-politics/
https://namawinelake.wordpress.com/2012/01/22/ecb-says-a-bomb-will-go-off-in-dublin-if-anglobondholders-are-not-paid-says-minister-varadkar/

[76] Sources: http://datatopics.worldbank.org/debt/ids/

https://data.worldbank.org/indicator/GC.XPN.INTP.RV.ZS?view=chart

[77] Sources: https://www.politico.eu/article/8-billionaires-own-the-same-as-half-the-world-bill-gates-jeff-bezos-mark-zuckerberg/?fbclid=IwAR2aSNHJ9imD_OgVZjEed201fXK9f7HYliVbr6-4cP3JKZsVzt__9FzDOnc

https://www.forbes.com/2010/03/09/worlds-richest-people-slim-gates-buffett-billionaires-2010-intro.html#baa0920141ab

https://www.forbes.com/real-time-billionaires/#3490aa1d3d78

https://www.businessinsider.com/worlds-richest-billionaires-net-worth-2017-6?r=US&IR=T

[78] Source: https://www.cnbc.com/2018/06/27/25-richest-families-in-the-world-are-worth-more-than-1-trillion.html

[79] An example is the article 'The Money Changers: Rothschild Banking Dynasty Said To Be Worth $100 Trillion' November 3, 2012 by Dean Henderson available at:
https://21stcenturywire.com/2012/11/03/the-money-changers-rothschild-banking-dynasty-said-to-be-worth-100-trillion/
https://geopolitics.co/2013/11/07/rothschilds-100-trillion-empire/
which states "the Eight Families who own majority stock in every private central bank in the world — Rothschild, Rockefeller, Kuhn Loeb, Lehman, Goldman Sachs, Warburg, Lazard and Israel Moses Seif. As cited in my Big Oil & Their Bankers… book and by others, the Eight Families own 52% of the New York Federal Reserve Bank, far and away the most powerful Fed Bank. Their ownership is disguised under names like JP Morgan Chase, Citigroup, Goldman Sachs and Morgan Stanley… with the Rothschilds being the most powerful. Their net worth alone is estimated at well over $100 trillion."

[80] Source: https://www.wsws.org/en/articles/2019/10/19/pers-o19.html

[81] Source: https://ellenbrown.com/2020/06/22/meet-blackrock-the-new-great-vampire-squid/

[82] Source: 'Covid 19: The Great Reset', by Klaus Schwab and Thierry Malleret, pg 246.

[83] Source: http://theeconomiccollapseblog.com/archives/who-runs-the-world-solid-proof-that-a-core-group-of-wealthy-elitists-is-pulling-the-strings

[84] Source: 'The Web of Debt' by E.H. Brown, pg 130. Second edition.

[85] Source: http://tapnewswire.com/2015/10/six-jewish-companies-control-96-of-the-worlds-media/

[86] Rockefeller's Fascism with a Democratic Face, The Campaigner, Vol.8, #1-2, November-December 1974, pg.72.

[87] Source: Tavistock Institute Social Engineering the Masses by Daniel Estulin, pg 31.

[88] Source: Tavistock Institute Social Engineering the Masses by Daniel Estulin, pg 97.

[89] Source: Tavistock Institute Social Engineering the Masses by Daniel Estulin, pg 214.

[90] Source: Tavistock Institute Social Engineering the Masses by Daniel Estulin, pg 116..

[91] Source: Tavistock Institute Social Engineering the Masses by Daniel Estulin, pg 151.

[92] Source: https://stockzoa.com/ticker/blk/

[93] Source: https://en.wikipedia.org/wiki/List_of_banking_families

According to Gerald Krefetz author of the book 'Jews and Money. The Myths and the Reality' (See Endnote [93])

> "The Rothschild banking concerns, however, were far from the only ones. Major Jewish investment banking organizations across Europe included those of the Seligmans, Oppenheimers, Habers, Speyers, Warburgs, Mendelssohns, Bleichroders, Eskeles, Arnsteins, Montagus, Goldsmids, Hambros, Sassoons, and others. The Jewish international banking network that floated state loans to finance European industry and railroads was wide: the five Rothschild brothers were in London, Paris, Vienna, Frankfort, and Naples. The Bleichroders were based in Berlin, the Warburgs in Hamburg, the Oppenheims in Cologne, the Sassoons in Bombay, the Guenzburgs in St. Petersburg. Jews were also influential in the creation of influential joint stock and commercial banks including two of Germany's largest -- the Deutsche Bank and the Dersdner Bank, as well as Credit Mobilier, Banque de Paris, Banca Commerciale Italiana, Credito Italiano, Creditanstalt-Bankverein, Banque de Bruxelles, among others."

[94] Source: https://en.wikipedia.org/wiki/Rothschild_family

Description of Jewish Economic Influence available at: http://holywar.org/jewishtr/06money.htm

[95] Source: https://en.wikipedia.org/wiki/Warburg_family

[96] Source: https://en.wikipedia.org/wiki/Goldman%E2%80%93Sachs_family

[97] Sources: https://en.wikipedia.org/wiki/Oppenheim_family
https://en.wikipedia.org/wiki/Sal._Oppenheim

[98] Silbiger, S., 2000, p. 78-79.

[99] Source: 'When Victims Rule – A Critique of Jewish Pre-eminence in America', Chapter 22. Wall Street. Available at: http://holywar.org/jewishtr/22wallst.htm

[100] Source: Article on the website 'My Jewish Learning', which was launched in 2003 and is part of 70 Faces Media, the largest non-profit, nondenominational Jewish media organization in North America. Available at: https://www.myjewishlearning.com/article/usury-and-moneylending-in-judaism/

[101] Meyer, Michael A., Ed. Brenner, Michael, Assoc. Ed. Mordecai Breuer, Michael Graetz. German-Jewish History in Modern Times. V. 1 Tradition and Enlightenment, 1600-1780. Page 106. Columbia University Press, NY, NY, 1996

[102] Lazare, Bernard. Antisemitism. Its History and Causes. p. 173. Britons Publishing Co., London, 1967

[103] Source: https://www.ijs.org.au/modern-judaism-orthodox-conservative-and-progressive/

[104] Source: https://www.myjewishlearning.com/article/types-of-jews/ which states,

> "Ethnicities: Ashkenazi, Sephardic, Mizrahi Etc. Jews from different parts of the world have developed distinct cultures and customs. Jews from Germany and Eastern Europe are known as Ashkenazim. Much of what, in America, is thought of as Jewish — bagels, Yiddish, black hats — are actually specific to Ashkenazi culture."

[105] Source: https://en.wikipedia.org/wiki/Judaism_and_politics

[106] Sources: https://concisepolitics.com/2018/07/03/talmud-quotes-related-to-hate-and-superiority-over-and-inequality-versus-non-jews/

http://www.talmudunmasked.com/chapter15.htm

In Abhodah Zarah (26b, Tosephoth) it says: "Even the best of the Goim (Non-Jews) should be killed"

https://www.youtube.com/watch?v=NfEmAaZ5g5c

[107] For example, the book 'When Victims Rule - A Critique of Jewish Pre-eminence in America' Chapter 6. Jewish Money and Economic Influence'. Available at: http://holywar.org/jewishtr/06money.htm and http://holywar.org/jewishtr/22wallst.htm

For example, the website 'Who Controls America?' available at https://thezog.wordpress.com/

[108] Sources: Hertzler, J. O. The Sociology of Antisemitism Through History. In Graeber, page 88, and 62-99; and Siegel, Richard/ Rheims, Carl. The Jewish Almanac, p. 127-129. Bantom Books, NY 1980

[109] For example, the following articles describe Khazarian mafia infiltration of Judaism, Banking, Politics, and Christianity:

http://stateofthenation.co/?p=21172 by Benjamin Fulford.

https://www.veteranstoday.com/2020/08/21/most-controversial-document-in-internet-history-the-hidden-history-of-the-incredibly-evil-khazarian-mafia/ by Mike Harris, who served as a technical advisor to the Committee on Science and Technology of the US Congress.

https://geopolitics.co/2015/05/01/the-khazarian-mafia-part-2/

https://sarahwestall.com/most-controversial-document-in-internet-history-the-hidden-history-of-the-incredibly-evil-khazarian-mafia/

[110] Source: 'Europa - The Last Battle' documentary at: https://www.bitchute.com/video/s1nPYDj7KBEQ/

[111] See Arthur Koestler, 13th tribe; also Dr Schlomo Sand's award-winning book reviewed on:
http://www.haaretz.com/hasen/spages/959229.html
http://www.gilad.co.uk/writings/the-wandering-who-by-gilad-atzmon.html
http://www.khazaria.com

"The Fallacy of Biological Judaism", By Robert Pollack, on: http://www.forward.com/articles/9406/

[112] Source: http://www.globalresearch.ca/world-bank-whistleblower-reveals-how-the-global-elite-rule-the-world/5353130

[113] Sources: http://john-f-kennedy.net/executiveorder11110.htm
https://en.wikipedia.org/wiki/Executive_Order_11110

[114] Sources: http://datatopics.worldbank.org/debt/ids/

https://data.worldbank.org/indicator/GC.XPN.INTP.RV.ZS?view=chart

[115] An example of a PRTR is the Norwegian PRTR. The website lists the pollutants released in various sectors of society. The website and database available at:
https://www.norskeutslipp.no/en/Frontpage/

The following document lists the pollutant groups covered by the PRTR Protocol.

https://www.unece.org/fileadmin/DAM/env/pp/prtr/guidance/PRTR_May_2008_for_CD.pdf

[116] Source: *United Nations Environmental Programme Year Book 2009: New Science and Developments in Our Changing Environment*

[117] Olson R. (1995) Sustainability as a social vision. Journal of Social Issues Winter v51 n4 p15(21) Page 1 Galegroup.

[118] Hartwick, J.M. (1977) *Intergenerational equity and the investing of rents from exhaustive resources*. American Economic Review 67. pp 972-974.

[119] RESEARCH ON THE SCIENTIFIC BASIS FOR SUSTAINABILITY (RSBS) (2006) Science on Sustainability Summary Report. RSBS Secretariat. Available at: http://www.sos2006.jp/english/rsbs_summary_e/about-rsbs.html

[120] Foundation for the Economics of Sustainability - The economic challenge of sustainability 'The Problem with Sustainable Development'. Available at: http://www.feasta.org/documents/landhousing/CORI_RD_EOS.html

[121] The United Nations Brundtland Report, *Our Common Future*, is available at:
https://sustainabledevelopment.un.org/content/documents/5987our-common-future.pdf

[122] Sources: Perman, R. and Stern, D. I., 2003. Evidence from panel unit root and cointegration tests that the environmental Kuznets curve does not exist. Australian Journal of Agricultural and Resource Economics, Vol. 47
Dasgupta, S., Laplante, B., Wang, H., and Wheeler, D., 2002. Confronting the environmental Kuznets curve. Journal of Economic Perspectives, 16: 147-168.

[123] The *'Prosperity without Growth'* report is available at:
http://www.sd-commission.org.uk/publications.php?id=914
http://www.sd-commission.org.uk/data/files/publications/prosperity_without_growth_report.pdf

[124] Source: https://medium.com/insurge-intelligence/green-economic-growth-is-an-article-of-faith-devoid-of-scientific-evidence-5e63c4c0bb5e

[125] Solow, Robert M. (1974). "Intergenerational Equity and Exhaustible Resources". Review of Economic Studies (Symposium): 29–46.

[126] Perman R., Common M., Mcgilvray J., Ma Y. (2003) Natural Resource and Environmental Economics. 3rd Ed. Pearson Education Limited., pg 37

[127] The Report of the UN's Secretary General's High Level Panel on Global Sustainability is available at: http://www.un.org/gsp/sites/default/files/attachments/GSPReport_unformatted_30Jan.pdf

[128] Eco-innovation – putting the EU on the path to a resource efficient and energy efficient economy, Wuppertal Institute for Climate, Environment and Energy 2009. Available at: http://www.wupperinst.org/en/home/index.html and at http://mpra.ub.uni-muenchen.de/19939/1/WI-Eco-Inno-09.pdf

[129] Information on UNECE's Committee on Economic Cooperation and Integration is available at: http://www.unece.org/ceci/welcome.html

[130] Available at: http://www.unmultimedia.org/tv/webcast/2012/03/general-assembly-briefing-by-the-secretary-general-on-the-final-report-of-his-high-level-panel-on-global-sustainability-english.html - http://www.un.org/ga/search/view_doc.asp?symbol=A/66/700

[131] A Note by the Secretary general at the Sixty-sixth session General Assemby, Agenda item 19 (a) Sustainable development: implementation of Agenda 21, the Programme for the Further Implementation of Agenda 21 and the outcomes of the World Summit on Sustainable Development Resilient people, resilient planet: a future worth choosing, includes a Letter dated 30 January 2012 from the Co-Chairs of the High-level Panel on Global Sustainability addressed to the Secretary-General and is available at: http://www.un.org/ga/search/view_doc.asp?symbol=A/66/700

[132] Source: *Tavistock Institute Social Engineering the Masses* by Daniel Estulin, pg 223. According to Estulin the members of the Club of Rome consist of the descendants of the richest and most ancient of all European families who controlled and ran Genoa and Venice in the XII century.

[133] Biopiracy quotation source: http://www.i-sis.org.uk/conventiononknowledge.php

[134] Source: https://www.investopedia.com/terms/c/company.asp

[135] 'Alternatives to Economic Globalisation'. Edited by John Cavanaugh and Gerry Mander. Pg 17.

[136] Dawson, J., (2006) Schumacher Briefing "Ecovillages: New Frontiers for Sustainability". Pg 75, 76. 1st Ed. UK. Green Books

[137] ROBERT, K-H. and MACK, M. (n.d). The Natural Step: A Vision for Sustainable Societies. Reflections. The SoL Journal of Knowledge, Learning and Change, 7 (3), pp. 9-14.

[138] Source: An article by Peter Koenig at: https://www.globalresearch.ca/insanity-sustainability/5725348

[139] Source: *Spiritual Economics Lessons from the Bhagavad Gita* by Dhanesvara das. Available at: http://spiritual-econ.blogspot.com/

[140] Examples of publications by *The Centre for Research on Globalisation* are available at:
http://www.globalresearch.ca/index.php?context=va&aid=15622
http://www.globalresearch.ca/index.php?context=theme&themeId=1

[141] This study was released by the Structural Adjustment Participatory Review International Network (SAPRIN). SAPRIN, *The Policy Roots of Economic Crisis and Poverty: A Multi-Country Participatory Assessment of Structural Adjustment*, April 2002, Executive Summary, p.21.

[142] The book *Food Fascism* by Dr Sahadeva Dasa, Pg 87-98.

[143] The book *Food Fascism* by Dr Sahadeva Dasa, Pg 70.

[144] The book *Ireland 1845- 1850: The Perfect Holocaust and Who Kept It "Perfect"* by Chris Fogarty, is available at:www.irishholocaust.org

[145] Source: www.foreignpolicy.com, April 27th, 2011

[146] Source: https://en.wikipedia.org/wiki/Peak_oil

[147] See the paper: "Tipping Point Near-Term Systemic Implications of a Peak in Global Oil Production" An Outline Review by David Korowicz, Feasta & The Risk/Resilience Network available at: http://www.feasta.org/documents/risk_resilience/Tipping_Point.pdf

[148] The report by the government of Finland is available at: http://tupa.gtk.fi/raportti/arkisto/70_2019.pdf

[149] Sources: https://www.vice.com/en_us/article/8848g5/government-agency-warns-global-oil-industry-is-on-the-brink-of-a-meltdown

[150] See articles at https://www.feasta.org/?s=clarke

[151] Source: https://mondediplo.com/outsidein/covid-19-oil

[152] The reset being discussed by the WEF at https://www.weforum.org/great-reset

[153] Scientist Jay Forrester. Sourced from the book *'Environmental problems and human behaviour'* by Gardner and Stern – pg 294

[154] The Science on Sustainability Report 2006 is available at: http://sustainabilityscience.org/content.html?contentid=1120 and at http://www.sos2006.jp/english/rsbs_summary_e/about-rsbs.html
www.sos2006.jp/english/rsbs_summary_e/ScienceOnSustainability2006.pdf, consulted 5 March. 2012.

[155] Source: https://course.oeru.org/csf101/learning-pathways/defining-sustainability-and-sustainable-development/summary-a-scientific-definition-of-success-for-humans/

[156] See a report by UNEP on chemicals available at:
www.chem.unep.ch/mercury/WGprep.1/Documents/k10_2%29/English/WG_Prep_1_INF2_PRTRs.doc, consulted 5 March. 2012.

[157] Broman G., Holmberg J., and Robèrt, K-H. (2000). Simplicity Without Reduction – Thinking Upstream Towards the Sustainable Society. Interfaces: International Journal of the Institute for Operations Research and the Management Sciences. 30(3).

[158] The Natural Step scientific conditions for sustainability are available at: www.naturalstep.org/~natural/the-system-conditions, consulted 5 March. 2012

[159] For example, the PRTR Protocol and the other agreements, such as the Stockholm Convention on Persistent Organic Pollutants, the Rotterdam Convention on the Prior Informed Consent Procedure for Certain Hazardous Chemicals and Pesticides in International Trade, and the Basel Convention on the Control of Transboundary Movements of Hazardous Wastes and Their Disposal. Information on the PRTR Protocol is available at:

www.unece.org/env/pp/prtr/docs/prtrtext.html, consulted 5 March. 2012.
www.unece.org/env/pp/prtr/guidancedev.html, consulted 5 March. 2012.

Note here that the PRTR Protocol incorrectly lists Co2 as a pollutant.

[160] McDonough, W., and Braungart, M. (2002) *Cradle to Cradle: Remaking the Way We Make Things*. 1st ed. New York: North Point Press.

[161] The Natural Step framework was pioneered by Professor Karl-Henrik Robert and is described in a number of books, including *The Natural Step – Toward a Sustainable Society by David Cook*. In additional, the framework is the basis of a Masters-level course in Strategic Sustainable Development at Blekinge Institute of Technology in Sweden.

[162] The writings of Dmitri Orlov are available at:

http://cluborlov.blogspot.com/2009/06/definancialisation-deglobalisation.html
http://fora.tv/2009/02/13/Dmitry_Orlov_Social_Collapse_Best_Practices

[163] For information on the eco-village at Cloughjordan in Ireland see http://www.thevillage.ie/

[164] Dawson, J., (2006) Schumacher Briefing "Ecovillages: New Frontiers for Sustainability". 1st Ed. UK. Green Books, pg 87

[165] Information on the Transition Towns network is available at http://transitionculture.org/

[166] The GEN database provides links to eco village resources and is available at: http://gen.ecovillage.org/iserviceces

[167] Information on the Sustainable Communities Network is available at: http://www.sustainable.org/

[168] "Permaculture is an approach to designing human settlements and perennial agricultural systems that mimics the relationships found in natural ecologies. It was first developed by Australians Bill Mollison and David Holmgren and their associates during the 1970s in a series of publications. The word permaculture is a portmanteau of permanent agriculture, as well as permanent culture."

Source: https://fr.wikipedia.org/wiki/Permaculture

[169] Relevant websites detailing bio-char and pyrolysis include:
http://www.css.cornell.edu/faculty/lehmann/biochar/Biochar_home.htm
http://www.biochar-international.org
http://www.bestenergies.com/companies/bestpyrolysis.html
http://www.biochar.org
http://www.abc.net.au/catalyst/stories/s2012892.htm
http://www.bbc.co.uk/science/horizon/2002/eldorado.shtml
http://www.eprida.com

[170] Source: *Vedic Ecology* by Ranchor Prime

[171] This is described in the book *Vedic Archaeology and Assorted Essays* by Stephen Rosen, on pg 72.

[172] Information on the Fiedler Ruling is available at http://axley.com/patrick-j-fiedler

[173] The article *"The Six Grand Illusions That Keep Us Enslaved to "The Matrix"* by Sigmund Fraud was published in 2015 and is available at: http://www.globalresearch.ca/the-6-grand-illusions-that-keep-us-enslaved-to-the-matrix/5429205

[174] Citation: Rees, W. 2010. What's blocking sustainability? Human nature, cognition, and denial. Sustainability: Science, Practice, & Policy 6(2):13-25. Available at: http://sspp.proquest.com/archives/vol6iss2/1001-012.rees.html Published online October 14, 2010

[175] Source: https://www.lucistrust.org/about_us/support_un

[176] Source: https://www.lucistrust.org/arcane_school/talks_and_articles/the_esoteric_meaning_lucifer

[177] Source: https://www.lucistrust.org/arcane_school/library/new_york_headquarters_library

Made in the USA
Columbia, SC
25 September 2022